CALABRIA

The Other Italy

CALABRIA
The Other Italy

KAREN HAID

Mill City Press, Minneapolis

Mill City Press, Inc.
322 First Avenue N, 5th floor
Minneapolis, MN 55401
612.455.2293
www.millcitypublishing.com

ISBN-13: 978-1-63413-230-5
LCCN: 2014921196

Maps by Debbie Scott at Snappymap.com
Photos by the author
Typeset by Mary Kristin Ross

Printed in the United States of America

In memory of my mother, mistress of the delightful missive, and in appreciation of my father's steadfast support

CONTENTS

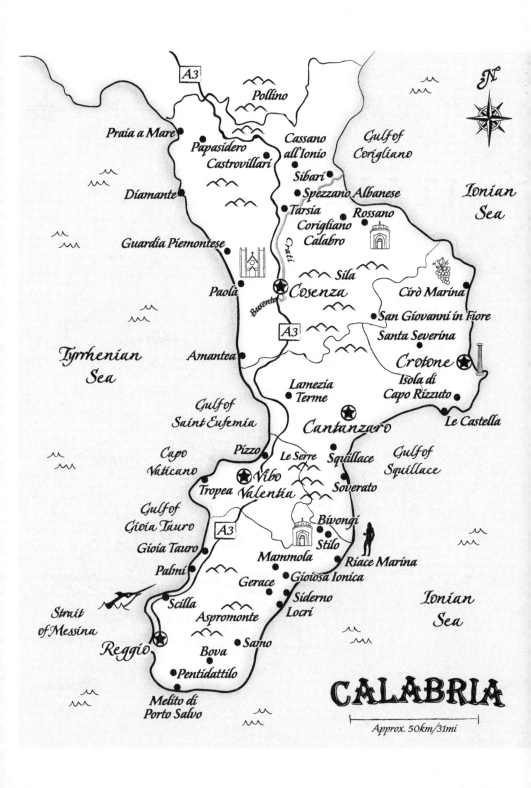

N

A3

Pollino

Praia a Mare

Papasidero
Castrovillari

Cassano
all'Ionio

Gulf of
Corigliano

Diamante

Sibari

Spezzano Albanese

Ionian
Sea

Tarsia

Rossano

Corigliano
Calabro

Guardia Piemontese

Sila

Paolà

Cosenza

Cirò Marina

Busento

Crati

San Giovanni in Fiore

A3

Santa Severina

Tyrrhenian
Sea

Amantea

Crotone

Lamezia
Terme

Isola di
Capo Rizzuto

Gulf of
Saint Eufemia

Cantanzaro

Le Castella

Capo
Vaticano

Pizzo

Le Serre

Squillace

Gulf of
Squillace

Vibo
Valentia

Soverato

Tropea

Gulf of
Gioia Tauro

A3

Bivongi

Gioia Tauro

Stilo

Palmi

Mammola

Riace Marina

Gerace

Gioiosa Ionica

Scilla

Siderno
Locri

Ionian
Sea

Strait
of Messina

Aspromonte

Reggio

Bova

Samo

Pentidattilo

CALABRIA

Melito di
Porto Salvo

Approx. 50km/31mi

INTRODUCTION

ON MY FIRST VISIT TO ITALY, I explored Rome and the hill towns of Umbria. My second was an extended stay in Florence, a study-vacation focusing on the Italian language and culture. I then branched out to Lucca and more of Tuscany. Venice, Milan, Naples, Sorrento, Taormina, the Cinque Terre and South Tyrol followed—always new places to discover, people to meet, meals to relish. My trips became longer as the periods between them shortened, and I soon realized that the time had come for a full immersion.

Teaching English to Italians appeared to be the most practical approach to support a residence in Italy. After garnering certification, I searched many months for a job, first from the United States and then from within Italy. An interview via Skype landed me an offer from a public school in a mid-sized town in northern Italy. A lesson demonstration resulted in a proposal from a rather large private school chain in Rome. Initial hopes were soon dashed, however, as the insurmountable obstacle of obtaining a work visa blocked any chance for my hiring. I came to the conclusion that what was described as difficult by the *Teach English as a Foreign Language* websites was really next to impossible. The only option seemed to be working illegally at private schools desperate for warm, mother-tongue-English bodies to fill the classrooms in larger cities where the hourly wage was not sufficient to cover modest living expenses.

I was staying with friends in Rieti, a provincial capital

northeast of Rome in Italy's exact geographical center. The Italians with whom I came in contact were as incredulous as my would-be-legitimate employers regarding the complications I faced as an American in their country. Friends trotted me around various government offices and police stations, convinced that the key to success within the Italian bureaucracy was knowing the right person.

Amalia knew everyone in town. She was from Rieti. She taught elementary school for over thirty years. I would not be surprised if she had a connection with the ancient Sabines or with the Romans who built the salt road through Rieti and over the Apennines to the Adriatic. We went from office to office, shaking hands and drinking coffee with her many acquaintances. However, as we stood face to face with a nonnative government worker whose Italian was noticeably weaker than mine, Amalia began to grasp my predicament. We had just finished explaining my situation. The young man sat in silence for a few moments as he tried to wrap his brain around the particulars of my case. He finally looked up and said as if he didn't quite believe it himself, "You're an *extracomunitaria*" (not a member of the European Community), to which Amalia vociferously responded, "No, she most certainly is not!"

I tried to calm her, explaining that the United States wasn't part of the European Union and that this foreign worker wasn't trying to insult me. In Italy, I had already learned that the word *extracomunitario* came with decidedly negative connotations, most often associated with people arriving in dinghies or hidden in trucks and cargo holds. I was a friend, however. My country was a strong ally and over the years had been a refuge to five and a half million Italian immigrants. How could I, a good American looking for a job as a mother-tongue English teacher, be categorized by such a term? In reality and somewhat shocking to many an Italian, my poor foreign counterparts entering Italy to clean houses or be nursemaids to the elderly had a much greater possibility of working legally.

The number of overall work visas ebbs and flows, depending on the annual total set yearly by the government. I happened to arrive on the scene during a severe retrenchment phase, in which being legally hired to teach English without already having a work permit was outside the realm of possibility. Not wanting to subsidize an under-the-table, full-time teaching job with my savings, I was coming to terms with abandoning my Italian experience before it started. A few months earlier a recruiter had urged me to consider Japan as an option, and a school in Italy had contacted me saying they wouldn't be able to hire me, but recommended a supervisor post in their Guatemalan location. However, I didn't speak Japanese or Spanish, not to mention the fact that I had my heart set on Italy.

Then on a Sunday evening in mid-October when I thought all schools would have already begun classes, I received a two-line email asking if I was still interested in a job at a school in Locri, Calabria. I recalled the position as an apartment was included, and had emailed my materials twice, once from the U.S. and a second time from Rieti when I noticed that the job had been re-advertised. I remembered googling Locri, a beach town, settled by the Greeks and something to do with the Mafia.

A copy of the school's proposed contract was attached to the message addressed "Dear teacher." I responded positively with a few initial questions, "a.s.a.p." as their note prompted me, along with who knows how many other "teachers." A short email correspondence pursued, and I learned that already being in the country fit in nicely with their seemingly urgent need for a teacher to arrive within the week. The school's director assured me that the spacious, two-bedroom apartment was completely furnished, including linens, promised a full refrigerator upon arrival and sent along at least twenty-five photos. The living room popped with brightly colored furniture and very shiny floors. My friends and I sort of wondered why the front door featured so prominently in a number of the pictures, prompting such tongue-in-cheek comments as, "It's Calabria, maybe they want to show you that there *is* a front door!" Such remarks revealed the popular concerns with life in Italy's deep south. The well-known presence of the Mafia in the Locri area wasn't the most auspicious of endorsements, either. However, the fact that I could move in with just one suitcase in tow made it definitely worth the go. What did I have to lose?

I would spend four years teaching English in Calabria, first in Locri and then in Reggio Calabria, its provincial capital. Emails became my main form of general communication with family and friends, at times humorous, at others less so, but all opened up a window on everyday life in southern Italy, at times ordinary, often extraordinary.

1

WELCOME TO CALABRIA

CHINALEA FISHING VILLAGE, SCILLA

THE JOURNEY

"They steal in Naples." "They board the trains, break into your compartment and rob you." Upon the strong recommendation of the school's director I was on a regional train, direct from Rome's main station to Locri, and these alarming declarations made by fellow travelers were far from comforting.

The journey of about 325 miles as the crow flew took roughly nine and a half hours by train. 'Direct' simply meant that I wouldn't have to change trains, and this option was only available on the overnight. The sleeper compartments ranged from two to six people. I had a ticket for one with four berths and was told that the sleeper cars were separated by sex. The bathroom and dressing room were on the hallway.

My first thought on approaching the track was that the train didn't appear to be new, noticeably absent were the smooth, sleek lines of the modern locomotives pictured on the *Trenitalia* website. No smiling faces, either, although in all fairness, it was a late night departure, which of course made the warnings about Naples even scarier. The train was quite long and pulled out of the station without a full load. The all-female carriage didn't exist, with men overwhelmingly outnumbering my cabin companion and I. A dentist from Calabria living in Rome, she made the journey frequently, was a fountain of information regarding the trip and unfortunately confirmed the Naples' rumors.

As we got underway, the conductor knocked on our door, asked us for our tickets and said that he would keep them so as not to bother us during the night. He recommended locking our door, cautioning us about theft in Naples. We didn't have to worry about anyone else joining us as there would only be the two of us in the cabin. At first, I didn't see how the compartment could even be called a sleeper—three seats faced three seats. Our suitcases filled the space between them. I soon learned that berths were created simply by lifting a few pairs of armrests. A long piece of scratchy gauze folded in half and a pillow with the same abrasive covering completed the transformation from well-worn seats to well-worn beds, 'linens' included.

The affable Calabrian dentist and I chatted for about an hour before putting the lights out. On account of the primitive sanitary conditions on board, the necessary lavatory visit in anticipation of our self-preserving lockdown seemed about as frightening as being robbed in your sleep by a Neapolitan. Curiously, the bathroom had been designed with running water in mind as there was a sign stating it wasn't potable. However, the only things running near that privy were the rails under the toilet. The dressing room was much less terrifying as the only piece of equipment that ever appeared to have been installed was a piece of rectangular metal at head level that had long since lost any reflective ability. Nevertheless, I avoided that chamber as well.

Having bolted the door, pushing our suitcases up against it, an exhaustion came over me as I lay my head on my handbag. I was afraid of falling asleep. Naples was only another hour away. Sleep? The train shuddered violently above three kilometers per hour. The accompanying clamor battered my senses like a metal-beaked woodpecker. How had the train not spontaneously fallen to pieces?

Stop and go. Stop and go. Hushed-voiced passengers brushed past the door, scraping their luggage along the walls. No announcements were made. The train stopped, bodies scurried up and down the corridors, the voices got louder. My heart began to beat faster. Suddenly, everyone was yelling. The dentist appeared to be sleeping. My heart was pounding as I wrapped my arms around my head, clutching my purse. We were in Naples. Dialectal shrieks had replaced the metallic din. I waited and listened—yelling, thudding, frantic scrambling and slamming— attentive to every sound, every movement. Suddenly, a quiet calm. Had we dodged the pillaging? The train lurched forward, triggering its disquieting vibrations, chattering its metallic teeth. I was not robbed. I would be jostled only by the train itself. I could sleep.

Correction. The man in the berth with whom I shared a paper-thin wall could sleep. This additional disturbance added an unpredictable dimension to the train's rhythmic inconveniences. His colossal snoring vibrated the wall and the bunk itself, as if the cabin partition was just a bed divider from a 1950s film. Perhaps what my fellow travelers were trying to convey was that in Naples, they rob you of your sleep. Even mother nature joined in with a powerful tempest as we convulsed southwards.

After what seemed to be a routine stop at 3:30 in the morning, the train started bucking like a mule catching itself in a stagger. This iron horse scenario lasted fifteen minutes before the train finally fell back into its familiar cadence. We were somewhere in Calabria, Italy's most southerly region on the mainland, in the toe of the boot. The trip followed Italy's western border along the Tyrrhenian Sea, from Rome in the region of Lazio, through Naples and Salerno in Campagna, briefly traversing Basilicata's limited Tyrrhenian access, and into Calabria, crossing at its narrowest from Lamezia Terme to Cantazaro Lido in order to reach the Ionian Sea and continuing southward to Locri.

The dentist left me in Catanzaro, the region's capital. The train continued along the coast, hugging its shoreline, flanking a flat, uninterrupted beach protected by banks of pines. Small, nondescript towns popped up on the other side. This land was to be my home for the next eight months. I checked the time frequently, as I didn't want to miss the station. I hadn't thought to get a map and there weren't any official communications via a loud speaker that would have been installed years before, along with the running water in the bathroom and the fragment of a shade that dangled by a thread over the cabin window.

Shortly before the scheduled arrival time printed on my ticket, I dragged my bag to the nearest door. The car appeared to be all but empty. I strained to see the names on signs as we slowed into the stations, names that I didn't recognize, and then LOCRI. The door didn't open automatically, no simple push-button, a heavy, complicated affair with a large wheel and big handle. I called the conductor who was sitting in his private compartment around the corner, urgently asking him to open the door. "I'll take care of it when it's time," he said. "I need to get off in Locri." "In 10 minutes." I thought that perhaps Locri was spread out with multiple depots as he seemed so sure that this wasn't my station. After two more stops, the conductor approached me, asking, "Did you want to get off in Locri?" "Yes." "We already passed Locri." "I told you when I saw the sign." "You told me after Locri." "No, I didn't." "Yes, you did." I felt as though I was back in my childhood home in New Jersey arguing with my sister about who was supposed to have taken the garbage out as the sanitation truck lumbered by. I finally broke in with, "It doesn't matter whose fault it is, just tell me how and when I can get back to Locri!" This railroad employee who obviously hadn't slept any better than I had was also clearly not from southern Calabria. Locri—Ardore—Bovalino—Bianco—, I now know every stop on the single rail line between Locri and Reggio Calabria by heart. He scratched his head, got off the train with me in Bianco and began searching for an informational board.

Returning in the other direction, the train's aisle space didn't allow me to keep my bag at my side. "Leave it by the door—it's safe," I was told. We were a long way from Naples. When the conductor asked me for my ticket, I produced the one from Rome and started babbling about what had happened. He looked at me as though I had just dropped down from another planet and smiled. After ten and a half hours, I had arrived at my destination.

LOCRI

IF ITALY IS EUROPE'S BOOT, Locri would be its bunion. Geography aside, negative characterizations are common for this Mafia-ridden locale situated in one of the nation's poorest regions. Hosting a courthouse, hospital, museum and bishop's seat, this mid-sized town of about 13,000 residents serves as an administrative, religious and cultural center of what is known as the Locride, an area that encompasses forty-two communities on the Ionian side of the province of Reggio Calabria.

Architecturally, Locri doesn't conform to an American's conception of what an Italian town should look like. Where were the old buildings? For a place founded seven centuries before Christ, the structures seemed rather modern. In actuality, the center of the once thriving Greek city-state was a few kilometers down the coast. However, as a result of the Roman conquest, invasions by the Saracens and Turks, and problems with malaria, the ancient settlement was ultimately abandoned and the people moved to safer territory in the hills. This flight to higher lands occurred all over Calabria. In Locri's case, the town was called Gerace. In the nineteenth century, the citizenry began moving back to coastal communities, reinforced by the budding railroad lines, and Gerace Marina eventually became independent, taking its new name from the original Greek colony.

Driving down the main street, Mario, the school's director, pointed out various stores, eateries and a few local landmarks— the piazzas, churches, the courthouse, municipal building, movie theater, and most importantly, the bars. Of course, in Italy when you talk of bars, you're talking about coffee. In Calabria, you can add pastries, and often gelato, and you never have to go very far to stumble upon another one. In Locri, elegant, modern bars lay behind many of the town's undistinguished, boxy, cement facades.

Coming from the train station, we stopped off in a lovely bar with a tearoom. Mario had originally spoken of another teacher arriving on the same train, but she changed her mind. Vacillation on the part of prospective mother-tongue English teachers was apparently not uncommon in Locri, to the point that when I missed my stop, Mario figured I was probably just another teacher not showing up. Perhaps these would-be educators either never figured out how to open the train door or they never made it past Naples.

So I was to be alone in the apartment, awaiting the arrival of the school's other teacher. Rather nice, the building sat in a courtyard off the main street. The doors were, in fact, quite solid; however, I was to learn that in the south of Italy the most important feature of any living quarters or workspace wasn't the security, but the southern exposure. Between the nonexistent or inadequate heating systems and poorly insulated windows, that balmy, 50-degree, outdoor winter temperature wasn't all that mild when experienced indoors.

I arrived in late October, however, with beautiful, Indian summer weather, perfect for long walks along the deserted beachfront. The flocks of vacationers, overwhelmingly Italian, had long since returned to the cities. The seaside businesses had packed up their lounge chairs, umbrellas, dressing cabins, bathrooms and entire restaurants and nightclubs, all stored away in an undisclosed location, to be taken out and reconstructed again the following June. One large, abandoned central building and a lone fisherman's shelter were left behind. On Sundays this 'men's only' beach refuge boasted animated conversation and card games. During the week, the occasional net was repaired, and boat cleaned and painted. At the other end of the beach, a group of fishing boats pulled up onto the sand served as an ad hoc fishmonger, where early birds could buy fresh fish from the briny hands of those who had caught them. Nearby, an unsmiling, kerchiefed old woman sat out in front of her house in cold weather, her back to the sea, her black clothes absorbing the warmth of the sun as it reflected off her bright, white wall.

Another summer had passed. Plants in public flower boxes were left to die, residents returned to their routines and children went back to school. I taught in a private, educational center for the study of English with mother-tongue teachers. The school occupied a roomy flat on the fourth floor of one of the taller buildings in town. Businesses as well as private apartments filled the five-story structure. At first, I taught in the school's larger classroom with a sea view. With the pleasant October temperature, I hadn't noticed the lack of centralized heating. As winter set in, I learned that the afternoon sun on the smaller room was far more effective than the inefficient space heater that consistently overloaded the power source. From January through March, my view inside the classroom was a sea of parkas.

The apartment had central heating, but it didn't carry very far into the room—radiators that didn't radiate. The cold began to set in around mid-November, which locals claimed was unheard of. I was experiencing the coldest winter on record. They would continue to say the same thing over the next few years.

Instruction began the week after my arrival with an Italian-Canadian married to a local filling in on the overflow. With 100% Calabrian blood, Sabrina had been waiting several years for her work visa to be approved. Mario sifted through resumes—all British. I had been an exception as my curriculum vitae showed European experience, plus I spoke Italian. No one seemed concerned that an American was an *extracomunitario* in the Locride.

AMERICANA AMERICANA

IS EVERYONE STARING OR is it just my imagination? I felt as though I had been dropped into a world where mothers never told their children it was impolite to stare.

Walking down the street, I had never seen so many heads turn. Had I all of a sudden become beautiful or was this merely part of small town living? Old men were the worst. They would stop in their tracks at a distance of a few feet or a few meters, depending on the strength of their prescription eyewear, mouth agape, as if stunned by my presence. Only their eyes followed my movements as I approached. Then as I passed, first the head, then the shoulders, hips, and finally they had to shuffle their feet 180 degrees to complete the ritual.

Initially, I thought this behavior was due to their having lost any inhibitions they may have once had, but then I realized that they were just doing what they had always done, what their fathers had done, and their grandfathers—old men occupying benches in the piazza, loitering in front of bars and standing in bars; middle-aged men positioning themselves in front of businesses, in stores, in bars; young men and boys hanging out in the piazza, in pizzerias, on soccer fields, in discotheques, in bars.

Calabria is full of males in groups *chiacchierando*–chatting. And the women? They're at home cooking, at least the older ones.

Staring from inside a vehicle is also a popular pastime. In Calabria, automakers could bring back the bench seat to facilitate rubbernecking. Drivers' heads bop all over the car trying to get a better look. These oglers feel invisible, as if they're behind windows in a police station interrogation room. Speeding cars suddenly slow down, which at times, can actually make crossing the street easier. Horn blowing is also an essential tactic in getting the object of interest to turn and look.

On Locri's beach drive, the U-turn is a common maneuver during the off-season. First, the driver slows, then passes at a good distance, turns around and positions himself for optimal viewing. Mario said that they were harmless, just curious to see an outsider. Sometimes they would try to engage me in conversation, but more often than not they were simply taking a long look. An attractive Ukrainian friend got herself a large dog to walk with.

I stuck out, not only wasn't I from the area, I didn't look

Italian. Tall and fair—the tourists were all gone, so who *was* I and what was I doing there? Gradually, the brothers with the fruit and vegetable stand, the man planted at the entranceway to his perfume shop and others began to ask these questions.

"I'm American." "*Un'americana?*" they'd respond inquisitively. I didn't look anything like the Americans they knew, Aunt Teresa and Cousin Anthony. "You're an *americana americana!*" they would exclaim. I was a real American. Italians often repeat words for emphasis.

The simplest reply was to just smile and say, "Yes." Perhaps a bit more complicated was explaining that we were all real Americans, any citizen of the United States of America, no matter where we came from or what we looked like, of course with the caveat that only Native Americans could claim indigenous resident status. Mention of my predominantly German heritage met with approval by those who thought I resembled the German tourists they observed in the summers, without the backpack and walking stick, that is.

Where in America did I come from? "I was born and raised in New Jersey." "*BELLO!*" An instinctive and completely different response from one you normally would hear in the states. Everyone had a relative or friend in the Garden State.

Why Italy? Why Calabria? Why Locri? "Beautiful country, wonderful food, friendly people." I occasionally told of my parents' connection with Italy, that my father had a degree from Rome's *La Sapienza* University. My parents lived in Rome for five years in the 1950s, my father a student, my mother working as a secretary and interpreter for Coca Cola. Interestingly, even the mighty multinational wasn't able to procure a work visa for my mother, a highly skilled, valued employee. Excessive bureaucracy has always made this issue and its avoidance fairly normal in Italy.

My parents' lives were enriched by their Italian experience. I grew up with an appreciation for Italy, particularly its food, eating more pasta than sauerkraut and knowing what *al dente* meant before it was in vogue. I was an *americana americana* with an affinity for the Italian culture.

When I arrived in Calabria, I already spoke Italian fairly well as I had been studying the language for a number of years, first on my own with books and recordings, and then in intensive language schools. I had spent a month at a time on study-vacations in Rome, Florence, Lucca, Sorrento and Taormina, opting for homestay accommodations to have the maximum opportunity of interacting with local people. I had passed an authorized language test at the level needed to study at an Italian university. After four years in Calabria, I passed an officially accredited examination certifying proficiency at the highest level of Italian for foreigners, equivalent to a mother-tongue speaker with a good cultural background. I'm not so presumptuous to liken myself to a native Italian speaker, but *me la cavo* (I get by).

Once engaged in dialogue, Italians show a great interest in the United States and Americans. Conversation piques curiosity, and Calabrians have a healthy inquisitiveness regarding the affairs of others. For many, no question is off-limits when couched by, "if I'm not being indiscreet." Of course, once that phrase has been uttered, the line has already been crossed, most often harmlessly, but best not to fan the flames. Information spreads quickly. The two questions asked most often by complete strangers: Are you married? Do you have children?

Less interest is generally shown in what you do. Incredibly, confusion sometimes arose as to my mother tongue and nationality. My first presentation at the Anglo-Italian Club of Reggio Calabria was entitled "An American in Italy." After speaking for an hour about my experiences in the United States and in Italy, I fielded the unbelievable question, "Are you British?" "No, I'm American." "But I understood you and I don't understand the Americans." Between film dialogue and pop music lyrics, we apparently have a reputation of unintelligibility. Admittedly, I have, on occasion, sought out the subtitle button while watching a Scottish or an Irish film, so I can appreciate their bewilderment.

An American teaching English also brought on some head scratching. "But you're American." I explain that we share the English language with the British. Considering the minor differences and to be more specific, I say that I speak American English. However, it's true. Logically, an *americana americana* should speak *americano*.

HAVE YOU GOT . . . ?

"HAVE YOU GOT A RUBBER?" "What? Excuse me?" "Have you got a rubber?" repeated the little girl with the pink glasses. She could see my confusion as it was my first day, so she showed me where it was. I smiled. The eight-year-old was only asking for something that would erase her pencil markings. Eraser=rubber, elevator=lift, truck=lorry, eggplant=aubergine. Maybe I do speak *Americano*. Knowing the common vocabulary differences between American and British English and using them in context were two separate matters.

The way in which the child phrased her question also set a distinct linguistic tone for me. In the United States, whenever someone started out with "Have you got . . . ," I immediately felt that I was probably going to want to put some distance between myself and the dubious stranger who was asking me for a cigarette, a light, some spare change, a dollar. In Italy, I had to get used to asking: "Have you got a brother?" "Have you got a dog?" "Have you got a bicycle?"

Why all the UK English? They've been around longer and they're in the European Union. English instruction now begins in elementary schools and sometimes in preschools. In Italy's high school English classes, they study Geoffrey Chaucer through Oscar Wilde, whether they can read at that level or not. What's more, the internationally recognized achievement exams normally taken in Italy are British. Of course, when someone wants to study outside of the EU, other tests are available.

My students did very well on the British examinations, despite my Americanness. I tried to use Britishisms consistently with beginning and lower intermediate pupils, especially when writing on the board, for example: John plays with his *favourite* toys *at* the weekend. Unfortunately, much is made of the differences by those who lack flexibility or don't know what the dissimilarities really are, thereby fostering the idea of 'American' as a separate language. I remember one simpleton insisting that American and British ambassadors needed translators to communicate with each other.

Americans, Canadians, Australians, New Zealanders and principally those from the United Kingdom and Ireland make up the mother-tongue work force in private English schools found all over Italy. Most public school English teaching is done in Italian, so these independent institutions offer students the opportunity of lessons completely in the target language with mother-tongue speakers. As Italians tend to study a great deal of grammar in their schools, I generally focused on communicative skills, putting into practice what they had often been taught in a very mechanical manner.

Mother-tongue English schools come in all sizes, and there are many chains, franchises, as well as individual institutions throughout the cities and towns of Italy. Calabria has numerous schools, many enrolling fewer than one hundred students. My school in Locri had around seventy-five, from preschool age through adult. Most of the classes were small, with about six participants, and adults often enrolled in individual instruction, called one-to-one in EFL/ESL (English as a Foreign/Second Language) parlance.

School children were grouped by age in Locri, which is common in Italy. Theoretically, as the younger pupils all study English at school, age should define the level. As I said, theoretically. In Calabria mixing an elementary student with middle school students or a middle school student with high school students and vice versa would not, as a rule, be considered. Italians put great stock in being graduated from one educational institution and proceeding to the next.

Up through the 1960s and even into the 1970s when poorer families sacrificed to send their children to school, these scholastic landmarks had a significance that still holds today, albeit without the sacrifice. In the 1960s, for example, although eight years of schooling was obligatory, many students dropped out of school before completing the compulsory education, giving value to a middle school diploma, particularly as opportunities for further study often didn't exist. And even through the end of the last century, only a high school diploma with a qualifying exam was needed to teach in a primary school.

Secondary school choices are rather varied in Italy, from the *Liceo* (High School) that can focus on the classics (Latin and Greek), science, languages, pedagogy or the arts, to the *Istituto tecnico* (Technical Institute) that follows a more practical course such as business and marketing or technological studies, and the *Istituto professionale* (Professional or Vocational Institute) that prepares students directly for the workplace in service industries or manufacturing and craft sectors. For instance, many of the high school age students at my English school in Locri went to the local *Liceo Scientifico* and the *Liceo Classico*. Although all students must take a basic course of study, the coursework is very directed in these institutions and Italians put these diplomas on their resumes even if they also attend college.

The secondary schools are located in larger towns and cities, and commutes can be quite long from small villages. In the province of Reggio Calabria (that includes the Locride), the public transportation system serves as the school bus, so schedules are set to coincide with student travel. Taking a bus or train during these hours can be quite unpleasant. Once on a train in Reggio, a group of 'students' ripped a pair of seats off their base and threw them out the window in a tunnel. Needless to say, I didn't see any Homer or Virgil amongst their belongings. Luckily, my students were the types who carried physics, Latin and philosophy books.

The Locri English school had a general, no-homework policy except when nearing their final exams. This approach set the expectation bar rather low. The thinking was that they already received more than enough homework from their regular schools. I worked through their texts in class, supplementing with as much interactive material as possible and hoping for a modicum of retention. Classes met twice weekly for an hour and twenty minutes each, an hour for the younger ones, and twenty to thirty minutes for the preschoolers. On the whole, the students were attentive and over time showed improvement. I suppose I couldn't have asked for more. Other than, have you got your homework?

THE MARKET

"*BELLA!*" THE MERCHANTS WEREN'T only staring, but they were shouting as well. "*Bella signora!*" I really must be more attractive than I thought, and that was a woman calling out to me. "*Bellissima!*" Well, I guess that clinches it.

Friday was market day in Locri, when the covered, open-air farmers' market spilled out to include the surrounding streets behind the town hall in the municipality's center. The streets were buzzing and the vendors were actively pedaling their wares. "These are from my garden." "I made the sausage myself, from my own pig." "I picked it this morning." "Taste my cheese."

I do like cheese. "What kind is it?" "*Pecorino.*" (Sheep's cheese.) It was good, aromatic but delicate. "What's that one?" "*Pecorino.*" They looked different, but the cheese-maker didn't volunteer information. Its rind was darker and was a bit firmer, a slightly stronger taste. It had been aged longer. "And that one?" "*Pecorino, da grattugiare*" (for grating). Calabrians eat a lot of *pecorino*. I went for the younger cheese, receiving a piece decidedly larger than I had indicated. I had to be firm on portion sizes or I'd always end up with extra. When it comes to food, Calabrians think big, family size.

With that cheese came a sampling of his father's *capocollo*, a cold cut made from the pig's neck. (*capo*=head, *collo*=neck) *Capicollo* or *capicolla* in English, the Calabrian variety has the Protected Designation of Origin (PDO) status given by the European Union to guarantee and protect quality regional products (in Italian, *Denominazione di origine protetta—DOP*). To produce, the meat is salted and massaged to both tenderize and distribute the salt, local herbs and spices, put in an intestinal casing and cured for up to six months, traditionally in a rough cloth. *Capicollo* has a subtle flavor, is a bit fatty in texture and is usually sliced very thinly, served as an appetizer, on a pizza or in sandwiches. Although the cheese maker's father massaged a delicious *capicollo*, I bought it by the slice at the *salumeria* (delicatessen).

Once a vendor has your attention, he or she tries to sell you everything he or one of his relatives in a nearby booth has to offer. At a certain point I had to smile, thank them and walk away, as dialogue wouldn't end naturally until I was staggering under the weight of my purchases.

"*Soppressata!*" Another merchant was waving a sharp knife with a slice of skewered salami in my direction. He had graciously pulled off the casing, so I tried the rustic-looking creation, a slightly crushed cylindrical shape, orange-red with flecks of white that had a strong flavor, slightly spicy, lightly smoked. This type of *soppressata* is found throughout southern Italy and is another PDO pork product of Calabria. Made from the best thigh meat, minced with pieces of lard, salt, pepper and *peperoncino* (hot pepper), possibly cumin and fennel depending on the locality, stuffed in a large intestine (thoroughly cleaned), the salami takes its name and shape from the pressing it undergoes during the drying process before its five- to six-month aging. Praised as far back as the eighteenth century by the famed Venetian adventurer Casanova, the *soppressata* stands up to the robust Calabrian red wines and is most often served as an appetizer with other meats, cheeses and bread.

Another product seen all over Calabria and sold in great abundance at grocery stores, specialty and tourist shops, as well as open-air markets is the *peperoncino* (hot pepper), a New World fruit long appreciated by the Calabrians and written about by travelers to the region as early as the seventeenth century. The climate suits the plant, yielding a quality product that Calabrians consume in ample quantities. Used in many of their sausage and cold cuts, in pasta sauces, and on pizza and *bruschetta*, the *peperoncino* is found on tables as a general condiment, fresh, in oil or dried. Many add a spoonful of what is often packaged for tourists as the "*bomba calabrese*" to whatever they eat—a mixture of finely chopped vegetables with a healthy dose of peperoncino in oil. Personally, dark chocolate with *peperoncino* is one of my favorites. At the market, I bought a scoop of the dried flakes to make the well-known *aglio* (garlic), *olio* (olive oil), *peperoncino* sauce for pasta.

I tended to buy my fruits and vegetables from the daily vendors, people who always managed to be the cousin of someone I knew. Calabria has wonderful greens— beet greens, turnip greens, chicory, an infinite variety of escarole, spinach, Swiss chard, bok choy, to name a few. Sometimes a farmer would have a pile of mystery greens splayed out on a table or in plastic bags in the back of his car, mumbling a name in dialect, assuring me they were extremely tender, had the most delicate flavor possible and were picked that morning— usually, all true. Calabrians from the older generations will boil up anything green, at least once. When faced with a pile of unfamiliar greens, I would ask how to trim them, what was edible, and the female farmers would always trim up a few stalks to demonstrate.

The male fishmongers would scratch their heads as I explained that I didn't really have a good knife and if they could not only clean the calamari but slice it for pan frying the rings, I would greatly appreciate it. They, too, weren't shy about giving basic cooking recipes for their fish. With the size of their anchovies, however, I, for one, couldn't fry them up and not worry about the bones.

Before heading back to my apartment, I purchased my favorite fall fruit—the persimmon. Although native to Asia, the *cachi* has been grown in Italy for about 150 years and is rather common. (By the way, *cachi* is invariable in Italian: 1 *cachi*, 2 *cachi*. The tree is also a *cachi*, but so is the color khaki!) I remembered them from my childhood when my parents would bring home the one or two decent persimmons they could find. We would wait until my father pronounced one to be ripe. He would then slice it open, rationing out a spoonful of the sweet, juicy pulp to each of us. Every so often, the spoonful would melt in your mouth, exquisite. In Italy, the experience is a matter of course. However, this round, red-orange fruit, the size of a large apple, must be eaten quite ripe or it can result in a strange, dry sensation, causing your tongue to stick to the roof of your mouth. Several different types exist, notably the yellower *vaniglia*, which is highly praised, although I prefer the classic variety. The persimmon isn't cultivated on a grand scale in Calabria, but you may just stumble upon a friend or local farmer who has a tree in his backyard.

On Friday mornings the merchants in Locri vary from very small-scale, a tiny table with one or two products to sell, to sizable operations that pull up in tractor trucks opening out to reveal complete, stainless steel butcher counters with rotisseries and grills, selling both raw and cooked meat. These bigger, commercial ventures follow the schedule of market days in the larger coastal towns.

As found all over Italy, Locri also features a nonfood open-air market, known for its Chinese merchandise and foreign vendors. I noted that "*bella*" wasn't used as liberally in that atmosphere. As I figured it, either I wasn't beautiful in that context or those markets weren't where the beautiful people went to shop. Either way, for nonfood items I frequented regular retail establishments, as those markets weren't where I wanted to be.

2

INITIAL EXPLORATIONS

ASPROMONTE MOUNTAINS

FIRST VISIT TO REGGIO

AFTER A FEW WEEKS WITHIN Locri's perimeters, I decided it was time to branch out. The employees at the visitor information center were sympathetic, but limited with regard to sightseeing particulars in the off-season, especially without a car. As a consolation, one industrious member of the staff invited me to the neighboring bar where I drank a pear juice and he, a Campari at 10 o'clock in the morning.

Looking over confusing bus routes and schedules of the Locride, I opted on the rails for my first outing as the choice was either north or south. It was my birthday, a sunny Saturday morning in November, and I was headed for Reggio Calabria, an hour and a half ride along the Ionian coast. The train was from the same era as the one I had taken from Rome. The efficient conductor, positioning his brightly striped glasses on the end of his nose from their place of rest on the cord around his neck, punched the de rigueur hole in the ticket I had bought at a travel agent's the day before. He seemed surprised, informing me that in the absence of an active ticket window, such as in Locri, tickets could be purchased on the train as only a handful of the larger stations had personnel staffing them. He then rattled off that evening's return schedule and sold me an open ticket to go back.

The sea was calm. The gray-green Aspromonte Mountains rose on the other side of the tracks, beyond the seaside towns and the hills, forming a barrier between the Ionian and Tyrrhenian Seas. About halfway through the trip I saw what seemed to be a peak amidst clouds. I wasn't aware of such a prominent mountain behind Reggio. Then it dawned on me that the mountain was a volcano and I was looking at Mt. Etna and the coastline of Sicily. Spectacular. We had traveled south, then west, and as we turned north around the toe toward Reggio, the volcano receded over my left shoulder as the train progressed along the Strait of Messina.

Reggio di Calabria, also called Reggio Calabria or simply Reggio, is the capital of the province with the same name, Reggio Calabria. With a population of over 186,000 and more than 270,000 in the metropolitan area, it is Calabria's largest urban center. The city takes its name from Rhegion, the Greek colony founded on the spot eight centuries before Christ, the first in present-day Calabria. However, between earthquakes and invasions, not much of the ancient peoples is still visible. Over one hundred years since the catastrophic 1908 earthquake and its accompanying tsunami that devastated Reggio and Messina from its epicenter in the Strait, Reggio's downtown appears relatively modern by Italian standards, with lovely art nouveau architecture flanking the main street, Corso Garibaldi, and along the coastal road, Via Marina.

The central train station faces none other than Piazza Garibaldi, more of a parking lot and bus depot than an English speaker's romanticized idea of what a piazza should look like. The obligatory statue of the "hero of two worlds" stands at its center, pigeons gracing its head. Corso Garibaldi runs along the other end of the piazza, continuing the length of downtown for about two kilometers, becoming a pedestrian zone at the Villa Comunale, the city park, until ending up at Piazza De Nava and the Museo Archeologico Nazionale di Reggio Calabria.

The archeological museum is often referred to as the museum of Magna Graecia or Greater Greece, as the collection focuses on the period of Greek expansion and colonization in Calabria. When I arrived in Locri, I was lucky to get to know the museum before its extended closing due to renovations. On this, my first visit, I had planned on spending several hours viewing the exhibits, so I fortified myself with a chocolate *cornetto* (croissant) and a pot of tea on my walk from the station. Opposite the piazza with its statue of the local, turn-of-the-last-century politician Giuseppe De Nava (and his pigeons), I entered the world of Magna Graecia through the doors of an impressive Fascist edifice with a frieze of ancient coins sculpted into its Travertine marble facade.

After using the restroom, which in itself would have caused the building's closure in the U.S. due to health and safety regulations, I went into the first hall dedicated to the local population before the Greeks' arrival. The guard I had passed at the entrance approached me, talking enthusiastically about the collection and offering to guide me through the museum. Was I on candid camera? Or was this just Calabria's bizarre twist on the surly Italian museum guard? I thought, "Aren't you supposed to be out back smoking, mumbling in a disgruntled fashion?" Now if he had a colleague who wasn't as informed about the exhibits but wanted to go 'above and beyond' cleaning the bathrooms, they would have really had something.

Joking aside, the museum possesses a wealth of culture and my guide gave me the perspective to appreciate it. The artistic quality of the artifacts is remarkable—from the decorative pottery and the bronze and iron implements of the indigenous people through the articles made by the Greeks and Romans. Many visitors race to see the famous Bronzes of Riace, largely ignoring the bulk of the exhibits; however, before the two magnificent life-size bronze statues were discovered, restored and put on display in Reggio, the museum already had a world-class collection. Many items on display come from Locri Epizephyrii, including large temple statues in marble, bronze tablets in ancient Greek, terracotta pictures from religious ceremonies, and small household articles and funerary objects in bronze, terracotta, ivory and bone. The city of Rhegion is also well represented, most notably with the marble Kouros, a young boy with a mysterious smile and curly red hair from the sixth century BC and two bronze heads discovered off the coast of nearby Porticello. Other ancient Greek colonies in Calabria are also represented, such as Metauros (present-day Gioia Tauro), Medma (Rosarno), Hipponion (Vibo Valentia), Kaulon (Monasterace Marina), Laos (Marcellina) and Krimissa (Cirò Marina). However, a move is underway to restore some of the artifacts to the towns of their origin, and today, when new relics are uncovered, they often remain within their communities with the establishment of new museums.

My guide had a lot of stamina and I suppose I did too, but after about three or four hours of intense concentration as he was speaking extremely quickly and was throwing a fair amount of new vocabulary at me, we agreed to take a break and I went out for lunch. Many restaurants didn't seem to be serving lunch, so I entered the first sit-down place I came across on Via Marina. I had one of the specials, *pasta e fagioli con le cozze*, a variation on the classic pasta and beans with the addition of mussels. Often this dish is listed as a soup in the U.S. as it is a *pasta a minestra* or pasta in soup, as opposed to *pasta asciutta*, literally dry pasta, signifying a non-liquid sauce, such as *spaghetti al pomodoro* (with tomato sauce) or *tagliatelle alla bolognese* (with a meat and tomato sauce from Bologna). Pasta and soup are considered *primi piatti* (first courses) in an Italian restaurant and would usually be followed by a *secondo piatto* (second course) of meat or fish. I didn't want to overeat, so I ordered a *contorno* (side dish) of grilled zucchini and eggplant as an abbreviated 'second.'

Having immersed myself in the art and history of Magna Graecia that morning, to accompany my meal I chose a beverage that dated back to the Greek period, a dry, white, local wine made from the greco bianco grape, originally planted in Calabria several millennia ago. As I was finishing, an assorted group of five adults with one small child came in and sat down at the table next to mine. The woman who appeared to be the leader looked me right in the eye, so I smiled and greeted her. Several sentences passed between us and she insisted that I join them. As at the market or in any situation, for that matter, once I got into a conversation with someone, I had trouble interrupting and excusing myself—not that I had anywhere to go, but my intention hadn't been to crash their luncheon. However, these friends and colleagues wanted to offer me their hospitality, welcoming me to their homeland, as curious about where I came from as they were eager to share their backgrounds and traditions. And if in doubt a good time was had by all, there was the evidence of the two empty bottles of *spumante* (sparkling wine), allegedly consumed in honor of my birthday.

Being sure to avail myself of the restaurant's facilities before I left, I returned to the museum until the shops opened up. Everything closed down from about 1 to 5 p.m., like a ghost town, and then within half an hour not a parking space was to be found. Returning to the station, I weaved in and out of the Saturday evening crowd or maybe I was just weaving on my own accord. Window shopping along Corso Garibaldi, Reggio's fashionable pedestrian street, I reflected on the delightful day I had passed, looking forward to my next visit and the experiences the provincial capital and its citizens had to offer.

THE LOCAL POST OFFICE OR TAKING CARE OF BUSINESS, JUST NOT YOURS

I KNOW ABOUT MUSSOLINI and the trains, but I don't remember hearing his success with package delivery bandied about. Americans take pleasure in bellyaching about their postal workers, but in comparison to the employees down in the tip of the boot, our "Newmans" are fairly efficient. When you walk into an Italian post office today, things appear to be fairly well organized. There's a bright yellow machine from which you select the service you require. Out pops a slip of paper with a letter and a number on it and you wait until your combination materializes on a screen that directs you to the appropriate window. Not just for the mail and your odd money order, the post office has banking, bill pay and collects some taxes, which I suppose was calculated to minimize the risk of loss if the payments were sent through their system.

One sunny, autumn day, all I wanted was a few stamps. It was usually easier to get them from the tobacco shops that sold everything from chewing gum to lottery tickets. The one on the main street in Locri even had a slot machine, but they didn't know anything about stamps for out of the country and they only had one choice of stamp to go with the ten choices of birthday cards they had to offer. Surprisingly, they were all Hallmarks and it looked as though they had been around for a while as they were up on the rack still in their little bags of about ten each. I suppose you could say that the store was really prepared for approximately 100 birthdays. It looked as though the little bags had either been in the store for a number of years or someone had taken them out and kicked them around the beach for a while, as it was hard not to soil the card after touching the bag.

So with my Hallmark in hand, I set off for the local post office. Upon arrival, I located the bright yellow machine, pressed the button next to the picture of an envelope and I then became P76 for the next 45 minutes. When I entered P68 was being served, so the future didn't seem all that bleak. Of course as P68 stood at the window having what only seemed to be an occasional interaction with the woman behind the glass, I couldn't help but think that maybe it was P68 who was holding up the works not having filled out his forms correctly. However, after P68 left, there wasn't any action whatsoever at window 8. Window 7 just next door was the postal business window. A young man stood at that counter for a while. He seemed to have lists of things. When he left, the older woman with glasses on a chain working that window made an initial effort to look busy. She straightened a few piles of paper, looked at her equipment for a spell, and we all waited for P69 to appear over window 7, as the woman at window

8 must have gone on a break. The woman with the glasses on the chain obviously would have needed to put them up to her face to have noticed the group of people waiting. However, she retired to the back room, so maybe it was her break time, too.

There was also a window 9 with a woman sitting behind it. The number 9 had been covered up and the box above the window with the lighted number seemed to be permanently disabled. I didn't know what her job was, but when the locals who announced they were in a hurry approached her glass partition, she showed that she was very important, indeed, and P77 and P78 realized that they had to wait with the rest of us. (Of course, windows 1 through 6 were for other business and although there were very few customers on that side of the building, obviously none of those employees had the training to help out in the difficult task of selling stamps and giving out packages.)

All I can say is that it was good that P71 and P72 decided to leave or I certainly wouldn't have been served at all that day. When I finally got up to the counter, the woman had to look in a book for the postage rates to the U.S. She then retrieved a large notebook from a shelf with cellophane pages under which there were stamps of different denominations and she began searching for the stamps she needed. After that she wrote the following on a piece of paper:

1 x 1,50 €
1 x 0,65 €

for the two stamps to the US. Next, she got one stamp out for Europe and took out a fresh piece of paper and wrote:

1 x 0,85 €
1 x 1,50 €
1 x 0,65 €

I'm not sure why the European stamp price couldn't have been added to the prices of the stamps for the U.S. She took out a calculator and did the arithmetic. I slipped my coins under the partition. She slipped back a few in change and I was finally on my way. She wasn't an unpleasant person.

That evening, the school secretary handed me a postal slip that was put in the mailbox most likely at the same time I was standing on line at the post office. I was happy that I would be able to tell my sister that her package had arrived after a month or so of "not yet." That night I looked closer at the slip and saw that there was a charge of 11,29 € for what appeared to be my signature and that I was directed to retrieve the package at the non-existent window number 9. I also reflected on the secretary's comment that it was good I spoke Italian as the postal employees weren't averse to pulling an occasional fast one on unsuspecting clients. These thoughts didn't make for a restful sleep.

The following morning, I made my way back to the post office. I was P21. The light in window 8 was not functioning and when I entered there was an old man standing at the window with a middle-aged man "assisting" him. The employee walked away after about 2 minutes and never returned. P20 tried to tell the elderly gentleman that no one was ever going to come back as apparently that computer didn't work, but he never budged, like a dog waiting for his owner, and to use the expression loosely, business carried on as usual.

I went up to the woman behind the glass in window 9 and said I was there to pick up a package. She said that she didn't do that. I said that she needed to tell that to whoever filled out the postal slips, as both P20 and I had pieces of paper directing us to window 9. She made no response. After about 5 minutes, the same woman who eventually waited on me the day before approached window 7 and number P20 lit up above. P20 approached the counter and without a word the woman walked away. She came back a few minutes later with a generic spray bottle marked "alcohol" that was filled with a pink liquid. She then systematically squirted the contents of said plastic container all over her workplace, not leaving a millimeter to chance. Obviously, one of her coworkers must have had the cooties. When she had finished her leisurely, yet deliberate wiping, she turned her attention to P20, taking his slip and disappearing once again into the back room from where she eventually emerged with a solitary letter. Judging by the number of signatures P20 left behind and the multiple rubber stamps brought into play, that must have been one important little envelope he walked away with that day.

P21. I slid the slip under the glass and she asked me for ID. I passed her my driver's license and she wrote down everything but my height and weight, most likely because she didn't understand the English measurements. She then started saying something about a charge. I said that there must be a mistake. I'm sure that the person in the U.S. paid the correct amount. She said that it was a charge for customs. I said that on the slip, the customs spot was not filled out. She then pulled out the customs form stuck on top of the box. The charges:

Postal charges:	2.50 € for presentation in customs
	3.00 € for postal expenses
Customs charges:	0.93 € duty (4% of claimed value of item)
	4.86 € tax (20% of claimed value of item)

The box had also been opened, so I asked her if there was actually anything still inside. The customs people had obviously cut the tape and then stuck the flaps back into the little USPO box. She opened the flap and a little package wrapped in my sister's characteristic style slipped out along with a small card. So, I paid the lady and went around to the box area, because the security glass didn't allow for more than a thick envelope. The postal worker turned the big hand crank to open the door and placed the little box of an inch in height and a six-inch width into a space that could have held a medium-sized refrigerator. Walking away with package in hand after the first attempt, I had apparently met with success on my visit. For a simple deposit the secretary had spent almost three hours there with her grandmother a few days earlier. On that occasion, the other side of the building was full of people and the mail division hardly had any clients.

Maybe that old man had been hired to stand in front of the window with the broken computer in order to make the employees look busy. He had been instructed to wait wherever there seemed to be the most confusion.

God Bless the USPS.

SIDERNO

HOME OF THE LONGEST *SGUTA* IN THE WORLD, a 520-meter (1706-foot) Calabrian Easter bread filled with eggs, hard-boiled right into the dough, Siderno displays its specialty on little tables arranged in a line down the center of the main street, closed to traffic for Pasquetta and other festivals, as well as the popular Saturday night stroll. As with Locri, Siderno Marina developed in the nineteenth century from its historic nucleus in the hills four kilometers away. Siderno Superiore, as it is referred to, retains its medieval layout and several Baroque buildings even after the destructive earthquake that shook most of Calabria in 1783.

The coastal town, now just called Siderno, is a small industrial center producing bricks, cement, soap, pasta and handicrafts, and its beautiful beach makes it a hub of tourism in the summer. Boasting the largest population of the Locride, about 18,000, Siderno also has the most comprehensive downtown shopping area, strongly recommended to me by the good citizens of Locri. There's also an indoor swimming pool and a mall in the outskirts.

Ever in the search of a comfortable shoe, I decided to take the five-minute train ride to this neighboring town and see what the talk was all about. One morning a little before ten, three rather tall policemen and I got onto the train going north. Quite a few people were standing due to the unaccounted for presence of numerous teenagers during school hours. I pantomimed a ticket transaction in the direction of the green-jacketed conductor at the end of the compartment, but he didn't budge from his seat. As I pondered pushing past the passengers in the aisle, the train arrived and I exited with an extra Euro in my pocket.

Siderno's downtown was larger and more visually pleasing than Locri's. I tried on several pairs of everyday shoes in a no-frills store, deciding on an Italian-made casual that seemed fairly comfortable. I also thought that the style might have helped me blend better, although I doubt that all the heads turning on the street were motivated by my footwear. I didn't question the 10-Euro discount the salesman gave me. Italians never make a mistake in the customer's favor, so he must have had his reasons. Perhaps he figured that I didn't know how to ask for a discount and he didn't want to hold it against me. Calabrians aren't shy about requesting a *sconto*.

I then stumbled upon a clothing store with big sale signs in the window, of the "everything must go" variety. I lucked upon two pairs of wool pants that would turn out to be lifesavers in cold classrooms and apartments.

My next stop was the pharmacy. The small grocery stores had a limited selection of personal products, and I wanted a facial soap with an exfoliant. The only product fitting my basic parameters scanned at 10.50. I was surprised at the price and must have shown a reaction, as the clerk/pharmacist immediately gave me a Euro discount. These Euros were starting to add up. I would discover that many drug stores gave small discounts on nonprescription products—all you had to do was ask.

At that point, I was starting to get hungry and asked the pharmacist where I could have a nice lunch for a good price—a perfectly normal question in Italian. As she started describing a restaurant, a woman who had just walked in piped up with a different place. We started talking and after a few minutes she said, "Why don't you come to my house for lunch?" Of course, I thanked her, saying I couldn't impose, etc. She insisted, even speaking some English as she had lived in upstate New York for seven years. I thought, "She seems nice, why not?" The only catch was that she lived in the countryside outside of town, although she said that she would bring me back to either the Siderno station or directly to Locri. We ran into her mother and a cousin from Australia as we were leaving the pharmacy, then another cousin sitting outside in a car.

As we approached Marisa's car, a gypsy came up to us with her hand out. I thought, "Siderno must be more affluent, as I haven't seen any panhandlers in Locri." This Rom, politically correct term for gypsy that I never heard in Calabria, started whining about how many mouths she had to feed. Marisa responded, "I can't help you, I have five children of my own." As we turned away, I said to her, "I thought you told me you had four children." "Yes, I have four." To me, four should have been an impressive enough number to ward off alms requests, but I suppose she felt five had more impact.

As I was weighing this numerical discrepancy, Marisa gestured towards a car with two men in the front seat. They weren't the most refined looking characters I'd ever seen, and I began questioning my safety. She introduced her son as the driver and her husband in the passenger seat. I found comfort in their discomfort. Only Marisa seemed unfazed by it all. The younger man navigated the incredibly pitted dirt roads as though they had been newly paved. We arrived quickly. They lived on a farm, a modest, one-story, contemporary house amidst fields, cows, vegetable plants.

We entered the great room, a modern kitchen with a sizable workspace at one end, a long, wide, heavy wooden table down the middle and a fireplace and television at the other end. Her husband Cosimo walked in and switched on the TV, turning up the volume. Either he was hard of hearing or he didn't want to talk. He then proceeded to start a fire by lighting pieces of paper at the gas stove and carrying the little blazing balls 200 feet across the room.

Marisa began getting things out of the refrigerator, handing Cosimo what looked like a plastic pitcher for lemonade. I set the table for four with plastic cups and plates, and Cosimo returned from the workroom next door with the container full of homemade wine. Their older son had just dropped us off, but their youngest, a 10-year-old, ate lunch at home as Italian schools usually finish around 1 p.m. so children can eat with their families. Their daughters were studying at a university in the north.

Although our place settings were store-bought, the food on them was not. We started out with an antipasto consisting of various vegetables from their garden that had been marinated in their own olive oil. Calabria is well known for its products *sotto olio* (under oil), such as eggplant, sundried tomatoes, perperoncino, olives, mushrooms, Tropean onions, artichokes, wild chicory and mixed vegetables. Historically a method of preserving vegetables, these products are now eaten as an antipasto, served with bread, cheese and cured meats. We ate Marisa's *verdura sott'olio* with local cheese—pecorino, and her homemade bread—not from a machine.

Although our spaghetti came out of a box as very few people still make their own pasta for everyday consumption, Marisa prepared it with tomato sauce from her own *passata di pomodoro* (tomato puree). The veal that followed had been cooked in the pasta sauce, a common relationship between the first and second courses. The calf had until recently lived in the barn a stone's throw from our table. We were literally eating off the land and everything was quite flavorful. Cosimo turned the volume down on the TV, and conversation flowed.

After we ate, the other son came back and I believe I had my first taste of an extended use of the Calabrian dialect—I felt lost. Cosimo was signing a pile of papers, and I had the vague impression that some cows had been sold. I helped Marisa with the washing up, quite a bit despite the paper plates. The Australian relatives stopped by, more dialect, a little Italian, some English, and they accompanied me back to my apartment in Locri (another Euro pocketed).

Marisa and her family had gone out of their way to welcome me. "*L'ospite è sacro.*" The guest is sacred. This Italian expression comes from the Greeks who believed it was man's duty to welcome strangers. Calabrians feel as though they own this proverb through their heritage, and often the hospitality involves food in great quantities.

I doubt the Locresi had such an adventure in mind when they had encouraged me to visit Siderno—apart from the pants and shoes, that is. Neighboring towns can be competitive. Whether you come from Locri or Siderno makes a difference, although the people come together to share a province and a region, particularly once they step outside of Calabria. Later that evening when I told the school's secretary of my wonderful day, mentioning the need to have my slacks hemmed, she informed me her aunt was a seamstress. Naturally, I brought them to her. You keep it all in the family, just as Mario's sister-in-law cut my hair.

3

CULTURAL DISTINCTIONS

FRONT DOOR OF A PRIVATE DWELLING IN BOVA

ROOMMATES AND COWORKERS

"I'VE BEEN USING YOUR TOOTHPASTE. I'll get some more when we finish this." The joys of having a roommate—I felt a little lonely before she arrived, but this sort of togetherness was more than I could handle.

"Cheers!" Yes, she was from the UK. The first time we walked down the street together, some of the people who hadn't ever addressed me smiled and greeted me. Perhaps escorting a guest gave me a sense of permanency. Either that or my new coworker's Che Guevara-look may have caught their attention. She was most likely the first woman seen in the Locride wearing a red beret together with black pants stuffed into army boots. In my new Italian shoes, I must have seemed like a local by comparison.

Italians often asked me how I felt, immersed in their culture, far from my homeland. They assumed that I would have had more in common with the British or other English-speakers than with the Italians. "Every group has their characteristics, but people are people," I would respond. In Calabria, I had British, Irish, Canadian and Australian colleagues, several of whom had blood ties to Italy. Some could barely say "hello" and "goodbye" in Italian, while others spoke fairly well. A few didn't even express themselves satisfactorily in English.

My roommate in Locri continued her antics, both in the apartment and at the school. After a month, her boyfriend arrived from England, compounding the irritation. I eventually moved into another apartment that I liked better, in the center of town across from the city park, a pleasant green area to walk through as I came and went. I was free from looking at the tomato stains on the wall where they had missed the garbage can or watching them blow smoke on our communal porch, their heads leaning up against my bedroom window. "Keep the toothpaste."

I was surprised what colleagues could get away with under the guise of cultural differences. The appropriation of your coworkers' school supplies was just considered idiosyncratic behavior. Since I was able to make myself understood, I couldn't possibly exhibit the quirky conduct of the fish out of water.

Charlie was my favorite colleague, a true English gentleman, the bumbling country type. Sometimes I wondered if he weren't playing the role. It was as if he had a list of eccentricities and when he got bored, he'd pick one. I don't think he knew how much hanging his socks on the clothesline without clothespins aggravated the landlord, for instance. How he got those socks to dance without falling, I'll never know. His socks weren't wanted in the garden below, however, and I'd be the one given the job of explaining to him the importance of the clothespin, and its use, if necessary.

I lived in four different apartments in Locri and three in Reggio. After the experience with the first roommate, I always had my own place. However, I wasn't immune to the cultural conflicts experienced between English teachers and property owners. Dear old Charlie wasn't the only one who inspired an Italian landlord to compose a list of house rules seeking my help with the English translation. Surprisingly, the number one complaint of offensive behavior committed by foreign teachers had to do with the windows. Rule number one: *Cambiare aria!* (Literally, change the air!) Although this expression can also refer to taking a break or having a change of scenery, the intent in this case was to air out the apartment. Italians generally do this on a daily basis, even in winter.

As it was often colder inside than out during the cooler

periods in Calabria, the frequent opening of the windows could only improve the living conditions. Most importantly, the level of humidity in many buildings made the opening of windows an absolute necessity. Problems with mold and mildew were rampant, as without centralized heating dampness was able to fester for months on end. Smells accumulated quickly, particularly in classrooms. I would have to hold myself back from saying to a colleague upon entering their room, "Why don't you open the window a bit?" Best left to an Italian. I just didn't want them to steal my books or whiteboard markers.

While opening the windows could have been considered more of a cultural rule, shutting off the lights was pure dollars and cents. Utilities are extremely expensive in Italy, and Calabrians are careful about their consumption. Some landlords took this to the extreme, forcing tenants to find the keyhole by the feel method while others understood normal usage for safety and convenience.

My apartment near the city park in Locri had a landlord with the personal touch, leaving bags of oranges from their property in the country on my front stoop, even inviting me to dinner with their family on occasion. A different type of personal touch was the hand of a landlord in Reggio inappropriately placed on my knee as we returned from what he called an obligatory trip to the appliance store. I needed to accompany him so I could supervise the delivery of the correct washing machine—the cheapest.

Of course, slamming doors is universal, but one landlord was particularly absorbed by the comings and goings of a colleague, seemingly because he opened and closed his door exceptionally quietly at what the proprietor considered odd hours. What must he have been doing, indeed? As long as he wasn't fouling my bathroom or hiding the class registers, I wasn't interested in the least.

THE COUNTRYSIDE

PRIMITIVE, UNDEVELOPED, SIMPLE, NATURAL—in Calabria, you have to take the good with the, well, not so good. How, uh, charming when a well-spoken, well-dressed adult reminisces of a childhood spent in the countryside, setting mousetraps in the fields, then roasting and eating the rather tasty morsels as a family affair. No need to remove the hair from the little creatures before cooking because the fire will take care of that straightaway.

At least a year before I ever thought about living in Calabria, I stumbled on a used paperback novel by a writer from the Locride at a Rome street market. Saverio Strati was born in 1924 in the inland village of Sant'Agata del Bianco and for 1 Euro I became acquainted with the struggles of the Calabrian poor. *Mani vuote* (*Empty Hands*, 1960) is set in the years just after the 1908 earthquake and is told through the eyes of a boy trying to survive in a primitive, brutal environment of peasant farmers and woodsmen, scoundrels and the economically advantaged. Despite carefully laid plans and working to complete exhaustion, the lad always came up empty handed in a world stacked against him.

A hundred years later, one stark reality has been exchanged for another. The dramatic slopes of the Aspromonte Mountains provide the backdrop, the rugged, beige and olive-green hills the middle ground and the narrow coastal plain is the new front line for many who migrated from their small villages. Unfortunately, stepping back to the sea, the erstwhile postcard view of the distant landscape is too often marred by unsightly abandoned construction, multilevel cement frameworks with rusted metal spikes reaching haphazardly skyward. Luckily, picturesque angles can still be found along the *Costa dei Gelsomini* or the *Riviera dei Gelsomini* (The Jasmine Coast or Riviera). The fragrant jasmine plant flourishes throughout the province and in particular along this strip of land along the Ionian coast between Capo Sparivento just south of Brancaleone and Punta Stilo in

Monasterace Marina. Taking advantage of the cheap labor, the delicate white flowers of this hardy climber were once cultivated in the area, harvested by women called *gelsominaie* and sold by weight to French perfumers.

The jasmine's sweet scent trails up into the hills amidst the unfinished construction projects also found in small towns and throughout the countryside. It would seem that the dream of every Calabrian parent is to add another level onto the family house for each child. Even the grown children who have long since left the area for jobs in the north need a place to stay when they return to their village for holidays and vacations, not to mention the relatives from abroad. Until funds are secured, the skeletal top floor serves as an excellent place to hang laundry, open on the sides for better drying and for all to see. Owners are immune to the exposed cinderblock of the rough fabrications. Neighbors become acclimatized to these eyesores, begun before they can remember and destined to remain works in progress long after they've gone.

Once leaving the better-paved streets of the larger coastal towns, the driver encounters more challenging roads leading to the villages and the mountains beyond. Residents bumpily speed over and around all of the obstacles in a manner that would be considered incredibly dangerous by ordinary American standards. Each and every driver negotiates the dips and curves as if he or she actually owns that strip of irregular gravel, even when confronted by an equally secure motorist barreling along in the opposite direction. No time to smell the jasmine.

Every once and a while, however, a commuter may be forced to inhale an odor a bit more earthy. In this case, lingering behind a flock of sheep isn't the same as slowly savoring a pungent *pecorino* cheese at dinner. Busy, modern lives don't leave extra time to wait for farm animals. I was taught that if you happen to get behind a flock of sheep, whatever you do, locate the shepherd and get as close behind him as quickly as possible. If not, you'll find yourself jostled about by a pack of ignorant creatures in a way that somehow just won't be as enjoyable as it seemed in your favorite foreign film.

The single donkey laden with his master's wares provides a much more pleasant agricultural tourism experience. Perhaps disappointingly, the beast's owner won't be dressed in the stereotypical clothing of the peasant farmer as in post second world war, neorealist Italian film productions. He may even be listening to an iPod. Back in town, the occasional herding of cows along the beach reinforces the quaint rural imagery, but only outside the tourist season when there's room to maneuver.

Off the beaten path, Calabria is not like Tuscany with its picture-perfect towns overlooking orderly olive groves, rows of exquisitely trimmed cypress trees and manicured villas. Calabria is untamed—eclectic architecture, wild banks of giant prickly pear cactus, fields of olives and oranges atop its irregular, undulating landscape and impenetrable, craggy mountains. Calabria has a beauty of its own, and winding up those erratic southern roads brings rewards of breathtaking views from the rough-hewn Aspromonte Mountains across the more hospitable hills to the sea. On a clear day and with the proper altitude, a bonus glimpse of Mount Etna can be had even from the Ionian side.

The mountains are well worth exploring, but if invited for an excursion, it's best to get all of the particulars straight before your departure. Don't underestimate a question, such as, "Do you have enough gas in that thing?" The type of Italian accustomed to actually living the occasional scene that we find so colorful, amusing, or even poignant when viewed on the big screen doesn't worry about a motorcycle running out of gas on the top of a snow-covered mountain on a late Sunday afternoon. And surprise, surprise, that blackberry doesn't get a signal. Of course, finding yourself in such a predicament on the peak is certainly preferable to being stranded facing a long ascent. But as anyone who's ever done the zigzags of a mountain road knows, it's not always a straight shot down. For the periodic inclines, Fred

Flintstone's stone-age vehicle would be much better suited for the type of pedaling required. The people were shorter in those days and clearly wouldn't have been able to reach the ground from the back seat of a motorcycle. I guess that's why this film would have to be called *An American in Calabria*, as without a pair of long, northern European legs scurrying along from the back seat, the adventure might not have been quite as successful.

4

Holidays

Ceramic Nativity figures from Seminara,
Ethnographic Museum in Palmi

CHRISTMAS

THE APPEARANCE OF DECORATIVE STREETLIGHTS symbolizes the coming of Christmas, in towns, cities and the smallest of villages. As I fumbled in the dark to find the lock on my front door, I thought, "Either the municipalities must pay a lower electric rate than its individual citizens or this expression of joy must be of utmost importance to city council members throughout the region."

December 8th, The Immaculate Conception, is a national holiday in Italy. My first year in Locri, I happened to be out walking that evening, when several loud noises and big sparks led me to join the small crowd assembled in the town square. The street had been closed off for the arrival of the event's protagonists, ceremoniously transported by a tractor customized with gray and beige sails, and large horns on the front and back.

Accompanied by the sorrowful tune of a lone, live trumpet, a girl in Goth attire evocatively danced around a simple May pole. Canned music then ushered in four young people on stilts, dressed in the same gray and beige as the tractor. The whole production had a very 'Cirque du soleil' atmosphere about it. The stilt-walkers waltzed around, occasionally shooting off fireworks from their hands. At one point, the Goth girl lit the four strands of the May pole and paced around with a little box that apparently had some representational purpose for the director, possibly the heavyset man who at times danced around and at other times focused on repositioning the tractor with the gear set in neutral. The lighting of a suspended string of fireworks signaled the grand finale and received the requisite smattering of applause—an auspicious heralding of the season and a favorable first encounter with the Calabrian artistic community.

"*Buon Natale!*" Merry Christmas! For schoolchildren and many throughout the peninsula the holiday season extends from several days before Christmas through Epiphany, January 6th. In this period, Calabrians move en masse toward their hometowns, boarding overcrowded trains and driving congested highways as they head south from northern Italy and Europe. Recent overseas transplants make the journey from the Americas and Australia.

Many Italians attend Catholic Mass on Christmas Eve and/or Christmas Day, especially in Calabria. Most celebrate with family. However, 100% honor the period gastronomically. On my first Christmas in Calabria, I became a part of that custom, beginning with a *cenone* (big dinner) on Christmas Eve at Mario's—or at least that's what I thought when he invited me.

I had anticipated a traditional meal of fish; however, when I arrived, apart from two small, active children, the house lacked the usual holiday bustle and more importantly was devoid of even a hint of aroma to presage the evening's meal. As Mario showed me around his spacious, brand-new condominium, I came to the conclusion that we were going out. I had misunderstood. The kitchen was spotless; the marble countertops gleamed. I wasn't yet used to the late dinner hour, and just when I thought I was going to faint from hunger, his home was invaded by what seemed to be an unending stream of old people carrying huge trays full of food. It was his in-laws and assorted elderly relatives. He and his wife had built above her parents, who lived on the ground floor and cooked in the large basement kitchen—a common home feature in the area.

With this whirlwind of activity, the dinner had begun. The

antipasto was a Christmas Eve classic, *le zeppole** (also called *crespelle*), fried dough balls filled with anchovies or cheese (also plain, with sundried tomatoes, olives or other fillings). Although delicious, I only put one on my plate knowing that I was going to have to survive several courses. My hosts convinced me to try one of each, which turned out to be dangerous as the serving method was to lift the tray and let the balls start rolling. I ended up with five, each one with a diameter of about three inches. Being a guest wasn't always easy in Calabria.

Pasta with a tomato-based seafood sauce was followed by a second course of the seafood that had been cooked in and given flavor to the sauce. An abundant platter of assorted fried fish came next. I was happy for the light salad of shredded lettuce and fennel, although Mario had been hoping for a more substantial side dish, joking that he could have eaten the vegetables through a straw. Perhaps he was looking for cauliflower, in-season at that time of year and often served fried on Christmas menus.

Panettone, the well-known, tall sweetbread with raisins and candied citron and orange, was served for dessert. Originally from Milan, the panettone is made and consumed all over Italy. During the holiday season, panettoni in recognizable boxes from large, commercial factories and in specialty gift-wrapped packages from small, artisan bakeries are stored on shelves and sideboards, in closets and cupboards all over Italian homes. On Christmas Day, a big family may have as many as ten different panettoni from which to choose, with variations such as cream, chocolate or even filled with gelato. I prefer the classic, of a handmade variety.

Nuts and spumante completed the meal. Italians look for any excuse to toast an occasion with sparkling wine. Opening a bottle is so commonplace that on that evening, the

---

* *Zeppole* come in both savory and sweet varieties. Methods of preparation and traditions associated with this food vary from town to province to region. In other parts of the south, the *zeppola di San Giuseppe* is a popular sweet for Saint Joseph's Day on March 19th, Father's Day in Italy.

spumante was uncorked by a 6-year-old boy, no towel to catch the stopper.

Stuffed to the gills, I couldn't rest with one lavish repast, as the *cenoni* would continue over the next two days. I spent a very pleasant Christmas Day at a student's home with another mouthwatering meal: an appetizer of assorted deli meats, cheese and olives, homemade ravioli in a tomato sauce, a nontraditional turkey with a radicchio and pea stuffing, a green salad, homemade bread, panettone, dried figs stuffed with walnuts (a Calabrian specialty), spumante, and two exquisite home-stilled liqueurs made from blueberry and licorice.

I learned that Christmas would not be complete without card games—with the whole family, between siblings and cousins, amongst friends. When I asked what they were going to do for the holidays, children often responded, "Play cards!" Many games are played with the Italian 40-card deck; two of the most popular at Christmas are "7½," similar to "21," and *stoppa*, a betting game with some aspects like poker that is played more often in the south. Three trick-taking games are enjoyed throughout the year: *scopa*, which means broom or sweep because of the motion of clearing the cards from the table, *briscola*, designating trump as in the winning suit, and *tressette*, a game based on gathering aces that has many regional variations. *Tombola*, the Italian bingo, is also frequently played at Christmas. Naturally, good-natured banter is an essential part of the amusement.

The third consecutive day of eating celebrates San Stefano on the 26th of December, a national holiday. Although Saint Stephen was the first Christian martyr, the festivities associated with him have anything but an air of sacrifice about them. I spent the day with my friends in Siderno and twenty-one of their 500 relatives, including those in the United States and Australia.

The stovetops were bubbling when I arrived. Two pastas were on the menu—one with a sauce of wild boar that Cosimo had shot himself, and the other with a sauce of chicken and other miscellaneous birds, also felled by my host. The second courses consisted of the boar and fowl. The big serving dish of the latter was a bit of a confusion for me, as I didn't know what to take. Cosimo pulled out and identified a *tordo* (thrush) and handed it to me. The little thing's eyes had long since disintegrated into the sauce but the body was intact, so I sort of waved it around like it was flying. He explained how to eat it and my general impression was that you approached these small birds like you would a lobster—pull it apart, suck the flavor out of what you can, eat whatever meat you can find, and if you feel like chewing up the little wings, by all means, chew.

The flavor of the delicate songbird balanced nicely with that of the more robust wild pig. Likewise, the accompanying table conversation matched up the more refined Italian language with the coarser Calabrian dialect, at least to my ears. Without distinction as to the ending of one sentence and the beginning of the next, it can be challenging diving into a discourse amongst relatives or friends. No pause is made, no space given. One idea must overlap the other. The family was very welcoming, however, wanting to hear about America and my impressions of Calabria. When in doubt, I could always talk about the food, a subject Italians never weary of.

All of those tiny birds, not to mention the chickens, had to be deplumed. The work of a hunter-farmer's wife was demanding. Just helping to clean the mounds of garden greens for all those people was an incredible chore. That evening, I assisted her son as he put together his new Legos and looked over some English of one of her college-age daughters. As I left, Marisa pressed a 1½-liter water bottle filled with wine into my hand. It had been a long day for me. I couldn't imagine the days of preparation for Marisa, facing all those little, pellet-ridden corpses, but she never complained. She was happy to serve her family. Perhaps the spirit of Saint Stephen *was* represented at the feast that day.

THE NEW YEAR AND WINTER TRADITIONS

"Where were you last Wednesday?" "My grandfather killed a pig." "Okay." A perfectly valid excuse for not showing up to class—a pig had been killed. The whole family had to drop whatever they were doing, run to his house in the country and eat it.

From antiquity, swine have been king of the Calabrian table. The killing of a pig became ritualistic, an occasion for celebration amongst family, relatives and friends invited to help in the processing and preparation of the meat for consumption, both in the moment and in the future. Nothing was thrown away: the pork was cured in various forms, the fats congealed, the hooves and ears became aspics, and the blood was mixed with chocolate to create a dessert called *sanguinaccio* (blood pudding).

Even today, cold weather in Calabria inspires the slaughter of pigs. Many families purchase one in the spring to be ready for this winter tradition. While Mardi Gras is generally the most precarious time of year for the porcine creatures, in Reggio, swine are also butchered for the *Festa della Madonna* in September. Included in the various methods of cooking and preservation is the pig boil. On Saturdays and during holiday periods, butcher shops place a large cauldron on the sidewalk in front of their stores for the purpose. Even the solidified remains scraped up from the bottom of the pot—suet and scraps—are sold in blocks or slices, most commonly eaten with eggs.

For those with some land and a house in the country, the home-style pig boil is an event. Big bones with residual meat attached are brought to the table. You hear your host asking, "Would you like the heart?" You look up to see a giant, dark hunk of meat on an enormous serving fork waving in your direction, and you respond, "Just a small piece for me, thank you," as though the question were as normal as, "Would you

like a gelato?" and you were limiting yourself to just one scoop
of the treat.

Attendance at a pig boil reveals the flurry of activity set
off by the slaughter of an animal—from its sectioning to the
making of sausage and salami. Many basements have workspace
for such pursuits, an area for drying or smoking meat, as well as
a wood oven for making bread and pizza. As the whole family
participates in this agrarian activity, the meal frequently takes
place amidst its rustic setting.

The centerpiece of the pig boil is the *frittole*†, or *frìttuli* in
Calabrian dialect. In addition to the innards and other lesser-
prized parts of the animal, the plate's focus is the boiled skin,
which is tasty if you like soft pork rinds. I ate a chunk and thought
how much my father would have enjoyed it. The richness of the
fatty pork is cut by a serving of the *giardiniera*, assorted chopped
vegetables such as carrots, cauliflower, celery and onions, boiled
and preserved in vinegar. The *frittole* is also served as a simple
sandwich and always washed down by a glass of the local red
wine. Oranges or other citrus plucked from a nearby tree make
the perfect dessert.

Although the countryside may seem a world apart, its
bucolic atmosphere isn't immune to the modern bangs and
blasts of New Year's. Italians love fireworks, particularly men
and boys. The piazzas are full of young people shooting off all
kinds of firecrackers that make a 6-year-old opening up a bottle
of champagne seem quite safe. In towns and cities, I was told to
stay away from windows that faced onto the street to avoid any
stray projectiles from New Year's Eve street shooting—pistols,
rifles, and even bazookas. Happily, in my first year in Calabria, I
spent New Year's in a hillside town, ten kilometers from the sea,
removed from the more aggressive celebratory bursts of firearms.

My visit to Samo was a living history lesson of a common

---

† The *frittole* is a traditional Calabrian pork dish, most typically from
the province of Reggio Calabria, not to be confused with a similar veal dish
from Palermo or a pastry from the Veneto region.

Calabrian saga. Tracing its roots to the Greeks five centuries before Christ, the medieval burg, known as Precacore, was destroyed by the earthquakes of 1783 and 1908, the latter just a few days before the New Year. 100 years later, this town with a young face but an ancient heritage remembered its past, along with many other communities throughout the province that had suffered the same fate. Today, living in nondescript cement houses away from the ruins, Samo's 1000 inhabitants make efforts to preserve the stone buildings of their ancestors. They lead contemporary lives while finding comfort in their collective history, filling their water bottles from the same fresh springs as their forebears and enjoying their enviable position on the edge of the Aspromonte National Park.

I rang in the New Year with a very satisfying meal of baked ziti, stuffed shells, a pork roast and lentils, which are a symbol of luck and obligatory at Italian New Year's tables. Naturally, panettone and spumante followed suit.

Young people eat important meals and toast the holidays with their families, after which they go out and celebrate with their friends. Larger towns furnish their citizens with fireworks displays, whereas smaller municipalities and villages often feature traditional bonfires in the town square. Samo's was constructed with gargantuan tree trunks and in addition to its festive atmosphere provided warmth for the men and youths chatting within the bounds of its glow.

The hill town also sprang for professional entertainment in the square, the headline performer being a female impersonator interpreting a Calabrian grandmother. Only picking up the basic scenario, I was clearly in the minority as young and old laughed along with the dialect, gleefully following the action as it unfolded. At the end of his performance, the impersonator deftly rattled off his list of future engagements. He seemed professional, but I would never have guessed that his circuit was international. But of course, he was a businessman. There are two million Calabrians in Calabria, but how many in the world?

5

CRIMINALITY, UP CLOSE

'NDRANGHETA, PART 1

ONE DAY I HAD MORE TROUBLE THAN USUAL settling
the children down to begin a lesson. It was a good class, polite
and attentive. On that afternoon, however, they were quite high-
strung, jabbering away in Italian, boys and girls together, even
those who usually kept to themselves. After several unsuccessful
attempts at getting their attention in English, I decided to listen
to what they were actually saying. Words catapulted from the
boy in the center, "My friend's father was shot! He was shot! He's
in my class. He doesn't have a father anymore. My classmate's
father is dead."

I had eaten my lunch and come to school as usual. At that
hour the stores were closed, so I hadn't seen or spoken to anyone
on the way. I hadn't heard of the incident. I hadn't heard the shots
fired amidst screaming mothers and children. Five shots, to be
precise, at point-blank range, two to the head, face blown away
by 7.65-caliber bullets, instant death. The assassinated man had
been standing in front of his son's middle school in Locri, as he
had done every day, awaiting the ringing of the bell, the reunion
with his son, lunch with the family. The assassin had simply
approached from behind and unloaded his pistol.

The national news reported the episode as a card game
gone bad. The killer was retaliating for the ill treatment his
father had received at the hands of the victim, an aggressive
man accustomed to barroom brawls. Further, the murderer and
the murdered were family friends. They were members of the

Calabrian mafia, the 'Ndrangheta, but it was the slap. The father of my student's friend was executed in broad daylight, putting women and children in danger, because he had slapped someone in a public bar. As the nephew of local crime bosses, he had exercised his right to demand "respect," without considering the possibility of repercussions.

This barbaric social climate isn't readily apparent to visitors of the Locride. While a certain Mafioso comportment may be occasionally witnessed, life appears relatively normal. Businesses function as anywhere else, that is, just like other places in which the proprietor must pay a tax not only to the government, but to the neighborhood criminal organization as well. To my surprise, locals rarely talked about this insidious presence, and if called upon to do so, there were those who grew uneasy and suddenly began to whisper. Every so often a protest march was held, although I doubt that extortions were put on hold or drug sales took a hiatus for its duration.

There is habitual complaining as to the lack of opportunity and the insurmountable difficulties of entrepreneurship, about insufficient and deficient public services, and regarding the complete failure of the political system. Many young people go north for work. Some choose to stay, and a few make a stance. Gianluca Congiusta was one of the latter, an honest citizen, a cancer survivor, and a young man who wanted to lead his life to the fullest in his hometown of Siderno.

I met Gianluca through the eyes of his father, Mario Congiusta, who couldn't rest in the face of his son's brutal murder, a cold-blooded shotgun blast to the head. I would translate a film documenting his struggle to obtain justice for his son and thirty-two other homicide victims in the Locride. *La Guerra di Mario* (*Mario's War*) is a passionate appeal, urgently calling for action. I hadn't ever typed so many exclamation points, all warranted. Only thirty-two years old when he was murdered, Gianluca had been too successful to be ignored. Greatly expanding his father's business, he had already established three thriving cell phone stores in adjacent towns along the Ionian coast, Locri, Siderno and Marina di Gioiosa Ionica, with numerous subsidiary affiliates the entire length of the province, from Reggio to Soverato. He promoted and sponsored initiatives for the betterment of his community, the development of tourism, and in support of children and the disabled. His main store in Siderno was a point of reference for the citizenry, not just for purchasing phones, but also for a friendly encounter, a piece of advice, or to share in his enthusiasm. Over the course of one year, however, the Locri location was robbed at gunpoint three times. Receiving police protection after refusing to acquiesce to regular intimidation and demands of *il pizzo* (protection money), the family ultimately closed the store in resignation, concentrating on the other outlets where they hadn't been threatened.

In the end, Siderno wasn't any different and Gianluca would be added to the list of fallen in the fight against the mafia. Through persistence on the part of his family and law enforcement, his assassins were brought to justice, to the extent possible. The majority of cases remain unresolved.

In Italy, when talking about the mafia, specific names are used as the organizations operate independently, such as the Camorra in Campania (the region with Naples as its capital) and Cosa Nostra in Sicily. Calabria's 'Ndrangheta may not be as well known, but is one of the most powerful criminal organizations in the world. Begun in the province of Reggio Calabria, the crime syndicate extends throughout Calabria and wherever Calabrians have emigrated—from northern Italy, to other European countries, the Americas, Australia and even Africa. To get an idea of their dealings, in 2008, the 'Ndrangheta's business volume was estimated to be about 44 billion Euros or 3% of Italy's Gross Domestic Product. Drugs are by far their main activity, followed by commercial enterprise and public contracts, extortion, prostitution and arms trafficking.

Clan families are very tight knit, by blood, making infiltration extremely difficult. San Luca, an Aspromonte mountain village in the Locride is the historic seat, where heads of the local organizations from all over the world meet once a year in a nearby Christian sanctuary. Many Italians view the whole area with trepidation. Once, returning from Reggio by train, I got into a conversation with a young man from Catania, Sicily, a city with a considerable criminal element. He had recently moved to Locri where he was living with his fiancée's family. His Sicilian parents were against the relocation—they feared for him. He said that at first he felt like a gumshoe in a B movie, cautiously looking around corners before he rounded them, literally expecting to be confronted with illicit activity at every turn. However, suspicious looks were all he observed. Upon entering a barbershop, for example, conversation would immediately stop until he identified who had sent him, and only then would the cold mistrust begin to recede from their eyes.

Acceptance may take longer than in other places, but once brought into the fold, bonds would become very close. I was warmly greeted by the owners of businesses I frequented, certainly not for the small quantity of merchandise purchased. Conversing with a proprietor or a sales clerk, I couldn't help but notice the raised eyebrows of locals whose acquaintance I hadn't yet made. Who could this foreigner on such good terms with Signora Valeria be? The young children seemed unusually innocent despite growing up in such a complicated social environment. I was surprised and moved by their reaction when I announced my leaving—tears lasting for over an hour. These children weren't used to people coming into their lives from the outside, the casual visitor. I had been accepted and they had become attached. They had embraced me. I, too, was fond of them.

6

LOCAL HISTORY

IMAGE OF PEGASUS FROM AN ANCIENT COIN OF LOCRI
EPIZEPHYRII, DECORATIVE MARBLE ON FACADE OF
NATIONAL ARCHEOLOGICAL MUSEUM IN REGGIO

LOCRI EPIZEPHYRII

WITH ALL OF THE BAD PRESS this poor Italian region receives, Calabrians capitalize on anything for which they can feel
proud, especially if their soccer team isn't doing well. They often hearken back to a time when Calabria wasn't at the foot of
a country or a union of countries, but to an era when their land
was at the center of the known world, the hub of the Mediterranean, a crossroads.

Calabria's native son Corrado Alvaro portrayed the territory
as the *"regione più misteriosa e inesplorata"* (most mysterious
and unexplored region) of Italy, a phrase frequently quoted by
tourist boards. Compared with better-known regions such as
Tuscany and Sicily, Calabria is relatively obscure. Its challenging
topography and undeveloped road system have contributed
to the mystique with which promoters hope to allure visitors.
Alvaro (1895-1956) would have experienced this isolation
firsthand, having been born in San Luca at the heart of both the
Aspromonte Mountains and the 'Ndrangheta.

In previous millennia, however, the ancients had already
explored the region, founded thriving settlements and begun
the process of demystification. Numerous civilizations came
and went; a few brought wealth while others merely exploited
resources. The region's geographic location at times gave it power,
at others made it vulnerable. Of the territory's long history,
Calabrians hold the most nostalgia for the period of Greek
colonization. In contrast to the collective memory of the arduous

peasant life in recent centuries, *Magna Grecia* or Greater Greece is looked on as an epoch of glory and prosperity, evidenced by the many artifacts on display in museums throughout Calabria and the world.

Visitors to Berlin's Pergamon or Rome's National Museum, for example, have the opportunity to view two magnificent marble statues from the fifth century BC that have their origins in Locri Epizephyrii: the larger-than-life goddess Persephone and the Ludovisi Throne (named after a former owner). These masterpieces are exemplars of the sophisticated civilization that existed in Calabria thousands of years ago.

The Greeks began colonization in the eighth century BC, looking to develop commercial interests as well as to resolve difficulties in feeding their growing population. After expansion into the Aegean Sea, they turned to southern Italy with the first colony on the island of Ischia, off the coast of present-day Naples. Control of the Strait of Messina came early on with Rhegion (Reggio) and Zancle (Messina). Although Sicily was also colonized by the Greeks, some historians only include Calabria, Basilicata, Puglia and Campania with the term Greater Greece while others embrace Sicily in the nomenclature. The Greeks didn't establish colonies nationally; rather, individual cities settled the new territories, which in turn, set up sub-colonies.

Locri Epizephyrii was founded in the seventh century BC by women from Locris in central Greece. According to Aristotle, during a long period in which their men were off fighting a war with Sparta, the ladies escaped with their slaves and established the colony. This version of events is generally accepted by today's historians and helps explain why Locri Epizephyrii was the only matriarchal society in the Greek world. Absorbing the indigenous population, the colony flourished for about 500 years before its fall with the encroachment of the Romans in the third century BC. The area was gradually abandoned as a city center. Building materials were carted away and the ancient society was left under the soil for future generations to discover.

Many travelers mentioned Locri Epizephyrii in their diaries, but scientific excavations didn't begin until the nineteenth century. Noted Italian archeologist Paolo Orsi (1859-1935) worked many years in Locri as well as other localities of the region, in particular, the present-day Reggio Calabria, Crotone, Sibari, Rosarno, Vibo Valentia and Cirò Marina, and is considered the father of Calabrian archeology.

I was introduced to the treasures of Locri Epizephyrii with my first visit to the archeological museum in Reggio, but Locri also had a museum of its own on the site of this ancient Greek settlement. The visitor information center had told me that there were buses for the summer tourists, but in the winter, the only option was a taxi. Walking the three kilometers along state road 106 wasn't recommended, as without a decent shoulder and with just one lane in each direction, this coastal route was dangerous, especially with all of the Italians driving like Italians. To avoid an exorbitant taxi fare, as 20 Euros seemed to be a standard rate for just getting into a cab, I studied bus routes to no avail, called the bus companies who never responded, and finally asked several drivers. Not a regular stop, only certain buses at specific hours would work, and for the return trip, wildly waving my arms on the edge of the road to halt a speeding coach would be my best bet.

Locri Epizephyrii encompasses a vast area and I would visit again with a car. The colony was founded on a natural bay with a wide plain and hills beyond, a perfect gradation for the planned urban center. Regular, rectangular lots for houses were set on parallel streets that ran from a higher elevation down to the sea for the easy flow of water. Interpretive signs tell of the excavations carried out in the area designated the *Centocamere*. I waded through weeds waste deep to view this craftsmen's quarter near the sea, using every ounce of my imagination to envision a bustling community in this large zone filled with stone foundations. Potters had lived in the modest, Mediterranean-style houses with multi-use courtyards, often with small porches. At least eighteen varying-sized kilns churned out terracotta objects ranging from small statuettes to large containers. I climbed up onto a section of the original wall that encircled the settlement with seven kilometers of massive boulders.

The public buildings were conceived on a grand scale. Remaining today are the ruins of several temples, from which large statues can be seen in the Reggio museum along with architectural pieces decorated with multi-color paint testifying to the vibrant, visual environment. A theater, restructured by the Romans, hosts summer performances of ancient Greek plays in Italian.

Many of the exhibits in both the Locri and Reggio museums come from the cemeteries that were established outside the city walls. For example, the Lucifero necropolis excavated by Orsi had about 1700 tombs, both simple burials and cremations, dating from the colony's inception to the second century BC. Objects from earlier periods were often imported from Greece, such as ointment receptacles from Corinth and painted vases from Athens. However, Locri soon developed its own skilled artisans who were particularly noted for their work in bronze. Women's tombs held small cosmetic containers and beautiful bronze mirrors with elaborate handles, men's, items representing banquets and athletics such as drinking cups and metal tools for scraping sand and oil off the skin when practicing sport. Children were sepulchered with toys and objects in miniature.

Also outside the walls, the sanctuary dedicated to Persephone revealed a wealth of archeological finds relevant to the goddess' cult that was quite important for the Locrians. Daughter of Zeus, king of the gods and Demetra, goddess of the harvest, Persephone was abducted by Hades and taken to his underworld where she would spend the winter, returning to earth in the spring as the personification of vegetation. Many small statues of Persephone as well as other votive donations were found in the area. Unique in the Greek world, however, the *pinakes* were one of the site's most important discoveries.

The rectangular tablets in terracotta with bas-relief illustrations represent the cult's myth and rituals.

Locally produced, the *pinakes* were painted bright colors and made from molds that depicted about 130 different scenes. When a Locrian maiden was ready to get married, she would donate a *pinakes* in the hope of receiving Persephone's protection during the transition from young girl to womanhood. The *pinakes* couldn't be reutilized and were broken after use. They were thus unearthed in more than 5000 pieces. Most of the *pinakes* were created in the fourth and fifth centuries BC. They show scenes of daily life with people, animals and objects of both mythical and cultural importance. The kidnapping of Persephone is the scene most often portrayed, and representations of marriage preparations are also frequently pictured. The *pinakes* are on display in both Locri and Reggio.

Another significant archeological find sheds light on the economic and political situation in Locri Epizephyrii—a strongbox full of bronze tablets that record loans made from the sanctuary of Zeus Olympus to the city. Written in ancient Greek between the fourth and third centuries BC, these contracts give a picture of the city's administrative and financial practices, its calendar and even its name day. Interestingly, outstanding debt seemed to carry over centuries. The tablets are on display in Reggio.

Commerce, agriculture, art, literature and philosophy were highly developed throughout Greater Greece. Their athletes participated in the Olympic Games, and Locri Epizephyrii had several champions, most notably in boxing. In the course of its history, this city-state also gave birth to several renowned intellectuals, in particular, Zaleukos, the first Western lawmaker and Nossis, a celebrated poetess.

Before Zaleukos, written laws didn't exist. Judges ruled arbitrarily, and punishment was therefore not administered equally. The Greek world greatly admired his code of law, of which only a handful of statutes remain today. He covered a wide range of topics, for instance:

♦ Locrians are not allowed to own slaves.
♦ Women are forbidden to wear gilded or silk clothes and to elegantly adorn themselves unless they are looking for a husband.
♦ Thieves should be condemned to death.

Twelve short works of Nossis have survived by way of a Byzantine anthology of Greek epigrams. It has been conjectured that she emulated Sappho, the Greek poetess from the island of Lesbos of which the capital is Mytilene. The following is one of Nossis' extant poems, thought to be her own epitaph:

> *Stranger, if you set sail for Mytilene of the beautiful choruses,*
> *To pluck the flowers blossoming by the grace of Sappho,*
> *Say that I was dear to the Muses and was begotten*
> *by the Locrian earth.*
> *Remember, my name is Nossis. Now go!*

With allusions to lesbianism added to the documented practice of sacred prostitution connected with the temple of Aphrodite, Locri Epizefirii certainly did have mysterious and unexplored areas for tourists to look into. The excavations have only scratched the surface of this fascinating culture.

Prospering for half a millennium, Locri Epizephyrii established sub-colonies at Medma (Rosarno) and Hipponion (Vibo Valentia) on the Tyrrhenian coast in the sixth century BC to maintain a balance of power and to ensure survival amidst fluctuating alliances and armed conflicts. However, all of Greater Greece would eventually succumb to the Romans.

The ruins of the two cultures overlap throughout the excavation site, and a nineteenth-century manor farm set in the middle of the archeological park even incorporates historic Greek and Roman architectural elements into its relatively contemporary construction. Much of the bygone settlements still remain under the surface, as life has continued to move forward.

LIFE BEYOND THE GREEKS

GREATER GREECE RECEIVES SO MUCH historical attention in Calabria that the question often arises as to what happened to its thriving culture. Where did the people go? What transpired during those thousand odd years after its demise? Alliances, aggressions, wars, pacts, dominations, disease and more of the same—survival was precarious.

In Locri Epizephyrii's case, much had to do with wars that sound folkloric today. The Peloponnesian (431-404 BC) resulted in a very close alliance with Syracuse that ultimately led to Locri Epizephyrii's acceptance of Rome's military protection in the face of threats from various indigenous populations. The First Punic War (264-241 BC) saw the expansion of Rome's influence with a growing malcontent throughout Greater Greece. The Second Punic War (218-201 BC) brought the famous Carthaginian Hannibal and his elephants over the Alps, down the peninsula and all the way to Calabria. Locri Epizephyrii switched its allegiance to Carthage in order to avoid attack, suffering much destruction at the hands of the Romans when finally retaken in 205 BC, and experiencing a considerable economic and demographic loss in the following century. Although no longer autonomous, the city-state retained its importance on a local level through the third century AD. However, with the weakening of Rome, the need for an administrative center lessened and the urban population declined as settlements spread out into the surrounding territory.

During the Roman period, Locri Epizephyrii became a center for the large agricultural complexes that emerged along the coast and in the hinterlands of the Locride. One such landed estate was discovered in Gioiosa Ionica, a town about fifteen kilometers to the north. Built at the end of the first century BC and reaching the height of its splendor in the third century AD, the Roman Villa Naniglio has only been partially excavated and is noteworthy for its underground cistern with vaulted ceiling that formed part of a thermal bath complex.

The word "villa" undoubtedly brings to mind an elegant manor house surrounded by beautiful gardens. With a 2500-year-old archeological site, however, just the evidence of the existence of such a villa is exciting. I visited Naniglio on a group tour from Reggio shortly after the public unveiling of its multicolored mosaic floors. We were accompanied by at least one expert from the Calabrian Department of Archeological Heritage and were met by the head archeologist of this particular excavation. Several local personalities were on hand to lend significance to the occasion—the town's mayor, its head of tourism and a few others took time from their busy schedules to show up and look important. I don't know why we had to stand in the sun and listen to politicians congratulating themselves, but that is how things are done in Calabria. If the event had been indoors, a long table covered in a frilly cloth would have been set up front with all of the dignitaries facing their public, each one given ample opportunity to speak at a proceeding that had already started late and at which their recitation had never been figured into the timetable.

Needless to say, my German friend who had accompanied me on the tour was beside herself. In my experience, I explained, the two most important things on a Calabrian day trip were the people and the food, and not necessarily in that order. The chances are high that something won't go as planned, so you have to approach the trip as time spent with friends. With a nice lunch and good company, everything else is gravy. We were behind and we would get even more behind as the day progressed, but the lunch was good. Still, I couldn't help but wondering that between all the VIPs and hostesses in attendance that day, why someone couldn't have ventured on the other side of the ropes to pull out the weeds growing between the antique tiles.

We also visited the Villa Casignana between the towns of Bovalino and Bianco about twelve kilometers south of Locri Epizephyrii. Dating from the first century AD, the villa occupied a vast area that today straddles state coastal road 106, a circumstance that has certainly complicated excavations. The estate would have belonged to an important personage, a wealthy landowner or even a Roman consul. Discovered by chance in 1963, the archeological site has revealed opulent living quarters as well as two large thermal spas and is noted for its exquisite mosaics. Although the villa's peak was most likely reached in the fourth century, evidence exists of habitation for an additional three hundred years.

The economic impact of Rome's decline on Locri Epizephyrii brought about the gradual abandonment of the city's nucleus after the fifth century AD. The villas were replaced with large farms that cultivated wine grapes and olives, crops that continued to be profitable. The coastal lands were eventually vacated in the seventh and eighth centuries due to outbreaks of malaria and the threat of Arab incursions. The Locrians headed for the hills, to a strategic position on a cliff that had been occupied since prehistoric times. Gerace held an excellent view of the surrounding low-lying areas and of the sea. This vantage point would protect its inhabitants for centuries to come. By the time the Locrians had fled to this stronghold, the Byzantines had already arrived, as had the Middle Ages.

Calabrian history in the following thousand years would consist of one foreign domination after another, a land under constant siege. While southern Calabria was part of the Byzantine Empire that established the Eastern Orthodox religion, the north fell to the Lombards who took up the Roman Catholic Church. With the Arab foothold in Sicily during the ninth and tenth centuries, Calabria was also a border between the Muslim and Christian worlds and was constantly under attack. Fortifications were built all over the region, to be modified, strengthened or supplanted by each successive victor.

Conquering Calabria in the mid-eleventh century, the Normans instituted feudalism, were tolerant with regard to religious worship, and left their architectural mark in the form of imposing castle remains found throughout the region. The house of Hohenstaufen followed (1194), most notably with a period of prosperity, culture and civility under the Holy Roman Emperor Frederick II. The reigns of the Angevins (1266) and Aragons (1442) were characterized by general economic decline with excessive power in the hands of the barons. Raids by pirates and Turks increased into the Spanish Dominion (1504) under the Kingdom of Naples. Lacking naval protection on both the Tyrrhenian and Ionian Seas, the long coastline was very susceptible to attack. Towers were constructed and castles were reinforced throughout the territory with a system of notification that at least gave the population a chance to flea inland to avoid assault. Natural disasters including earthquakes, pestilence and famine further impoverished the territory, and the expulsion of the Jews in 1540 contributed to the commercial deterioration.

Rule of the Kingdom of Naples was passed to the Austrians (1707) and then the Bourbons (1734) who began to launch reform; however, the defining historical event in Calabria in the eighteenth century was the 1783 earthquake that devastated the entire region. The French Revolution and the Napoleonic presence in Italy interrupted the Bourbon control with the brief Parthenopaean Republic (1799-1801) and the reigns of Napoleon family members Joseph Bonaparte and Joachim Murat (1806-1815) that abolished feudalism and set other progressive ideas in motion. In 1816 the Bourbons returned with a reactionary regime that extended its southern dominion to include Sicily, thus presiding over the whole *mezzogiorno* (word that refers to the Italian south). With the capital still in Naples, the Kingdom of Two Sicilies would rule until the Italian unification in 1861.

Garibaldi had brought aspirations for change. However, beginning in the final decades of the nineteenth century, many Calabrians emigrated in search of a better life, settling principally in the United States. Some returned and some sent back money. After the Second World War they went to Canada, Australia, Europe and northern Italy. Although opportunity is still difficult to come by, the Calabria that these immigrants left has changed.

Today, coastal towers and castles perched on hills and promontories contribute to alluring panoramas, along the shoreline, in towns, cities and the countryside. Medieval settlements have been abandoned, some by choice and others by the force of nature. Over millennia, these houses, churches and fortifications in varying states of ruin have left a lasting testament to Calabria's complex history and its enduring spirit of survival.

7

HILL TOWNS OF THE LOCRIDE

CATHEDRAL OF THE ASSUMPTION, GERACE

STILO

I HAD BEEN LOOKING AT PICTURES of the Cattolica di Stilo for a year before seeing it in person. One of Calabria's architectural jewels, this Byzantine church features prominently in every guidebook and sightseeing website of the region. The attractive red brick structure topped with five tiled cupolas sits at the edge of a cliff nestled in the Calabrian Serre, a forested, hilly and mountainous zone between the Aspromonte and Sila ranges. Sooner or later, I expected to see a tourist advertisement with the Riace Bronzes attending church services there.

Heading northeast from Locri, the fifty-kilometer (thirty-one-mile) trip took longer than I would have thought, as do all excursions in Calabria; nonetheless, the travel books had good reason to show the Cattolica at every opportunity. I hadn't yet purchased my digital camera, but the image was worth snapping away without thinking about how many pictures remained on the roll. Perhaps it was the structure's compact symmetry amidst the terraced cliffs of untamed prickly pear cactus, or its lofty position overlooking the weathered rooftops of the town below and the rolling valley beyond, flanked by the dry, wide riverbed. The simple, cube-shaped edifice exuded an unpretentious elegance with its crown of tightly packed cylindrical domes modestly decorated with diamond-shaped bricks. Had the church developed this sense of stocky permanence over its thousand-year existence or had it been imbued with such perpetuity upon construction in the tenth or eleventh century?

My friend Phil and I were the monument's only visitors on a brisk winter morning. The other car belonged to the guard who appeared mute, perhaps afraid of a language barrier. As we approached and upon entering, we were surprised at how small the church was. If the six-foot-six-inch Riace Bronzes had been superimposed on one of the many publicity pictures, we may have had a better perspective. The interior was well lit from the arched windows in the cupolas, revealing the classic form of a Greek cross. Four archaic pillars, probably scavenged from a temple in nearby Kaulon, divided the space into nine compact squares. Only a few faded images remained of the once vibrant frescos. I decided to jump in and ask the attendant something about the wall paintings and to our surprise he immediately came to life, pointing out the different stratum of imagery from the Byzantine warrior saints of the tenth century to a mother and child from several centuries later when the church had changed from its Eastern orthodox origins to the Latin rite. Scholars differed about dates, particularly in regard to the church's construction; nevertheless, a few inscriptions in Arabic attested to the Cattolica's rich and varied history.

During the Byzantine Era, monks set up refuges in natural grottos of the Stilo valley, eventually building numerous monasteries and churches throughout the area. The Cattolica was founded by Basilian monks who followed the teachings of Saint Basil the Great of the Eastern Orthodox Church. In the nearby town of Bivongi, the Basilians also established the Monastery of San Giovanni Theristis in the eleventh century, an abbey in Byzantine-Norman style that flourished through the fifteenth century with an extensive library and valuable artistic treasures. Bivongi is also noted for the Cascata del Marmarico, Calabria's highest waterfall, but as January wasn't the best time of year for cascading water, we decided to visit a lesser-known site in the area and continue the Byzantine theme with a religious sanctuary in a mountain grotto.

Located outside the town of Pazzano, historically important

for the mining of iron, Santuario Santa Maria della Stella is situated on Mount Stella at an altitude of 682 meters, a beautiful drive, although a bit more complicated than described to us as, "five kilometers on state road 110 to the fork that takes you to the sanctuary." The mountain road twists and turns through the type of forest in which every bend resembles the one just passed, as if driving in circles. We didn't pass any other cars on our ascent through the quiet wood and at the summit were rewarded with a magnificent panorama of the surrounding valley and Ionian Sea. Our car was the only one in the parking lot of the eighteenth-century retreat, still functioning and available for use by reservation. Following signs, we quickly located access to the grotto, a deep, natural cave with jagged walls and sixty-two steps carved out of the stone that descended to the floor of the underground chamber. The small chapel at the bottom could be seen from above, six rows of chairs facing a raised altar set into the rock.

Holding regular Catholic Mass in the warmer months, the church grew out of a Basilian monks' refuge from at least the end of the tenth or the beginning of the eleventh century, based on the dating of the grotto's earliest wall painting. Interestingly, this image depicts Mary of Egypt, patron saint of penitents, rarely portrayed in southern Italy, leading some scholars to the conclusion that female ascetics may have inhabited the sanctuary during a period of its history. Our pondering on the lives passed and the events transpired was cut short by the cavern's winter dampness. Up in the parking lot, a forest ranger was sitting in his car, eyeing us a bit curiously and offering to lead us back out. We had thought we were alone, but were thankful for his assistance as our stomachs were telling us it was time for lunch.

Returning to Stilo proper, we entered the first eating establishment we came across, a typical, no-frills, family operation with the mother in the kitchen, the daughter waiting tables and the father at the cash register. The other patrons were all men—a large table of regulars. The pasta was a traditional homemade macaroni, made by spinning strips of dough around a *ferro* (iron, as a knitting needle), to form a medium-length shape with a very small hole down the center. For its sauce, I opted for the ragù with goat meat, a traditional dish. The flavor was subtle, similar to lamb but more delicate. Phil wasn't as adventurous and enjoyed his pasta with a tomato and eggplant sauce. Grilled, local sausage followed, washed down with a carafe of house wine from Bivongi, a dry, harmonious red. The classic goat sauce gave us a taste of the area's Greek heritage as well as the sense of Stilo's distance from the sea for most of its long history. The town's architectural past had been largely wiped away by the 1783 earthquake, but as seen all over Calabria, castle ruins remained, those in Stilo were of Norman style.

The surrounding hills and mountains had hosted scores of humble mystics seeking out the isolation and tranquility of this remote forested area. Centuries later, spirituality in communion with nature was an important theme for the Calabrian philosopher Tommaso Campanella, born in Stilo in 1568. Although of simple origins, Campanella traveled throughout Europe, leading a life that would transfer well to the big screen—encounters with the likes of Galileo Galilei and Cardinal Richelieau, condemnation for heresy by the Inquisition, multiple arrests and imprisonments, conspiracy against the Spanish crown and the feigning of madness. Returning to Stilo for a couple of years in his midlife, he was the spiritual leader of a peasant rebellion, or in Campanella's eyes, the organizer of a new republic—needless to say, squelched by the authorities. The unjust realities of life in his home territory influenced his beliefs and had an impact on his writings. He detailed his vision of a utopian society in his best-known work *La città del sole* (*The City of the Sun*).

By Campanella's figuring, only four hours a day of honest labor from every citizen would be necessary to take care of all the work in the world. Driving back toward the coastal road, I wondered whether those numbers would still have been valid or if we could have gotten by on three due to mechanization. I reflected that the unfortunate of Calabria had certainly come a long way since Campanella's time—he wouldn't have recognized them today. Turning south towards Locri, we passed the town of Riace, where the famous bronzes were found in 1972, submerged just off the coast. Medieval watchtowers dotted the shoreline. The road was deserted, as in Calabria the hours after lunch were perhaps the quietest of the day. Those who didn't need to work their four hours or who had flexible schedules were taking a *pisolino* (nap).

GERACE

MY FIRST VISIT TO GERACE was on a bad day for harvesting olives, as a student had offered to show me the town when he wasn't otherwise engaged in the fruit gathering process. Whether he was actually combing the olives from the trees, bending down to pick them out of the waiting nets or supervising the operation wasn't clear. The olive harvest in Calabria ranged from November through January, with the resultant oil being greener from olives gathered earlier in the season and more golden towards the end. Fortunate Calabrians with fields of olive trees in the countryside harvested their own olives (or presided over their harvest) and brought them to cooperatives for pressing, thus being able to enjoy their own, high quality, biological olive oil at the dinner table.

Unfortunately, that cold, overcast, windy day in December wasn't conducive to sightseeing, either, but we set out for Gerace all the same, arriving at the castle just as the first drops began to fall. From the former stronghold at the town's high point, we were able to survey the whole valley below. Only a tower and some of the wall remained of the Norman structure, built around 1050, complete with a drawbridge, an armory and a canalled system of rainwater collection. Earthquakes had destroyed the castle and innumerable churches that, according to legend, once numbered as many as 128. I would return on nicer days to have a better view of Gerace's charming medieval center with old stone buildings and historic churches of which only seventeen survive in various states of preservation. Edward Lear, British artist and writer, visiting the town in August 1847, remarked on the disreputable state of repair of many of Gerace's buildings due to the earthquake damage. Notwithstanding, he was also delighted with the town's visual impact, observing, "... each rock, shrine and building at Gerace seems arranged and coloured on purpose for artists, and the union of lines formed by nature and art is perfectly delicious."[*]

With its picturesque setting at the edge of the Aspromonte Mountains and its breathtaking panoramas reaching the sea, Gerace fits the profile of a quaint Italian village and is one of the must-sees of the Locride. For area residents, the historical nucleus is a pleasant place to take a Sunday stroll, before or after a meal at a restaurant or *agriturismo* in the vicinity.[†] During the summer, Gerace's altitude of 470 meters above sea level provides coastal dwellers a welcome break from the heat. In the Dark Ages, the citizens of Locri Epizephyrii fled to this outcropping for safety. Their descendants returned to the coast one thousand years later and settled Gerace Marina or the modern-day Locri. A visit to Gerace helps to fill this historical gap.

During most of the year, the day-tripper can wander the streets unencumbered, as the town's nearly 3000 residents must either stay indoors with the lights off or live much of the time elsewhere. When the tour buses start pulling up in the high season, however, the narrow lanes swell. The municipality even supplies an open-air, train-like vehicle reminiscent of those found

---

[*] Edward Lear in *Journal of a Landscape Painter in Southern Calabria*, 1852. Lear is best known for his popularization of what he called nonsense verses, subsequently referred to as limericks.

[†] *Agriturismo* or agricultural tourism refers to a restaurant that serves local produce and products, theoretically their own. The term can be translated as farm vacation, farm holiday, and the establishment can also be a form of bed and breakfast or hotel.

in children's parks that perilously whips people up and down the switchbacks from a parking lot to the upper village, which is the focus for most tours. However, the town has two levels. In the lower part, called Borgo Maggiore, a conglomeration of churches from diverse periods in various states of disrepair can be seen as well as dwellings dug right out of the volcanic rock, a few still containing ceramic workshops, an historic, local craft. The Borghetto, the upper village, features the castle, a number of churches including the cathedral and a few significant private mansions.

The plethora of religious buildings that once made up the fabric of Gerace testifies to the town's elevated ecclesiastic stature over the centuries. Evidence exists of churches dating to the Early Christian period. Many churches have Byzantine architectural roots, and the Greek rite survived up until 1480, when it was abolished in favor of the Latin service. Gerace's majestic Cattedrale dell'Assunta was built under the Normans over an eighth-century structure. One of the largest churches in Calabria, the Cathedral of the Assumption is in the form of a Latin cross in Byzantine-Romanesque-Norman style. The visitor's access is through one of the semicircular apses that opens to an evocative, Byzantine crypt divided by twenty-six columns, stripped from ancient Locri and subsequently crowned with nineteenth-century capitals. The cathedral's tiny museum is housed in an adjacent room. An exquisite, twelfth-century double-arm reliquary cross caps the collection. Above, the sanctuary is a long, three-nave structure divided by twenty columns of granite and marble, smooth and ribbed, with varying capitals. Any frescos or other embellishments have long since been covered or have disappeared. Unadorned, the simple church with its subtle diffusion of light from the small, high windows doesn't distract worshipers from their purpose. While the nearby castle fell centuries ago, the cathedral steadfastly remains, a striking example of the imposing Norman architecture testifying to the community's religious devotion.

Other churches of note include the tenth-century Chiesa di San Giovanni Crisostomo (Church of Saint John Chrysostom) that follows the Greek Orthodox rite and the fourteenth-century Chiesa di San Francesco (Church of Saint Francis of Assisi) in gothic style with a spectacular seventeenth-century polychrome, inlaid marble altar. Gerace was once full of churches, convents and monasteries. Patrician houses line the streets—picturesque, but certainly not at their prime. On my first visit to Gerace, I was too concentrated on not slipping on the wet stone pavement to take in the atmosphere as described by Lear. I saw a lot of the gray buildings he had mentioned, but not the lovely dove color of which he had written. On return visits I saw more colors, walking the medieval streets fit for the noble families and archbishops they once accommodated. Gerace boasted a rich history.

On more than one occasion, the street sign "*Via Caduti sul Lavoro*" caught my attention. Thought provoking, this guidepost paid memorial to those fallen or who died from work, to the people who built the churches and the stately homes, to the meek who attended Mass in the countless houses of worship and whose humble lodgings surely didn't weather the earthquakes, to the peasants on whose labor the more fortunate could prosper, and even to those who harvested the olives. Hopefully, they too, were able to take a moment and bask in the view through the stunning *Porta del Sole* (Door of the Sun), across the valley to the Ionian Sea, but I doubt the fallen workers ever thought that one day they would be remembered.

MAMMOLA

THROUGHOUT THE PROVINCE of Reggio Calabria, the word *pescestocco* or just *stocco* is pronounced with reverence, excitement, and even pride, such as, "My wife makes the best *stocco*!" Fishmongers display large signs in their windows, boasting their sale of the product. "*STOCCAFISSO!*" "*STOCCO.*" At first, I didn't bother asking what all the fuss was about as the fish that I saw wasn't fresh and the pieces looked too large for me to deal with.

I would stumble on the meaning of *pescestocco* when a friend of a friend of a friend invited me to lunch in Mammola, a town of about 3000 inhabitants located between the Aspromonte and the Serre ranges, approximately thirty kilometers (nineteen miles) north of Locri on state road 682. This highway cuts across the toe from the Ionian to the Tyrrhenian Sea, starting at Gioiosa Ionica and ending in Rosarno, passing through lovely, rolling terrain, although the long, tunneled portion is rumored to have been a dump for toxic waste during its construction. Notwithstanding the higher than normal levels of radioactivity in the tunnel, the landscape is beautiful, and highway 682 is usually faster than driving through the coastal towns on state road 106 to Reggio. Mammola is on the Ionian side and is the undisputed capital of *pescestocco* in Calabria. (Cittanova, at the foot of the Aspromonte on the Tyrrhenian side is also noted for its preparation of the fish, many crediting the town's high quality water.)

Italians have strong networks of family and friends. Being in an area without any prior connections, my friends started thinking about their possible acquaintances in the zone, resulting in multiple phone calls and a few encounters with, for all intents and purposes, perfect strangers. My trip to Mammola was one of those occasions. From my phone conversation with Stefano, the original plan had been to eat locally, but he then got the idea to share a provincial specialty, *lo stocco* with his foreign charge. This decision required a trip to Mammola, the Calabrian culinary destination for this particular delicacy.

Stefano wasn't a young man, but he was educated, made pleasant conversation and was knowledgeable about the area, although directions weren't his strong suit. I knew he had been a politician, and during the course of the drive, he explained that he was a little out of practice behind the wheel as he had had a car and driver for many years, not unusual for Italian elected officials.‡ Admittedly, the strong rain and accompanying fog did make visibility difficult.

At about 240 meters (787 feet) above sea level, Mammola is nestled between the slopes of two mountain chains and covers a vast territory that attracts outdoor enthusiasts with its many hiking trails. The Santuario di San Nicodemo dedicated to Saint Nicodemus of Mammola, a tenth-century Basilian monk, is a destination for religious pilgrims. Mammola also lives very much in the present with its Museo Santa Barbara, a museum and laboratory of contemporary art that exhibits its collections in a restructured Byzantine monastic complex and an open-air park. By capitalizing on its food culture and naturalistic setting, this historically agricultural community has reinvented itself. Gastronomic festivals include the mushroom in October, *ricotta affumicata* (smoked ricotta) in June, and the most important, the *Sagra dello stocco* (Festival of *stocco*) on August 9th.

The *stoccafisso* or stockfish is the centerpiece of Mammola's table. None other than dried Norwegian cod, this fish is sometimes confused with the similar *baccalà*, which is dried, salt-cured cod. *Stocco* is dried in the open air, resulting in a different flavor.§ Importation into Calabria began in the sixteenth century, reaching Mammola by way of old mule trails. The dried fish was then reconstituted in running water over a three-day period. Many traditional recipes were created, particularly in the province of Reggio Calabria where *lo stocco* has been customarily eaten on Fridays, especially on Good Friday and Christmas Eve. Today, the fish is hydrated following

‡ Italy is famous for what's referred to as the *auto blu*, state vehicle used by government employees from the highest of federal classification down to the local level. A big issue when looking at government cutbacks, this Italian practice infuriates taxpayers. In 2009, for example, Italy topped the international list of such vehicles with over 600,000 cars. The United States came in second with 72,000. Although Italy has reduced its tally over the past few years, its numbers remain out of proportion as compared with those of other countries.

§ Inexplicably, in the Veneto region *stoccafisso* is called *baccalà*. And amusingly, in the figurative sense *baccalà* means fool or moron.

time-honored traditions, and cherished recipes are passed from one generation to another.

Entering Mammola's narrow streets lined with small houses and the occasional Baroque mansion, we pulled into a tiny piazza and waited for the torrential rain to let up before getting out of the car and going into a small, non-descript restaurant with no more than six wooden tables. Stefano assured me that this wasn't the best-known establishment, but was the place that served the finest food. Like almost all Calabrians, he fancied himself a culinary expert. Unfortunately, as we went to sit down, the eatery's young waiter didn't seem to recognize Stefano or his name, prompting a decidedly awkward moment. As my lunch companion puffed himself up and began to inform the server that he should have known just who he was, I discretely vanished into the ladies room. When I came back, all was well and we proceeded to order. I didn't ever see a menu, which is normal in that type restaurant. Either the waiter just rattles off the options, looking around in a bored manner, or he describes each dish with the same loving care that is presumably given to its preparation, sure to please the palates of the most discriminating clients. Needless to say, after our seating debacle and in light of my host's apparent importance, our waiter had been transformed into an older gentleman, attentive and precise, the sort with a personal stake in the business, such as an owner or a family member.

The plan was to be dazzled by a string of appetizers – *stocco* prepared in every way imaginable, such as stocco salad (raw in oil, garlic, lemon and parsley), fried stocco, stocco fishballs, stocco frittata, stocco fritters, eggplant stuffed with stocco, as well as a tasting of assorted sausage and cheese, mushrooms from the area mountains in oil, *la pizzata* (Mammola's specialty cornbread), rustic bread and the local red wine—and dazzled I was. At no time did I have the sense that the poor fish I was eating had gone through an elaborate process of drying and hydrating. The cod was a flavorful whitefish, prepared to perfection, but we hadn't finished yet. The pasta was bucatini (long pasta with a small hole down the center) with stocco, cooked in a tomato sauce with onion, garlic, peperoncino and parsley. *Basta*! (Enough!) I couldn't go on to a second course, such as stocco alla mammolese (with potatoes, red onion, dried peppers, tomatoes and brined olives), grilled stocco basted with salmoriglio (oil, oregano, garlic, salt and lemon) or baked stocco. I couldn't eat another bite, and I also couldn't help noticing that Stefano paid about half of what I thought would have been the minimum price for the meal. As often is the case, there wasn't a written bill, but I overheard. I didn't react, but he brought it up, saying that his former position came with such perks. I filed it away.

Returning to the coast, Stefano mentioned that he hadn't had any connections with the mafia—just in case I had heard something about his family. I had, certainly not from my friend who had put me in touch with him, but after we had arranged to meet. Actually, I had also looked him up on the Internet. The situation wasn't clear. "If you make a deal with them once, they have you forever." He said that he had always been honest. Maybe so. I thought about the half-price meal. Perhaps he had sent the restaurateur a lot of business. He was from a respectable family. In Locri, black from white was sometimes difficult to distinguish. The *stocco* was good and he didn't get it for free.

8

BACK TO SCHOOL

LOCAL TRAIN IN REGGIO'S CENTRAL STATION

REGGIO'S UNIVERSITY FOR FOREIGNERS

WHEN I ARRIVED IN CALABRIA, I already had a solid foundation in the Italian language and my skills continued to improve. So in June of my first year I took an advanced certificate examination at the *Università per stranieri* (University for Foreigners) in Reggio. Several accredited organizations administer nationally recognized Italian tests all over the world. The exam responses are sent to a central location, in this case, Rome, for grading, which can take several months. When I inquired in person the following September, the results had not yet been tallied. I casually asked about the school's language classes and the administrative assistant told me that their teacher training course would be the only appropriate program available at my level. She strongly encouraged me to apply saying that they needed ten participants to run the course, and that if the class made, scholarships would be provided to cover the costs. The program focused on teaching, but the majority of the classes were cultural. She had the simple application form ready—no deposit, no commitment, so I filled it out. She told me I would be contacted by the end of October if they were going to have the course. I never heard from them and assumed that was the end of it.

Just before Christmas, I went to the university to pick up my certificate that had finally arrived. Out of curiosity, I asked what had happened with the course. As it turned out, I was "*in regola*" (in order). "Excuse me?" My one-page application form had been transferred to its own faded construction-paper folder together with a group of other faded construction-paper folders of various colors and they expected me for the entrance exam on the 11th of January. No letter, no email, no phone call and not much more information. No one was around to give me any particulars. Back in Locri, I went to the university's website, which hadn't been updated. The course name sounded impressive: *Corso di alta formazione per docenti di lingua italiana come lingua straniera* (Upper level training course for teachers of Italian as a foreign language). The program had been in existence for twenty years and seemed to cover a lot of material in six months. A free course—how often did that come along? I decided to show up and find out what it was all about.

The *Università per stranieri Dante Alighieri* is in the center of Reggio, behind the city theater just off the main pedestrian street. The stately building with its lovely, interior courtyard had been a convent. Today, smoking foreigners clutter the entranceway and former cloister before and after scheduled classes. On the day of the admissions test, I rose early, took the train to Reggio and joined a multicultural group of about twenty, assembled in a once elegant classroom to complete a rather difficult Italian exam. The proctor waltzed in and out over the three and a half hours, from time to time admonishing and threatening a young Ukrainian who was helping himself to his neighbors' answer sheets. I think she stepped out to give herself a break from his constant questioning and maybe even to let him cheat a bit.

The listening and speaking parts of the exam were held in the same room the following day. Two Italian ladies walked in, placed a boombox on the table, inserted a cassette tape and pressed PLAY, the entire operation performed to the accompaniment of a jackhammer. The school's main entrance had been blocked off that morning and the work was being carried out directly under our classroom. I looked around for the candid camera, but all I saw were the strained faces of my fellow applicants. The day before, one of the women had set up a tiny, electric space heater near my chair after I had inquired as to whether the building had heat. So after a minute, I took it upon myself to point out the absurdity of the situation. They looked at me a bit quizzically as if ambient noise was part of the listening experience, but finally decided to move to another room and start from the top. After the oral interviews, we were told that classes would begin the following morning. Ten students were accepted into the program, satisfying the number required for the school's operational funding, and unfortunately including the aforementioned Ukrainian with whose shenanigans we would be burdened until the bitter end.

The makeup of the class relied heavily on the citizens of former and current communist countries: two young Serbian women with Italian degrees from the University of Belgrade, a Polish tour guide and French teacher, an Hungarian English-language interpreter who fidgeted constantly, ostensibly in an attempt to keep warm although the twitching continued into the warmer weather, a young Chinese man with a computer science degree and strong English skills, a fast-talking Croat who cursed in Italian, Calabrian, Croatian, Serbian, Russian and English, and who had lived most of his life in Italy, attending high school and college there, and another Ukrainian who had studied at a high school in Reggio and an Orthodox seminary in his home country, dreamed of becoming a chef and liked to take a nip during the breaks, occasionally not making it back to class. A Colombian majoring in Italian at a university in Bogotá rounded out the group. On the second day of classes, he pulled me aside, gestured to the others and said with an air of confidentially, "They're not like us."

The schedule started out with classes from 9:00 to 10:30 and 11:00 to 12:30, Monday through Friday. My understanding was that they would be adding another from 1:00 to 2:30 in the afternoon. The notification of program specifics was an ongoing process, and the course list was a bit intimidating: General Linguistics, Italian Linguistics, Foreign Language Teaching,

Italian Literature, Literature of the Theater, Classic Literature, Philology, Early Modern to Contemporary Italian History, Art History, Philosophy, Italian Film, Archeology, Music History, Creative Writing, Folk Traditions, Calabrian Literature, Language of Special Sectors and Italian Conversation. With such a heavy load, I had thought about resigning my teaching position in Locri, as doing both would be backbreaking. However, my boss wasn't going to hear of it, saying he had already done his recruiting for the year. I thought if I showed my loyalty, that illusive work permit might eventually be my reward.

So I commuted from Locri, leaving on the 7:22 every morning. If the train arrived at Reggio's central station on time at 8:53 and I really hustled up the street, I would be five minutes late to my first class. More often than not, the train was behind schedule and I'd miss the first ten to thirty minutes. I doubt Mussolini's punctuality ever made it down to Calabria. When I got out of class at 12:30 I ate lunch at a *tavola calda* (literally "hot table," a small eatery with pre-prepared food) on the way to the 1:30 train, which was full of pushing, screaming students just let out of public school. When my class ended at 2:30, I'd leave a bit early and take the 2:37 train to arrive in Locri in time to teach. Shaving a few minutes off one end or the other didn't seem to bother anyone, as I noticed when I occasionally showed up on time, the room was empty.

Riding the train every day gave me a taste of the Italian commuter experience. I got to know my fellow travelers, some friendly, others less so. Several marveled at my reading material on such an uncomfortable conveyance—class work, naturally. I learned to sit in the front of any compartment so that when the well-dressed woman from Bovalino took it upon herself to open the window, as she was wont to do, I didn't have to suffer the wind in my face. Italians are preoccupied with drafts, vigilantly covering their necks and shoulders at the slightest cross wind and closing all windows on the hottest of days, but that aggressive woman from Bovalino knew how to squelch all but the most combatant travelers.

The seats were configured with pairs facing each other, making privacy impossible and legroom nonexistent. Perhaps two little, old Calabrian women could sit facing each other, not cramped or limited by the limbs of the person facing them, but I struggled with the arrangement on a daily basis. The Italians would also crowd together, systematically avoiding the Moroccans, one of the more visible minority groups in the area. One morning, a place with a solitary Moroccan appeared to be my best option. I didn't get up when his friends then filled in around me and across the aisle, talking at the volume needed to project in a North African bazaar. I didn't want to seem rude even though my head was ready to explode. At a certain point, climbing back and forth all over me, each one took his turn to use the restroom, just a hole over the tracks fitted with a toilet but no running water—an experience I avoided at all costs. When the man sitting directly across from me returned from his visit, I couldn't help but notice the drops of liquid on his brown, pointy-toed, lace-up dress shoes. I got up and sat with the woman from Bovalino.

One of my regular seat companions compared the train to the stagecoaches of the Wild West. Often just one carriage, the rectangular box on wheels sported green paint on the front and rear, a whitish wagon with a touch of blue and two passenger doors leading up several steps to the seating, all second-class, not in the sense of second-best, but second-rate, inferior. A third class didn't exist. Bumping and rattling its way along the Ionian coast's single track, the line was plagued with long delays, as when one locomotive had a problem, the approaching train also stopped, afraid of colliding even with a half hour or more between them. Cows on the track held us up for over an hour one afternoon. A drunk sleeping across the rails jolted us to a stop on a lazy Sunday morning. We accompanied him to the next station, waited forty-five minutes for a police car to pull up, watched the officers enter the bar for *un caffè* (an espresso) and finally board the train, saying, "*Amico* (friend), put your shoes on!" I had wanted to make that same request three quarters of an hour earlier. I avoided the pair of seats in which the sad boozer had left leaves and debris until they eventually blended with the others.

One morning, about a week into commuting, I heard, "*L'america-a-a-ana-a!*" I recognized the slurred delivery immediately and looked up to confirm its source in the form of my Italian literature professor. *Il professore* came across as the product of a film director's colorful imagination—suit, long coat, brown leather satchel, lively scarf, dress hat perched atop his head just a bit askew, moustache, all put together with sweeping physical gestures and accompanied by a theatrical drawling of the vowel sounds. At the end of his first class when he asked us if we had any questions, no one said anything. Most of my fellow students didn't even understand that he had posed a question. He must have stared at me for two straight minutes, squinting his eyes and pursing his lips, so I had to come up with something. I thought, "Could you possibly enunciate more clearly?" But instead, I asked him his name. He said he hadn't told us as he figured everyone already knew who he was. I thought, "We only know what the Croatian has told us."

"*L'america-a-a-a-ana-a-a!*" Either he started the morning with a shot of whiskey (as was the Croatian's contention) or he had a speech impediment. My feeling was some combination of the two, cultivating the loose pronunciation as part of the act. He and his friend were to rob me of my legroom that morning, and I was subjected to an extra forty minutes of his garbled speech mixed with Calabrian dialect. The pleasant man next to me tried to contribute to the conversation, but *il professore* squashed him with a conspicuous lack of acknowledgement and the glaring absence of a gesture.

The course ran for a grueling six months, back and forth on the train and teaching at night. My Italian improved, particularly my listening skills. Most of the teachers had a meticulous pronunciation. *Il professore* would prove a challenge. I remember a class early on, in which a few minutes remained until the end of the hour. *Il professore* gave what sounded like an expansive closing statement and then started to read the newspaper. I began gathering my things and had my coat on before I looked around and realized everyone was still sitting there silently in place, presumably waiting for the next pearl. They watched me put my coat on and stand up and still no one made a move. I said something like, "I've got a train to catch—until next time," as I walked away, wondering how long they all sat there looking straight ahead, watching him read the newspaper.

LESSONS LEARNED

THE GRADUATION CEREMONY FOR THE teacher training course was held on a hot, sunny morning in late June with the school's director presiding. I hadn't ever seen him before, even though his office was just down the hall from our classroom. As I had almost become accustomed, the formalities got under way late—forty minutes to be precise. The reason wasn't clear.

We had spent 555 hours in class. My goal had been to improve my Italian, an objective I had achieved, receiving a wealth of pedagogical, historical and cultural information along the way. Upon reflection, perhaps the strongest educational aspect of the program was untaught, the wisdom absorbed through experience.

The oral exam, for example, was a new type of test for me (outside language proficiency testing or a thesis defense in postgraduate school). In Italy, schoolchildren grow up with the system of *interrogazione*, in which the teacher questions each student individually in front of the whole class. The examiner has a lot of leeway with both the questioning and the assessment. The personalities of the student, the teacher and the class as a whole come into play. Verbal skills can affect a math or science result.

Grades are commonly posted for all to see. In the university course, almost all of the exams were oral. At first I assumed that preparation was similar to that of a test in English, but I gradually realized that the oral exam wasn't anything like the written exam. Essays give time for reflection; short answers and multiple-choice tests can evaluate an extensive range of information in a relatively short amount of time. Further, with written examinations, the whole class takes the same test at the same time.

Watching my fellow students, I couldn't help but notice that self-assuredness, even arrogance, counted for a lot. The Serbs, for example, were clearly comfortable with the process. They had an impressive ability of memorization and regurgitation, not pausing for an instant, a barrage of information, a vomiting of minutia. I saw that the students focused on an initial speaking topic, hoping to overwhelm the examiner with a specific subject matter from the outset and thus prove mastery of the overall material. Jockeying for position in the exam order was also a well thought out process. Innocently, my only concern was catching the train.

Some professors use the exam for grandstanding, wanting all students in attendance at every interrogation so as not to miss his demonstration of superior knowledge. Jumping in as the student pauses for a breath or to collect a thought, the examiner goes on and on, not allowing room for the student to pick up where he left off, as if he or she had been floundering and the professor saved a potentially awkward social moment. Instead of listening politely, the student is supposed to punctuate every one of the examiner's statements with, "In fact," or "Yes, indeed," to indicate being already abreast of whatever particular he is espousing. And if the examiner doesn't stop talking, the student should just cut in and talk over him. In the end, I concluded that studying for an oral exam was like preparing a discourse of an indeterminate length for an audience with a possible heckler. My shortest oral exam was about five to ten minutes, and my longest, an hour and a half.

Other situations that may arise in a school are more universal. For example, on the eve of one exam, I received the email message, "*Dobbiamo incontrarci con tranquillità.*" (We have to get together undisturbed!) As the prospect of meeting the professor in question outside of school made me feel anything but tranquil, I never responded, which certainly did not set an aura of tranquility at my oral exam.

Being unduly subjected to an instructor's personal beliefs is another educational hazard all too common in the field. Several professors and at least one custodian at the *Università per stranieri* were outspoken communists. *Il professore*, the notorious garbler with a penchant for the theatrical, carried a Soviet-style lighter with the bold hammer and sickle insignia and saw communism in the entirety of Italian literature. We were "*Compagno Cinese*" (Chinese Comrade) and "*Imperialista Americana*" (American Imperialist). His only saving grace was that he had the work ethic of a stereotypical communist worker and we were spared a minimum of twenty minutes of his jumbled rhetoric at the start of every class. The aforementioned custodian was fairly vigilant, however, with his habitual allegations of our overloading the building's electrical system with our wanton use of both the inefficient space heater and the overhead lights. He wasn't so alert in his duties regarding lavatory sanitation, and toilet paper was available on a strictly bring-your-own basis—very communist, indeed. For the first couple of months we thought our classroom was haunted as the lights mysteriously went on and off on their own, until we discovered that faulty wiring allowed the adjacent classroom's light switch to operate our fixtures.

Unfortunately, our *Compagno Cinese* wasn't with us on that final day as we received our diplomas. The earthquake that had shaken western China two months earlier had greatly upset him in the initial days following the catastrophe, especially when he had difficulty contacting his parents. Finally, his father assured him that his grandmother, who lived in the affected zone, was all right, but as it turned out, he was hiding the news of her death, as he wanted his son to finish the course. However, with his absence from the country, other relatives had homed in on his inheritance, so our *Compagno Cinese* had to go back to China and present himself in person. The part of the story most difficult for me to imagine was the idea of an old Chinese woman with money and a companion. *Il professore* also never made it to the ceremony. He was in the building, however, most likely drawling a correlation between "Da-a-a-ante" and communism.

9

WELCOME TO REGGIO

PROCESSION OF REGGIO'S PATRON SAINT, THE
MADONNA OF CONSOLATION

ON FOOT IN REGGIO DI CALABRIA

AFTER TWO YEARS OF TEACHING IN LOCRI, I decided to move to Reggio, finding a position in one of the provincial capital's numerous English language schools, once again, not an easy task as an American. Settling into the rhythm of the larger community, I would join the throngs of locals, streaming up and down Corso Garibaldi, the pedestrian-only shopping street, as well as its parallel coastal avenue. Seen and being seen was the order of the day, from the very young, proud to be walking with their parents, to the not so young, proud to still be participating in this longstanding social tradition. I once accompanied an older friend buying new glasses, and somewhat surprisingly for me, listened to her tell the optometrist that her main concern was being able to distinguish friends and acquaintances during the *passeggiata* (promenade).

This walk was a destination in itself, as going to the theater or out to dinner. Pedestrians didn't just throw anything on before leaving the house. These were strollers with a civic purpose. Old men dominated the weekday morning sauntering, arm in arm or side by side with hands clasped behind their backs. Teenagers through twenty-somethings flooded the streets on weekends and holidays, making key meeting points such as the *teatro comunale* (city theater) and the *tapis roulant* (moving walkway) almost impassable. Groups of teenage boys, dressed in black with slick, coiffed hair, roved boisterously in an effort to attract the attention of the clusters of girls tottering on their high heels, scarves artistically draped around their necks.

All manner of serious folk also played a role in the promenade, a pastime that appeared to be completely unaffected by the country's general financial crisis. While walking was free, il Corso's shopping certainly was not, and the hoards of young people spilling out of bars and nightclubs made me wonder just how long their grandparents' social security checks would hold out. The national news had story after story about people who weren't able to make it to the end of the month on their paycheck or pension, yet in one of the country's poorest regions, children crowded into pizzerias on Saturday nights—tables of teenyboppers all by themselves, ordering pizzas and Coca-colas, leaving half of what they had ordered uneaten on their plates. What would their great grandparents have thought?

Youth, for the most part, do not work in Calabria, even those from lower-income households. Odd jobs are generally done by *extracomunitari* (non European Union citizens) from poorer countries. Young people manage by living with their families at least until they get married, which is a rather costly affair. Calabrian weddings are no longer charming, home-cooked, country celebrations, but ornate, fully catered gatherings that often give rise to considerable debt as couples endeavor to emulate their smiling counterparts in brides' magazines for their closest two- to five-hundred relatives and friends. On beautiful days, these young hopefuls are frequently seen posing for formal wedding photos along the seaside.

The esplanade looks out over the Strait of Messina, the coastline of Sicily and on a clear day, Mount Etna—a truly spectacular panorama. The lower promenade is at sea level and in the summer is lined with beach concessions. At its midpoint are a modern amphitheater and a striking fascist-style monument of Athena in homage to Victor Emmanuel III (1869-1947), who on the very spot, first set foot on Italian soil as King of Italy at the death of his father in 1900. The waterfront was redesigned after the 1908 earthquake and again more recently when the railroad was repositioned under the street. The wide, upper level promenade flanks what is commonly referred to as Via Marina, a pair of coastal roads that run north in one direction and south in the other and are laid out in boulevard style. The approximate two-kilometer strip of land between serves as a lovely city park the length of the downtown area. Stately late-art nouveau mansions face the strait and this public garden. Welcoming shade from the midday sun is provided under and amidst its many exotic plants and trees, most notably the Moreton Bay Fig, a massive-trunked, Australian evergreen with an impressive aerial root system.

Walking the dog is a popular pastime in the waterfront area, although Reggio's usual windiness can become quite blustery in the colder months. My friends Franco and Luisa live with their three dogs in an elegant mansion on Via Marina. During my time in Reggio, I enjoyed many a pleasant walk with them and their dogs; however, I can attest to the fact that these magnificent homes and their inhabitants suffer during the winter with their frontline exposure to the meteorological elements whipping through the strait. Frigid, gale-like winds toss around residents, sending pedestrians up to il Corso and the bit of protection its buildings furnish from the blasts of winter weather. Deceivingly, the official temperature reading may be a moderate forty-five or fifty degrees Fahrenheit, but with the cold air blowing down from snow-topped Etna and the humidity whirling off the sea, even Via Marina's streetwalkers congregate in the somewhat protected cross streets.

Of the many significant shoreline structures, the neo-gothic Venetian-styled Villa Zerbi that was once home to a noble family, has at times served as an exhibit space, featuring art expositions and other displays with a local focus. The area's long history is preserved by a section of the ancient Greek city wall and part of a Roman bath complex along Via Marina. In nearby Piazza Italia on Corso Garibaldi archeological excavations have revealed six stratifications in the six meter dig: Hellenistic Greek, Imperial Roman, Byzantine, Norman, Angevin and the nineteenth century. Steps lead down to view part of a Roman road under the piazza. Above ground, the square is surrounded on three sides by handsome, early twentieth-century edifices, seats of the provincial and municipal administrations and the office of the prefect. In the next block, Reggio's theater, dedicated to opera composer Francesco Cilea (1866-1950) who was born just to the north in Palmi, presents a limited season of theater, ballet and music, and shares a roof with the city's small *pinacoteca* (picture museum) containing two works attributed to Antonello da Messina (1429/30-1479), a large painting by Mattia Preti (1613-1699), known as the *Cavaliere Calabrese* (Calabrian Knight) and a collection by regional artists.

The *Castello Aragonese* (Aragon Castle) also serves as an exhibition space. On a hill two blocks up from il Corso, the castle was founded in the Byzantine period, continually restored, modified and enlarged through the Spanish period, retaining the typical form of an Aragon defensive fortification through modern times. Surviving the 1908 earthquake intact, the majority of the structure was subsequently knocked down in the name of city planning. Today, the visitor practically needs a map to find the castle that has lost its former position of prominence. Seemingly in hiding outside of a block's range, the impressive edifice suddenly looms above with its two formidable cylindrical towers, often pictured in the city's publicity materials.

The *Chiesa degli Ottimati* (Church of the Nobles), one of the oldest religious institutions in Reggio, faces an angle of the castle. Although several antiquities remain, such as the geometric mosaic flooring in Byzantine style, as is the case with most of the city, the present structure was reconstructed in the twentieth century. Facing a large piazza-parking lot on il Corso, the nearby *Duomo* (Cathedral) or to use its full name, *Basilica Cattedrale Metropolitana di Maria Santissima Assunta in Cielo* was rebuilt in Romanesque Revival style following the 1908 earthquake and re-consecrated in 1928 almost one thousand years after its establishment. Christianity in Reggio dates back much further, however, to the spring of 61 AD, according to the Acts of the

Apostles 28:13. Coming from Siracusa (Syracuse), the Apostle Paul stopped at Reggio for a day. According to legend, Paul was given permission to speak to the pagans as long as the flame of a lamp continued to burn. Miraculously, when the lantern's flame extinguished, the stone column beneath it caught fire and the apostle spoke until the following morning. The fervor in Paul's words impassioned the hearts of the local people, converting them to Christianity and making Paul the founder of the church of Reggio and of the Christian faith in Calabria. What is left of this column can be viewed in the Chapel of Saint Paul to the right of the chancel in Reggio's Cathedral.

The story of the burning column may sound more folkloric than factual to twenty-first century skeptics, but the population's faith unwaveringly embraces miracles. Busloads of the devoted make regular pilgrimages to the sanctuaries of San Francesco in Paola, Calabria and Padre Pio in San Giovanni Rotondo, Puglia. Travel agents organize frequent trips to Our Lady of Lourdes in France. I was in Locri when the court of the European Union was deciding a case regarding crucifixes in the classroom. While the national media featured both pro and con viewpoints, with a leaning against their public display, one hundred percent of my students were in favor of keeping crosses in their schools.

Reggio has a host of churches, including several on il Corso amidst the stores, bars and banks. Parking can be a problem for those who have traveled to the province's center for shopping, strolling, and keeping in touch with friends and occasionally making new acquaintances. Upon passing a familiar face, it's okay to wave and keep walking, especially if one party is clearly on the way to an appointment or otherwise engaged in intensive conversation, particularly on the cell phone. However, a lengthier salutation is generally more acceptable, especially if the individual approaching is a relative or friend you haven't seen for a while. In any event, once stopped, the greeting must include a physical gesture, either a handshake for acquaintances and first encounters or kisses on both cheeks for family and close friends. This physical salutation must be performed both at the beginning and the end of the exchange, even if it lasts less than a minute. Going around a large group of people twice within such a short period of time seemed unnatural to me at first, but I realized that it was perfectly normal for Calabrians and a necessary component of the social experience.

While the aspect of stretching one's legs plays into the *passeggiata*, the promenade isn't meant to be strenuous. Participants go back and forth on the flat streets parallel to the sea. Wandering away from the waterfront area, the walker faces a rather steep hill, thus the construction of the aforementioned *tapis roulant* to take pedestrians up and down at the city's core. On more than one occasion my young students cited this moving walkway as an example of the modernity of their city. Surprised at first, I realized that by Italian standards Reggio was quite modern in the physical sense and they wouldn't have even needed to include this people mover to make their point. The city's face has changed many times over the centuries. Traditions such as the *passeggiata* and getting together in the town square, however, predate many an earthquake, and for the average citizen provide a more tangible connection to the past than the exposed Greek boulders on Via Marina.

REGGIO'S GUARDIAN ANGEL

BOOM! BOOM! Two CANON SHOTS announce the start of the procession for Reggio's patron saint, the Madonna of Consolation. Taking place annually on the second Saturday of September, this festival, *La festa della Madonna della consolazione* is one of Calabria's biggest celebrations and has been observed for almost five hundred years. A sixteenth-century painting of the mother and child has long provided its inspiration. As the legend goes, this representation of the Madonna mysteriously disappeared from its location in Reggio only to be discovered

by a young shepherd on a nearby hill. After several such miraculous relocations, the faithful built a church on the site where
the icon appeared to be most comfortable. Over the centuries,
the Madonna is credited with having saved the citizens of Reggio from various plagues, famine, Turkish siege and earthquakes.
Throughout their many natural disasters, the citizens have come
to rely on the Madonna as their protector, and their faith is reflected in the festival's substantial attendance.

After much preparation and a vigil at the Basilica of Eremo the
evening before, the religious procession sets forth from the icon's
home in the Eremo district and ends three and a half kilometers
(two miles) away at Reggio's *Duomo*, the city's cathedral on il
Corso in the center of town. Naturally, the cortege's centerpiece is
the icon itself, the Madonna and child flanked by Saint Francis and
Saint Anthony of Padua. Also featured are local bands, the clergy, a
group of cloaked *cavallieri* or knights (without horses, but notably
including a few women), and of course droves of townspeople,
several making the trek without shoes to either demonstrate their
thankfulness for a gift from or in appeal to the Madonna. As
for the shoeless, from my position on an acquaintance's balcony
overlooking il Corso, the ecclesiastics were certainly not counted
amongst them, sporting quite a varied array of footwear. The
upper echelons of church hierarchy were more uniform with basic,
conservative black slip-ons. The crispness of a garment's creases, a
prominent display of lace or a headpiece crowned with a pompom
also accentuated rank. Those whose attire included a wrap-around
belt of some sort, however, had on shoes ranging from orthopedic
sandals to royal blue sneakers.

A few days before the procession, loudspeakers were
mounted on il Corso's light fixtures. Pre-recorded prayers and
songs accompanied the column of devoted, resulting in the
occasional Charles Ives effect when an enthusiastic band or chorus
of voices neglected to take heed of the public address system's
selections and pacing. As in festival scenes of Sicilian films,
colorful, decorative bedspreads were hung from the balconies of

the prestigious apartments above il Corso's ground floor stores. My hosts chose a lovely nineteenth-century, emerald green silk brocade. Their home was equally elegant, with beautifully restored hand-painted ceilings, gilded antique furniture, and a stunning crystal chandelier in the salon that overlooked il Corso. For my first procession, I was lucky to have such a fine view from their corner apartment's wrap-around balcony, and as a cool refreshment on the hot, Indian summer day, my hosts offered large, silver platters overflowing with mounds of miniature ice cream cones, sold in combination pastry and gelato shops throughout the city.

The entire procession takes several hours to complete and much time is spent passing conversation in anticipation of the spectacle. From a distance as the Madonna moves down the street, she appears to proceed quite smoothly, but due to her apparent weight, she needs to stop for a rest every so often. Or better said, her carriers are obliged to take a break every few minutes, for as she approaches, it becomes clear that the mass of people directly surrounding the painting are supporting long wooden logs on their shoulders and that the manpower used to carry the painting is as original as the bedspreads adorning the balconies. A cadre of men in white, short-sleeved shirts and burgundy or other various shades of red neckerchiefs bears the icon's significant weight due to its elaborate silver-plated frame topped with a large crown. In this procession, hierarchies exist not only in the clergy, but also amongst the *portatori della vara* (carriers of the icon's structure). A *portatore* starts out at the end of the log behind the Madonna and over the years with enough staying power, gradually moves up to the front, and one day may even become the leader.

During the pauses, the *portatori* often turn the painting to face in one direction or another. They have also been known to stop and offer someone a cup of coffee. Theories are proffered as to why every year the Madonna faces a particular business or house, such as, a certain watchmaker fixed the timepieces of the carriers for free all year long. If true, of course, said watchmaker would no longer have been in business, as the carriers have to work in shifts and number in the hundreds. More likely, a *sconto* (discount) may have been extended. The *portatori's* frequent breaks also serve to give parents the opportunity of passing their babies down the row of carriers, until the *portatore* nearest the icon raises the child up and leans him or her in to kiss the picture, eliciting resounding cheers from the crowd. The bottom half of the canvas is covered by a see-through sneeze guard or grubby fingerprint shield for such gestures of affection.

The week of the festival is full of activities not directly associated with but in some way in celebration of the Madonna. Costumed dancers and musicians perform tarantellas in the streets and invite onlookers to join the whirling merriment, in which the old timers' seamless precision often outshines the more flamboyant style of the younger generations. The rapid 6/8 dance characterized by fast footwork is usually accompanied by a small accordion and a tambourine. The instrument perhaps the most interesting to see is the Calabrian bagpipe. Slung over the musician's shoulder or hugged to the body, the "bag" is composed of an entire goatskin, bloodstained spots and all. Other entertainments include a pair of humorous, dancing giants and carnival rides set up along the Strait of Messina with loudspeakers that blare American pop every evening until 4 a.m. (I "enjoyed" that aspect of the festival for an entire week staying at my friends Franco and Luisa's apartment on Via Marina.)

As in any Italian festival, food is involved, and the *frittole* features prominently. (See chapter 11.) Large quantities of Italian rolls filled with sausage and peppers, similar to a sandwich served at state fairs all over America, are also consumed. Oddly enough, many choose to substitute French fries for the peppers—right on the sandwich. Street stands sell colorfully decorated anise cookies called *'nzuddha*, as well as other sweets and nuts. Balloon vendors set up their carts throughout the downtown, such as in the middle of Piazza Duomo, thinking nothing of blocking the faithful's view of the passing icon.

The painting remains in Reggio's Duomo for two months before a procession brings it back up the hill on the Sunday after the twenty-first of November, a bit more of a physical effort for the return trip. Many Masses are celebrated in the cathedral and devotees pay their respects to the Madonna, often entering the cathedral, approaching the icon, maybe leaving some flowers, and then going on their way right in the midst of a liturgy. On the Tuesday following the weekend of the festival's start, the painting is taken out again and carried around the city for another couple of hours. Observing that procession from street level definitely gave a different sense of the humanity amidst a crowd on a hot evening. The icon's weight was also more apparent from the strained faces and the sweat-soaked neckerchiefs of the carriers, about a hundred men at a time not including those who help balance the weight from the opposite directions on all sides. To lift the icon and start moving, the *portatori* utter a short refrain in dialect, "*Eh, giràmulu tutti cu còri! Oggi e sempri, viva Maria!*" (We all shout from our hearts! Today and always, long live Maria!) The ding-a-ling of a little bell signals the moments of rest. I couldn't help but think, "Why don't they just use some wheels?"

Certainly, if the clergy had to transport this weighty icon, a mechanized system would have been put into place long ago. And even with the prayers that do seem repetitive during the length of the procession, most of the priests let the loudspeakers do the work, carrying on conversations with their colleagues and waving to their friends and parishioners in the crowd. The resultant procession is an odd mix of devotional and non-devotional, pomp and simplicity, black patent leathers and blue sport shoes, local knights and balloon salesmen, the devout mumbling prayers and distorted electronics disturbing the peace, the shoeless and the tarantella, a religious pilgrimage and an annual parade. The Calabrians practice a matter-of-fact religiosity. The Madonna is ever-present. There's time for both solemnity and a party.

CITY LIVING

WHO'S PRACTICING THE BASS TROMBONE IN THE MIDDLE OF THE NIGHT? Half asleep, partly awake, I listened to the rank beginner blat out a descending chromatic triplet, struggling to land squarely on his destination note and ending in a retching gurgle. BLAH-BLAH-BLAH-PPBLAHAHAHAUGH! Over and over, the metallic vibrations rattled my whole being. PBLAH-BLUH-BLUAH-P-P-B-BLUAUAHAHAUGH! "ENOUGH!" I was screaming at the top of my lungs, waking up not to a middle-school-band nightmare, but my own private nightmare, as I gradually became cognizant of the fact that no brass player, however inept, could ever have launched such an insufferable assault. At the very least, the trombonist's lips would have tired long before the onslaught ended.

I was lying in bed in one of several apartments I would rent in Reggio. The courtyard project that the realtor assured me had been abandoned had newly come to life at seven o'clock one morning shortly after I moved in. Particularly vexing, the hired hands only worked when I was present, never in the afternoon or evening while I was out teaching. My school classroom was the same, just when I was about to do a listening exercise, PRBLAH-BLUH-BLAH-PPBLAHAHAHAUGH! The racket emanated from the adjoining building; for the better part of a year, every day around 5 p.m. the infernal attack would begin. If I was doing an individual lesson, I had the option of switching to the closet cum studio that reeked of fish from the dumpsters directly under its window. Once, during an extended serenade, a high school student in a class often subjected to the absurdity shouted over the din, "One day we're going to walk outside and there'll be a castle next door!" I came to appreciate the hidden beauty in the abandoned construction projects throughout the region.

Calabria is full of buildings in need of renovation, wonderful undertakings in theory until you find yourself part of the never-ending process, as concrete seems to require a rather protracted, aggressive approach. The *martello pneumatico* (pneumatic drill), the *trapano elettrico* (electric drill) and all manner of power tools used to knock holes in concrete walls are inescapable aspects of daily life in Calabria. The *piccone* (pickaxe) is also frequently heard chipping away at cement walls, but with the noise level set by its more forceful counterparts, the manual implement is hardly noticeable. Upon reflection, the *passeggiata* may have more to do with escaping the awful racket inside homes and businesses than meeting up with friends on the street. I frequently found myself rising earlier than I wanted and going outside, which had another benefit—it was usually warmer. I could also take the opportunity to do my shopping.

Getting used to store hours was a challenge, with the extended lunchtime closing often catching me off guard. Accustomed to twenty-four hour availability every day of the week, I felt constrained by the possibility of forgetting something, only to be left on a Sunday, a holiday or any weekday evening without a basic necessity. In a moment of desperation, Reggio did have a few larger supermarkets outside the center that didn't close for lunch and were open on Sunday morning, but the bus schedule made it imprudent to travel the distance on off hours. And in all truth, I preferred the availability and quality of the local products, and usually, the informal conversation at the small mom-and-pops. Not to mention the fact that the seated cashiers in the larger chains didn't bag groceries and more often than not were rather surly.

I quickly discovered that anonymity wasn't advantageous for the Calabrian shopper. In small stores regular customers generally receive better service, and in popular businesses without a numbering system for serving customers, it helps to be recognized by the proprietor or assistant working behind the counter. Most Calabrians enter a store or bar bellowing out a hearty, "*Buon giorno!*" Often, a public demonstration of cordiality isn't the principle motivation behind such a salutation. Strongly addressing the assemblage forces everyone to acknowledge the well-wishers presence and his or her place in line. Not participating in this ritual puts a customer at risk of being invisible, as the 'me first' attitude is quite pervasive. Chivalry pops up occasionally when a man finds a woman attractive, insisting that she pass in front of him in order to get a better look. Short, old women of the sturdy variety have their own technique of jumping to the front of the line, squeezing past the legs of taller customers to ostensibly inspect the offerings in the display case. "Who's next?" "I am," the Lilliputian brazenly responds, not turning even the slightest one way or the other to acknowledge the presence of a shop full of people who clearly arrived before her.

Being on the shy side, I avoided establishments in which it was a struggle to be served. "*Ragazza!*" (Girl or young woman, a compliment for anyone over the age of 35.) *Il macellaio* (the butcher) was looking right at me with a huge smile. He had quality products and was always aware of the moment I entered his store. "*Bella biondina!*" (Beautiful blonde—he obviously liked my highlights.) *Il macellaio* tended toward the familiar, slightly overstepping grammatical boundaries, but was always polite. (The Italian language requires different forms of 'you' for formal and informal situations.) I introduced my friend Luisa to his shop and she's now a regular customer, although she did feel it necessary to establish social protocol early on, making a point of flinging around "*la dottoressa*" (female college graduate) and "*la professoressa*" (high school teacher or university professor) just to let him know that I merited a certain level of respect. Italians are partial to titles.

Il macellaio liked to give the impression that his meat came from animals practically cared for as family pets and humanely slaughtered for his illustrious customers' fine palates and sensibilities. The veal came from *his* calf or the eggs from *his* chickens, hand fed from *his* table. Many butcher shops also sold prepared food ready to throw in a pan or pop in the oven, such as *cotolette milanese* (breaded cutlets), *involtini di vitello* (stuffed veal roll-ups), *pollo ripieno* (stuffed chicken parts), *melanzane alla parmigiana* (eggplant parmigiana)—naturally, made by *his* wife, although it seemed more likely made by *his* Philippine or Moroccan worker using recipes of *his* wife. Sometimes *his* father helped out—a classic one-handed butcher who adroitly served up the *frittole* from the gleaming stainless-steel caldron placed on the sidewalk in front of the store on Saturday morning.

When I finally had enough of the noise, humidity and mold in my place near the central train station and moved to an apartment at the other end of *il Corso*, I discovered that the 25 cents *il macellaio* charged for *his* organic brown eggs was a bargain compared to the 50 cents for a similarly touted egg in a pricier location. I was told, "These eggs are from *my* chickens, they're *da bere* (for drinking raw)." As I had no intention of drinking my eggs, in my new neighborhood at the north end of *il Corso*, I passed up the eggs in little wicker baskets next to the cash registers, having to settle for a variety not hand-fed by the mother-in-law of anyone I knew. However, the apartment was worth the sacrifice, a lot more money but with a million dollar view. In the words of Luisa's husband, "*Che meraVIGLia! CHE MERAVI-I-I-IGLIA!*" (How marvelous!)

The corner building with functional-looking balconies up its six stories wasn't the most attractive on *il Corso*, but entering on the side street, taking the tiny elevator up to "A" for *attico* (attic) and opening the door that led to an enormous terrace, my little apartment and an incredible view of the entire Strait of Messina, my guests exclaimed with awe at the miraculous vision that made living there truly a pleasure. I never had to look for something special to do on my time off; I simply opened my rolling shutters and took in the panorama: Reggio's *lungomare* (waterfront), the currents of the strait with its passing ships and sailboats, windsurfers and the very occasional pod of dolphins or other cetaceans, and the city of Messina with the coastline and mountains of Sicily behind. Admittedly, I had to either stick my head out of the window or go out onto the terrace to see Mount Etna, but I even had the view from my bathroom! Most visible early in the morning as the volcano's cone attracted clouds as the day wore on, Etna was especially spectacular when snowcapped and I took countless pictures of the *meraviglia* (wonder). Sicily's enchanting night view glittered with the lights from Messina. As often as I stared out of my window, however, I never saw Reggio's legendary optical illusion, the *Fata Morgana*. This protagonist of myths and mysteries to which shipwrecks and other disasters have been attributed is caused by the refraction of images off water vapor, making the opposite coast seem closer than it is. Documented since ancient times, this phenomenon has lent Reggio one of its nicknames, "the City of the *Fata Morgana*."

The sea and the strait's peculiar atmospheric conditions did, however, conjure other images for me. Classic epic journeys flashed through my mind during big storms in the attic apartment, when the sea was rough and swollen, the strong winds whipped down the mountains and through the narrow passage, and the gales howled and rattled the loose metal gutters. Perched in the little rooftop structure, I was at the whim of the elements, tossed around the Mediterranean like Ulysses and other travelers before me, confronting the volatile environment.

I faced another of nature's forces one morning as I got out of the shower, catching myself in a slide, my slippers hydroplaning across the floor. I looked down to see my light-colored tiles covered in black. It took me a minute to realize that the window I habitually opened to let out humidity, on that day had let in volcanic ash. I hadn't opened the big rolling shutters in the living room or glanced out the small window in the bathroom before I hopped in the shower. By the time I surveyed the streaked, graying sky, similar to that of a large forest fire, Etna's peak was completely cloud covered. My friend Luisa swept ashes up from her balcony on Via Marina several times a day for a week, using the powder as plant fertilizer. In the open-air market, the vendors shrugged off the black dust landing on their prepared items, declaring the consumption of Etna's ash nutritious. The cinders certainly did wonders for the local fruits and vegetables.

On my upper floor, I was just happy to have water in which to take a shower. I could always clean up the ash—during the day, that is. A little while after I moved in, I suddenly didn't have water between 8 or 9 in the evening and 6 o'clock in the morning. This absence of what would normally be considered a necessity in any civilized country went on for several months straight and then occurred periodically for the rest of my stay. Having already had a no-water experience without any notification in my apartment near the train station, I was already aware of the city's insufficient supply. The secretary at my school told me that, as a child, she felt a kinship with America's Wild West. Pans and buckets of water were filled and saved for necessary washing and toilet flushing. I, too, learned to be prepared, although I did find myself washing my hair in a salad bowl filled with bottled water on a few occasions.

Numerous condominiums in Reggio had holding tanks that collected water for when it wasn't available. Some outskirts never had water after a certain hour. And incredibly, not only wasn't there enough water to see the residents through the entire day, but the quality of the precious commodity was also dubious. In many downtown locations, the water was extremely salty and seemed to have been pumped directly out of the strait. The plus side was that the pasta water didn't need any additional salt. As a renter, knowing the water situation before moving in didn't always help, as circumstances sometimes changed. The utility company could apparently turn the water off and on at their whim, only giving out information to tenacious customers who persisted with repeated phone calls and/or in-person visits to their offices. One unsympathetic landlady dismissed my difficulties with, "This isn't the north," a weak excuse that perpetuated the status quo of a stereotypical backward south. In the end, the only defense was preparedness, which included having water on hand.

I was able to have an ample supply of drinking water at the ready as my favorite, family-run quick shop delivered in the neighborhood. The mother also made a tasty, traditional *stoccafisso* with potatoes and olives every Friday, and other friends and acquaintances furnished her shop with baked goods, eggs and fresh ricotta on Monday, Wednesday and Friday. The store carried good, local olive oil in bulk, which I bought in their unmarked, green-glass, liter bottles. Sold similarly, their table wine wasn't bad either. That little ten by twenty-foot storefront one block up from *il Corso* had almost everything—fruits and vegetables, dried goods, a frozen case, but the real draw was the fresh bread. The wooden bins on the back wall were filled with an amazing assortment for such a small business that wasn't a *fornaio* (bread bakery). Their bread came from a variety of sources, the enormous loaves three feet in diameter or the large, dark, crusty sourdough baguettes from which they were always willing to cut me smaller pieces. For those new to the shop as well as for the regulars, the selection process required patience as the gloved mother or grown son would hold up different bread and rolls—whole wheat (*grano*), multi-grain (*integrale*), rye (*segale*) and naturally an assortment of white (*bianco*), in a myriad of sizes and shapes—while everyone waited their turn to go through the process. And in a country plagued by cheating, this mom and pop store always gave a valid, fiscal receipt even for one, tiny, fifteen-cent roll.

My other regular food haven was a family-run pizza place just past the museum. I tried to limit myself to one pizza a week, often entering with the idea of selecting from their *tavola calda* (table of hot prepared foods) of both first and second courses or a sandwich on their freshly baked bread, but ending up with my favorite of their menu items, the pizza with gorgonzola and apple. Perhaps that pizza was more popular with the take-out customers as I never saw anyone else eating it at one of the tables, and whenever one of the girls gave the order back to the *pizzaiolo* (pizza maker), he'd smile, look out and wave. Every once and a while I saw him duck out just after I'd ordered, no matter how busy they were, returning from the fruit stand next door with a green apple in his hand. He also baked delicious bergamot cookies, made from the rare citrus fruit that flourishes in the area. Those little gems seemed to be more generally appreciated than the gorgonzola and apple pizza.

I often ate my unusual pizza by myself, incomprehensible to the locals, as Calabrians didn't eat by themselves, especially women. Going to a casual lunch place that served workers who didn't have time to go home to eat with their families may have been marginally acceptable, but eating in a restaurant unaccompanied on a Sunday afternoon couldn't help but attract attention and provoke speculation. I was looking over the menu in just such a circumstance when a friendly waiter came up to my table with an apologetic smile and a narrow glass filled with a dark pink liquid. The Campari had been sent over by a lively table of middle-aged men who looked ready to cheer on their favorite soccer team. I reluctantly accepted, and over a period of time, they adopted me. The group was a fixture on Sundays and holidays, first meeting for a swim in the Strait, and then a few drinks before returning home to their families for dinner, leaving a clutter of the small, cone-shaped bottles and several empty platters with a few cold French fries on their table. Colorful, to say the least, they bounced between Calabrian dialect and Italian, and sported nicknames like Killer (apparently referring to his approach with the ladies), *Olé* (an homage to his Spanish surname), *Gigante* (Giant, naturally, a shorter fellow), *il Maestro* (the master, an amateur fiddle player) and Bud Spencer (for his resemblance to the burly Spaghetti Western actor). On holidays, *Mano lesta* (Light fingers), the *pasticciere* (pastry chef) supplied the group's appetizer. If Killer wanted to make sure I showed up, he'd arrange for *Mano lesta* to bring one of his seasonal specialties I couldn't turn down, nicely wrapped up for me to take home.

Reggio was an odd mix of positives and negatives. Living there, I was constantly faced with people who could care less about those around them and others who went out of their way to brighten someone's day—often, food was involved and needless to say, individuals did have their motives. People could be brutal, particularly when seemingly anonymous, such as working for a utility company, sitting behind the wheel of a car or grasping the handle of a pneumatic drill. The natural world also dealt out its own form of harshness. Mount Etna spewed her volcanic ash indiscriminately, destroying the paths of some and enriching the environment for others. Survival was for the fittest. Quality of life was a delicate balancing act in Reggio di Calabria.

A VISIT TO THE DOCTOR'S OFFICE

TO THE UNINITIATED, MY FRIEND'S massive fur coat may have seemed a bit excessive down in the toe of the Italian boot. However, anyone who has ever experienced the bone-chilling humidity and gelid winds blowing off Mt. Etna and whipping through the Strait of Messina understands that mild, official temperature readings and the presence of overloaded citrus trees can sometimes contribute to poor outerwear choices in this Mediterranean town. My friend Luisa and I were on our way to a gathering where she had been invited to speak about a recently deceased Italian translator of an obscure, late nineteenth-century British writer.

Upon arrival we were buzzed into an office building next door to one of the many economical Chinese clothing stores found throughout Italy. Traditional red lanterns running the length of these shops and restaurants draw attention to their presence despite the oft-tenuous relationship between this immigrant group and the Italian people. Curiously, native inhabitants of cities with large Chinese populations complain more of the exotic cooking odors emanating from individual apartments and eating establishments than the nation's economic loss due to the influx of cheap apparel and designer knockoffs.

We followed a few others up a flight of steps and entered what, according to the signage, was a doctor's office, complete with two fire-engine red ticket machines that would have been more suited to a butcher's or baker's. Greeted by the presiding MD, we were ushered into a good-sized, no-nonsense waiting room with molded, plastic, stackable chairs around its rectangular perimeter. Once seated, we began to read the information contained in the many health-related posters adorning the walls. "*Sinusite*" (sinusitis) featured prominently, and I wondered if this was the government health program's illness of the month or if the problem was endemic to Reggio, as I had suffered with an inordinate number of colds and related nasal issues since I had lived in the province. However, the most notable feature of the room was an oversized electronic sign placed high at one end. I didn't know if I was at a sporting event or my local DMV. Although not lit for our meeting, three boxes were ready to flash the numbers corresponding to the doctors whose names appeared above them—an offbeat setting for the cultural club of the citizens of the town of Cittanova living in Reggio di Calabria.

68 kilometers (42 miles) might not have seemed far to me, with Reggio being 4578 miles away from my birth place, but for the Calabrians whose origins were rooted to that particular hillside town northeast of the province's capital, the one-and-a-half-hour monthly meetings obviously provided a connection with their cultural heritage. And while the name George Gissing may not have meant anything to me at the time, it seemed as though everyone in the room had enthusiastically read their fellow Calabrian Francesco Badolato's translation of Gissing's 1901 travelogue *By the Ionian Sea: Notes of a Ramble in Southern Italy*.

Luisa kicked off the proceedings, warmly telling us of her encounters with the translator as well as with more contemporary British travelers to Reggio. An English instructor, a teacher trainer and longtime president of the Anglo-Italian Club of Reggio, Luisa was an excellent speaker who lent an old-world sophistication to her informative presentations. The program's main presenter, while an admirer of Gissing and his quest for the land where Magna Graecia once flourished, was more than a bit bothered by a few of the author's negative comments with regard to Naples, where his itinerary began, and Reggio, where the writer ended his journey. The speaker's criticism wasn't always well taken by many in the room, who could quote entire passages of the work from memory. Opposing remarks and discussions got quite heated, periodically obliterating those of the lecturer himself. To an English speaker unused to the Italian habit of talking over one another, the meeting would have appeared to have completely deteriorated, nothing salvageable out of the apparent bedlam; however, the thread remained solid and the group members weren't at all disturbed by such a lively exchange of ideas. Quite naturally, the participants took observations and perceived disparagements about their beloved homeland seriously.

When the program went past its scheduled time and it was clear that the presenters and their audience had far more to say than could be wrapped up in a few extra minutes, several club members started getting up to leave. Just as a foreign observer may have been at a loss during the impassioned discussion a short while earlier, the departure of those with allegedly pressing business elsewhere would have probably also raised an eyebrow amongst those unfamiliar with the region's customs. Calabrians don't enter or leave rooms quietly. They somehow feel obligated to greet everyone present, rather loudly excusing themselves for the interruption that is always more bothersome than the intrusion itself. They may even shake a few hands, and they more often than not hesitate an extra moment, holding a glance just a second or two longer on any stranger amongst them. Surprisingly, the speaker persevered through several departures, but was finally pressed to wrap up his presentation in order to give some time to the singer who was poised to give her contribution to the evening's fair.

She and her boombox delivered the musical selections with gusto, beginning with a familiar country and western number of which the only word I caught was "darling." The energetic performer followed up with "Calabria Mia" and ended with a popular Neapolitan song, both in their respective dialects. The doctor kept quite busy during that time, leaving the room and coming back, handing envelopes to various attendees. It seemed that the advantageous location of the meetings wasn't lost on those present.

As the doctor's waiting room didn't have any more heat than my school classroom, we hadn't removed our furs and down upon arrival, saving a step as we left. Down on street level, a frigid blast of wind whisked us out the door, and we hurried off to our late suppers in keeping with the southern Italian tradition.

A TRIP TO THE MOVIES

"BAM! BAM! BAM! *SCUSATEMI PER IL RITARDO!*" (Excuse me for my tardiness!) Very few students consistently arrived to class on time, and the general lack of punctuality was something I had trouble getting used to. I would say that Calabrians struggled with punctuality, except for the fact that no one seemed to be struggling at all. The first time I was the guest speaker at Reggio's Anglo-Italian Club, I arranged to meet the president (who would become my friend Luisa) at her house and walk to the nearby conference location together. Naturally, I arrived with plenty of time to spare; however, we somehow only set out for the meeting after its scheduled starting time. My uneasiness was mitigated by the fact that I was with the group's president, but what I found amazing was that this unpunctuality didn't seem to faze her in the least. Logically, living amongst a population with a propensity towards lateness, to arrive at a 9:00 appointment before 9:15 would be pointless, and in the end, a waste of time. For those individuals unaccustomed to adjusting their personal timetable according to the intricacies of the culture at hand, confusion arose on the rare occasions when the scheduled appointment time was really the same as the actual meeting time.

One Saturday evening Luisa and I had arranged to see a movie at 8:00. It probably would have been easier to walk, but her husband wanted her to take the car for the trip home even though returning on il Corso would have been perfectly safe, elbow to elbow with the usual Saturday night crowd. An analogous world on wheels presented itself on the parallel Via Marina, where cruisers drove, or more accurately inched up and down the coastal road. Despite its dramatic setting overlooking the Strait of Messina and the lovely greenery down its center, from inside one of the cars perpetually lined up during the city's rush hours or on foot, trying to cross the street in front of one of them, chaos reigned.

Knowing that it could take longer to drive than to walk, I arrived at Luisa's house at 7:30, and at 7:50 we were backing out of her driveway into the lineup. As we sat there amidst the honking, she told me that she knew a trick—no problem. In the park-like median strip there were turning lanes, some of which were the length of a city block. To expedite her maneuvers she sped down the bus lane, explaining that the express lane was also utilized for emergencies. "Luisa, what's our emergency?" I asked. "We're going to the movies, these people are just Sunday driving!"

Miraculously, we arrived in the area of the theater as it was turning 8. Cars were parked and double-parked. It didn't seem even remotely possible that we would be able to find a space, but she pinpointed a little gap on a corner in front of a butcher shop that was just closing and gently bumped a few teenage boys off a metal railing to get her nose a bit closer. We had found a space in record time and walked the short distance to the theater; however, her efforts seemed for naught as we faced the sea of people waiting in front of the ticket desk. Not a line, but an expanding mushroom cloud in which the same people always seemed to remain on the edge as their more dexterous compatriots managed to enter and work their way up to the front. I was already thinking of other possibilities for the evening when she said, "Come with me," and walked directly up to the young ticket-taker. "Are there still seats available?" she asked. "A few," he replied. "We'll check." We entered, found what seemed to be the last two places together near the back, sat down and watched the movie.

I thought, "What chutzpah!" Then after the movie, I found out that one of her cousins owned the theater.

We would go to that movie house several times. Usually, it was empty and Luisa could look around and identify a good number of the patrons. Once, she said, "Look, it's Judge So-and-So with his wife, without a security detail. Do you remember the bombings last year—one in his office and a few months later another one at his home?" "Yes, it was on the national news and they had the street blocked off for a long time," I replied. "He was one of my sister's students. He's looking a little tired." "Luisa, do you think maybe we should sit on the other side of the theater?" "No, the perpetrator is in jail." The large, round garbage can at the end of our row didn't seem to bother her or the judge. Was I overly cautious? Didn't the "perp" have cousins and associates? Where was his bodyguard to check it out? I suppose the judge had to live his life.

On the way home, Luisa wanted to stop by her sister's condo to drop something off. She found a parking space that wasn't a parking space, nestling the car halfway over a crosswalk and halfway in a handicap space. As I didn't know how to drive a manual, I offered to carry the parcel up so she could move the car in case a traffic cop were to pass, but she wanted to do it. I was to remain there and tell the officer she'd be right back. No problem—she told me to say that I wasn't able to walk very far due to my bunions. I had recently traded in my narrower, more stylish Italian-made footwear that I had purchased in Siderno for a pair of heavy, square-toed shoes. My new, bulky German boots would be proof enough for any Italian not to write up a ticket.

WHAT'S YOUR FAVORITE . . . ?

AS AN ENGLISH TEACHER, I had to ask a lot of questions.

"What's your favorite color?" elicited a one-word answer, sometimes two.

"What's your favorite sport?" prompted diverse responses, although "football" (British for soccer) was the overwhelming preference, especially amongst males. "Basket" (Italian for basketball) also had many followers, particularly in Reggio where American Kobe Bryant had spent several years as a boy while his father was coaching the local team. "Volleyball" was a sport they had all played, particularly in cities where schools lacked adequate gymnasiums, and physical education as described by many of my students, often consisted of setting up a net in the courtyard.

"What's your favorite food?" always generated smiles as Italians love talking about what they eat. Adults would go into incredible detail. Adolescents usually put either pizza or pasta in first place. Younger children preferred pizza, but some gave equal weight to pizza and chips. (Chips, British = French fries, American)

When I first posed the favorite food question, the most surprising responses for me were, "Pizza with chips," and "Pizza with chips and *Würstel.*" (*Würstel*, German = Hotdog) These extremely popular pizzas* were actually topped with French fries and hotdogs—horrifying to even look at! The pies were both cooked to order and pre-made, ready to be served by the slice to youngsters lined up for the treat. They didn't seem bothered by soggy French fries. Sadly, the famed Mediterranean diet floundered in many a pizzeria where standard appetizers consumed before the pizza were French fries (routinely eaten with mayonnaise squeezed out of little packets), *Würstel*, potato croquettes and fried cheese.

Occasionally, a child would veer from the norm, not

---

* The plural of pizza in Italian is *pizze.*

beguiled by greasy deep fryers and McDonald's Happy Meals, which were also popular amongst the younger set. One colorful lad who had the mannerisms of a bygone age kissed his cupped fingertips when describing a particularly mouthwatering liver dish and ecstatically whirled his raised hand with a gesture that radiated from his elbow as he conveyed a passionate enthusiasm for his grandmother's macaroni with goat sauce—the absolute best in the world!

With some students, trying to get a conversation going or to even exchange a few words in English was a bit like playing the game "20 Questions" or circulating at a lame cocktail party. Even the most loquacious of people could freeze up when addressed in a foreign language, particularly adults. Leo, a friendly twenty-something who followed the lessons with great interest was one such example. Over a month passed before he uttered his first word. Granted, he started out with a cold; however, he parlayed a touch of laryngitis into a fashion statement, as only an Italian could do, carefully protecting his neck with an expert wrapping meant to ward off all conversational approaches for as long as he could pull it off. When Leo finally spoke, he had an excellent pronunciation. His classmate Nino never did make his foray into the English language. As he told Leo whom he ran into during a *passeggiata*, his wife wasn't happy with him having a female teacher and made him drop the course early on.

The good-natured banter of the mother and son duo of Carmen and Raffaele lent a lively atmosphere to Leo's class. The pair exemplified Calabrian togetherness—working side by side in their family business, studying English in tandem, even sharing a book. However, as is the case with many Italians, pronunciation was a challenge for Carmen. The pure Italian vowels were part of her DNA. In addition, English's non-phonetic spelling, the seven extra vowel sounds used by the British and the forced multiculturalism in English as a Second Language textbooks just added to the confusion. Students would look at foreign names and logically try to pronounce them as if they were English.

So when "Juan" appeared in her elementary class text one day, Carmen articulated an English 'j' and gave the name two solid syllables, becoming Raffaele's favorite joke. Of course, everyone had his individual strengths.

One day, the class was learning how to say numbers in various forms, such as with prices and decimal points. The students were musing as to the whereabouts of the printed telephone numbers in their book, and I said that the one with the 212 area code was in Manhattan. Apparently, having this type of knowledge was inconceivable down in the toe of the Italian boot, so Raffaele pulled out his phone to test my assertion. *Ring. Ring.* "Hello?" responded a man's voice on speakerphone in what I assured them was a New York accent. Raffaele hung up. "Why did you hang up? We could have talked to him," I said. He redialed. *Ring.* "Hello?" This time Raffaele spoke resolutely, "I am Joo-*an!*" to which the respondent delivered the classic "A-a-and?" Amidst hysterical laughter Raffaele hung up a second time and I felt as though I had become part of a Bart Simsonesque prank call. Nevertheless, they were quite satisfied with their first authentic English interaction with a real New Yorker.

Another evening, fellow classmate Mimmo responded to his phone's vibration, apologizing profusely for the uncharacteristic interruption, but his friend was calling to say that the fish were biting. Obviously, to the question, "What's your favorite sport?" he would have undoubtedly responded, "Fishing." At 9 p.m. in the middle of winter, he raced to an undisclosed location along the shores of the Strait of Messina, and the next day I was the beneficiary of several *spatola* or *pesce sciabola* (cutlassfish), an extremely unattractive silver fish with an eel-like body, protruding lower jaw and menacing teeth. I sautéed the delicate white fish in olive oil with fresh tomatoes and parsley, and enjoyed the sauce with spaghetti, appreciating the very Italian way in which Mimmo combined his favorite sport with his favorite food.

10

ONLY IN CALABRIA

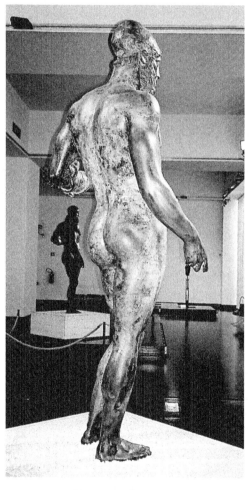

THE BRONZES OF RIACE, STATUE B IN FOREGROUND,
NATIONAL ARCHEOLOGICAL MUSEUM IN REGGIO

THE FAMOUS BRONZES

DURING MY TIME IN CALABRIA, the region unveiled a publicity campaign that was a bit controversial amongst its citizenry. At its center were *i Bronzi di Riace* (the Riace Bronzes) or as they're more commonly referred to both in Calabria and throughout Italy, simply *i bronzi*. Back in 1972 when they were fortuitously discovered by a diver in the Ionian Sea off the coast of Riace, a small town north of Locri, these 2500-year-old Greek statues in bronze were a spectacular archeological find even for a country like Italy in which historic artifacts were unearthed at practically every turn of the shovel.

After many years of restoration, both in Reggio and in a specialized laboratory in Florence, the Bronzes were first put on public display in exhibitions in Florence and Rome before making their permanent home in Reggio's Archeological Museum in 1981. Twenty-eight years later, the statues were scheduled to make a trip to the G8 Summit in Sardinia, much to the chagrin of many Calabrians who felt that if the Bronzes started to go out on tour, who would come to Calabria to see them? Was Michelangelo's David carted out of Florence's Accademia Gallery for political photo-ops? The issue was resolved by the conference's change in venue to Aquila, which was seen as too great a seismic risk, ironic for statues that lived in Reggio.

Calabrians are very protective of their beloved Bronzes. When they saw caricatures of the precious statues being used in national television spots to promote regional tourism, many felt embarrassed and distressed. From an American point of view, the ad was clever; however, for the average Calabrian the sight of the two male nudes bounding from the mountains to the sea was debasing. Trivializing masterworks was not how a population that already struggled with its self-image wished to be presented to the world.

"*Noi abbiamo i bronzi!*" (We have the Bronzes), small children would proudly proclaim when telling me of their hometown. While perhaps not comprehending the breadth of history and the artistic value of the statues, even the youngest Calabrians were well aware that the museum was home to something rare and special. They watched their older siblings move to the north to find work. On holidays, their aunts and uncles visited from Canada and Australia where they, too, had sought out a better life, but the Bronzes were there to stay.

These two celebrities from another era, having left their shields, spears and helmets behind, mythologically materialized from the bottom of the sea, encrusted with 2000 years of marine-life but quasi intact, to represent the city of Reggio and the region of Calabria. Were they gods, heroes, warriors or athletes? Had they been conceived as part of a group or just strangers who shared an unfortunate passage? These are questions that have yet to be answered; however, such quality, large-scale works sculpted in precious metal would have held great value in ancient Greece and would most likely have graced an important sanctuary or piazza.

Presently, for want of more specific information as to their identities, the Bronzes are referred to as Statues A and B. Standing at approximately six and a half feet tall and physically formed to perfection, the imposing statues transmit a magnificent strength. Although sculpted in similar poses—left arms bent as if holding shields, right hands grasping imaginary spears, straight right legs supporting their bodyweight and flexed left legs placed slightly forward, the two statues are actually quite different. Representing distinct stylistic periods, Statue A typifies an idealized perfection of the human form, while Statue B embodies a humanistic vision of man. Most Calabrians have a favorite.

Statue A was created first, in the Attica region of Greece circa 460-450 BC. Tense, more static, aggressive and younger, Statue A appears aloof and detached. He is a glorified image. His ivory eyes sans pupils gaze fixedly at his opponents. His proud, combative stance and determined jaw challenge onlookers with a vanity and refinement exemplified by his silver teeth, full copper lips and well-defined, curly locks and beard.

I prefer Statue B, sculpted in Greek's Peloponnese region about 430-420 BC. Staring vacantly from his remaining marble eye, Statue B has a more human aspect. He is more relaxed and has an older, softer physique. Statue B is also of a lighter green color, partly due to a higher copper content in his alloy and also because Statue A has a mysterious black patina covering half of his body. The anatomic detail is quite remarkable in both statues, particularly the veins beneath the skin, and equally charming are their rose-colored nipples!

The public had the occasion to view the Bronzes from a completely different angle when the museum was closed for renovation and the opportunity was seized upon to give the statues a refurbishment. Instead of locking them away in a laboratory, a glassed-in restoration studio was set up in Reggio's Palazzo Campanello, the seat of the regional government, thus allowing the public to watch the restorers at work. It is a curious vision, the two heroes lying on their backs, their imposing strength frozen in time, their legs and arms forever poised in an incongruous movement when viewed from a horizontal perspective. The position allowed visitors to see the openings in their feet, exposing the statues' hollow forms. As with people, checkups included surface examinations, x-rays and assorted interior probes and procedures. Over the course of various operations, more than 100 kilos (220 lbs.) of clay and soil originally used in their construction was removed from each statue and subsequently analyzed, as the restorations were and will continue to be both conservative interventions and exploratory in nature.

Most knowledge of Greek sculpture has been through Roman copies in marble, so from both a scientific and artistic standpoint, the Bronzes are rare and important. However, they are not solitary discoveries. Calabria's waters have revealed other treasures, including two bronze heads, also housed in Reggio's museum. Most noteworthy, the Head of the Philosopher dates from the last quarter of the fifth century BC and was found in 1969 off the coast of Cannitello, just north of Reggio. While the Bronzes were discovered all by themselves, the Philosopher was part of an ancient shipwreck. Thus, his left foot and left hand, his right knee and a large corner of a short cloak come together with his wrinkled forehead, long beard and concentrated expression to give the picture of a scholar or philosopher. Extraordinarily, looking into his face is like looking at a real person, slight comb-over and all. For this reason, the experts consider his likeness to be the portraiture of an actual person, and a very early example of such artistic realism.

The Riace Bronzes and the Head of the Philosopher represent the period in which Calabria was part of the illustrious society known as Greater Greece, a time when Calabria's ports attracted an uninterrupted flow of ships from the east, the Orient, the Balkan peninsula and Greece. The ferocious storms of Ulysses' lore hid riches off Calabria's shores. Some have already been discovered while others remain concealed, ready to enhance Calabria's already rich historical and artistic patrimony. The region's archeological heritage is a source of pride for its people and their children.

The museum's renovation was scheduled to take a year; its completion was to coincide with the 150th anniversary celebration of Italy's Unification. For four years the Bronzes remained on their backs, suspended, waiting for more funds to replace those that weren't ever enough, were misspent or had disappeared. The unification ceremonies came and went; the opening of the museum was announced and then retracted; accusations were made, investigations begun and in the end more money was secured. In late 2013, the Bronzes finally returned to their home along with a new filter chamber through which all visitors must pass. Although back on their feet, they sadly inaugurated an almost empty museum, to great fanfare, despite the great state of unreadiness of the rest of the collection. Just as the ancients had to carefully navigate around the tip of the Italian peninsula, contemporary society has to be attentive and adroitly steer through the intricate machinations of modern Calabria.

THE UNCOMMONLY COMMON BERGAMOT

BEFORE I WAS EVER AWARE OF CALABRIA, I unknowingly had a connection with the region through a few products commonly found in most American homes. However, as a child, how could I have known that the classic bottle of Chanel No. 5 that graced my mother's bedroom dresser contained an oil derived from the bergamot, a citrus fruit grown in Calabria? Likewise with the Earl Grey tea on the pantry shelf?

In Calabria, my acquaintance with the bergamot came shortly after my arrival. Looking for relief from a chronic upper respiratory tract infection, I decided to try the age-old remedy of tea with honey, as all those with whom I had come in contact had advised me. Locri's Calabrian food store was well stocked with a wide assortment of local honey, including varieties made from the eucalyptus, a mixed assortment of flowers (*millefiori*), chestnuts, lemons, oranges and citrus blends. When I asked the proprietor for a recommendation, she didn't hesitate, handing me a jar of *miele al bergamotto* (honey with bergamot). Unlike the other types of honey whose name referred to the type of nectar the bees had used, this particular jar was made with the addition of bergamot oil. For me, the taste was exquisite and I wasn't ever without a spoonful in my tea, even when my sinuses had cleared.

The store carried many other products made from the bergamot, such as candy, marmalade, cookies, liquors, soaps and a tonic that indicated effectiveness for everything from acne to psoriasis. Clearly, the bergamot is quite a versatile fruit. The exceedingly curious thing about the unusual citrus, however, is that Calabria is the only place where the plant really flourishes. Stranger still is that the area is limited to a narrow stretch of land less than one hundred miles long from Villa San Giovanni to Monasterace in the province of Reggio Calabria. The main area of cultivation is half the size, extending from Reggio to Bovalino, just south of Locri. While the plant can grow in other areas, it cannot produce fruit. In the few locations where the bergamot has had success—Africa, Brazil and Argentina, the fruit is of a lesser quality. Even right across the strait in Sicily, nurseries are able to grow the plants, but they must be transplanted to Calabria in order to bear fruit.

While the high humidity of the area may be a challenge for its human occupants, the province's damp climate with its relatively consistent temperature readings that don't usually dip below 50 F in the winter is perfectly suited to the bergamot. Resistant to the summer heat, the citruses are protected from the strait's strong winds by banks of coastal pines, the same trees that provide Calabrian beachgoers cool shade for their August picnics. Blossoms appear in April and the fruit is harvested between November and March. The bergamot is round, slightly larger than an orange and not as yellow as a lemon. The skin is thin and has a delicate fragrance while the interior is quite bitter; thus, the bergamot's principal use has been through its essential oil, which is obtained by pressing the skin. 90% of the bergamot oil on the world market comes from the province of Reggio Calabria, and France is its biggest importer.

While able to cultivate the highest quality fruit, Calabria hasn't been strong in manufacturing the raw material into marketable products and has historically sent its precious oil outside the region and the country, mainly to be used as an ingredient in the perfume industry. Coveted for both its scent as well as its attribute of prolonging a perfume's fragrance for as many as sixteen hours, the bergamot's essential oil was an important ingredient in the original Eau de Cologne, created by Italians living in Germany in 1709. Since that time, perfume makers and their clients have clamored for the exotic element, most notably Coco Chanel with her popular No. 5, spritzed by my mother in preparation for an evening at the opera.

Gastronomically, the bergamot was considered a delicacy by the Vatican as far back as 1536 when the famous chef Bartolomeo Scappi used it to prepare a candy that was served to Emperor Charles V. In a more popular vein, the bergamot's oil has lent its characteristic flavor to Britain's Earl Grey tea for almost two hundred years. In France, the *Bergamote de Nancy*, a hard candy made with the oil, has been manufactured since 1850, earning the PGI (Protected Geographical Indication) in 1996 to recognize its special place in French confectionary. In Calabria, local varieties of hard and soft candies made with bergamot oil are sold, but the region hasn't developed a branded foodstuff or perfume that has achieved any significant success past the territorial level. Today, Calabria exports 99% of its essential oil that was awarded the PDO (Protected Designation of Origin) in 2001.

To gather information on an article I was writing about the bergamot, I had the opportunity to make the acquaintance of the leaders of the *Consorzio di Bergamotto* (Bergamot Consortium), an organization founded in 1931 to manage and protect the essential oil. Meeting in their unassuming offices decorated with bergamot memorabilia at their factory in Pellaro, a town on Reggio's outskirts, I was impressed with their energy and scope of ideas. Not just focusing on the traditional oil, they were scrutinizing every aspect of the fruit and scientifically analyzing its components for eventual use in many different areas. Through developmental programs, scientific research and business initiatives, the Consortium's hope was that Calabria would someday be able to truly capitalize on their valuable commodity, exporting products as well as the raw material throughout the world.

Our discussion began with the bergamot's origins. Thinking logically, the Calabrians disregarded the various foreign hypotheses of the fruit's genesis, reasoning, if the tree couldn't bear fruit in Spain, China or Greece, or even survive in Italy's Bergamo, how could it have come from those locations? Thus, the bergamot was probably indigenous to Calabria, a genetic mutation involving a crossed pollination between various citruses. The first major grove was planted in the center of Reggio in 1750. In that period, the oil was obtained by manually squeezing the fruit into absorbent sponges. In 1844 a Reggio native invented the *macchina calabrese*, a machine that provided a quality oil and led to the true industrialization of the bergamot. By today's methods, 200 kilos of fruit yield one kilo of essential oil.

Historically, the bergamot has been used by Calabrians for centuries. While the fruit's bitter quality precludes eating it like an orange, the juice is traditionally used in cakes and cookies. The liquor *Bergamino* is also a classic, made from the bergamot's peel. As the rind hardens to a wooden consistency when dried, the hollowed-out skin was also used to make small lanterns and snuff boxes. The fruit's medicinal properties have long since been embraced by Calabrians as well. The oil was used as both insect repellent and as a cure for mosquito bites. To heal wounds, the fruit was cut open, gently heated and applied directly to affected areas. In the nineteenth century, the juice was used in the treatment of malaria. And as early as 1804, a Calabrian doctor presented his thesis at the University of Pavia documenting the bergamot's reparative properties with regard to lesions.

On the world market, this all-purpose fruit has been predominantly prized for its essential oil; however, the rare liquid has had its ups and downs. In 1964, one kilo of oil sold for 40,000 lira, an enormous sum when a Fiat 500 sold for about 468,000 lira. Exports and prices fell dramatically in the late seventies as a result of competition with synthetics and negative press due to the photosensitivity of the oil. Put directly on the skin, discoloration can occur when exposed to the sun. Ironically, this chemical reaction was actually exploited in some local suntan lotions in the 1960s and 70s. Now, bergamot products made for the skin undergo a distilling process to eliminate any problems with skin blemishing.

After a low of 42 Euros per kilo, the Consortium worked to stabilize prices and in 2010 was able to empty their warehouses of all their current oil and that of previous years. Selling at 80 Euros per kilo, the Consortium guaranteed a price fluctuation no greater than 3% over the following decade, hoping to stabilize the market, gradually expand production, and return to peak prices. Excited about the bergamot's favorable prospects and the resulting benefits for the region, the Consortium actively promotes the fruit and its genuine derivatives in the perfume, pharmaceutical and food sectors.

Medicinally, the bergamot's 358 chemical substances are recognized to possess antibacterial, antiviral and antifungal qualities. Successful research also indicates the fruit's application as an anti-depressant and a cholesterol inhibitor. Over the counter products boast a myriad of uses, such as in the case of wounds, infections, inflammations, headaches, sore throats, acne, herpes, psoriasis, rheumatism, muscular cramps, insect bites and as a general antiseptic for the skin and mouth. The Consortium intends to diversify in the pharmaceutical industry as well as in other areas, including the use of byproducts to make alcohol and to feed animals with the highly caloric and nutritious remains of the fruit after its pressing.

Of the many alcoholic drinks made from the bergamot including a grappa infused with the flavor, a bitter and a *digestivo* (after dinner drink to help with digestion), my favorite is the *crema di bergamotto* (bergamot cream), as the fruit's subtle character blends well with the velvety-textured liquor. A tasty soda is also being marketed in Calabria where residents have long appreciated the very refreshing bergamot gelato, a treat that has crossed international borders. As the pope's chefs experimented half a millennium ago, contemporary culinary innovators continue to create new gastronomic combinations, such as grated zest to flavor pasta, extra virgin olive oil infused with the essential oil or a few drops of juice to lighten the spicy Calabrian *'nduja* salami or to assuage the intensity of an anchovy dish.

The Consortium strives to nurture the bergamot at home, to encourage Calabrian agronomists, chefs, perfume makers and entrepreneurs to take an interest in the region's valuable commodity by launching technical and scientific initiatives for farming improvements, advocating the development of business ventures and through educational programs, such as a master's degree in perfumery, essences and food flavoring at the local university. By promoting and protecting the bergamot, its proponents aim to foster and safeguard the future of the region. Reggio Calabria is, after all, the *Città del Bergamotto* (Bergamot City).

The bergamot has stubbornly clung to Calabria's soil, with its "*testa dura*" (hard head) resistant to transplantation, just as the region's headstrong native sons have clutched onto their ideas and traditions and have often been disparaged by the moniker. For all one knows, the environment may be unique in the true sense of the word, affecting its living inhabitants in an uncommon way. Nevertheless, as a natural resource the bergamot patiently waits to be fully discovered and exploited for the benefit of its fellow residents. And perhaps one day while savoring one of the many aspects of the region's remarkable fruit, citizens of the world will prize the bergamot as a true Calabrian original.

CALABRIAN THEATER

THE FIRST TIME I SET FOOT IN *Teatro Siracusa*, a charming art-nouveau theater on Reggio's main shopping street, I didn't know what I was getting myself into. I had seen a poster out front for a play with free admission and I showed up at the appointed time. At first there weren't many people, but gradually the theater began to fill up, and we waited. And we waited. I read everything I had in my purse, and then set about to absorb my surroundings. My eye was drawn to the elegant wrought iron balustrades lining the balcony. Built in the early 1920s after the famous earthquake of 1908, the theater had a graceful simplicity about it.

After a half hour had passed, I thought to myself, "Just how long does one wait in a situation like this?" Finally, three-quarters of an hour after the scheduled starting time, someone walked out onto the stage and began talking into a microphone. The play had not commenced, but a series of thank-yous and congratulations had started, and they went on, and on. At that point, I began reasoning with myself, "I've already been here for over an hour. I've waited this long..."

And finally the production began. Huh? Come again? Did I miss the line on the poster that said the play was in dialect?? I struggled through the first act, feeling as though my Italian skills had reverted back to square one as I strained to make heads or tails of the dialogue. If pressed, my description of the work would have been general in nature, "A Calabrian parlor piece, similar to the English genre, only the characters talked louder and made more references to food." At the time, I'm sure I could have come up with more detail, but a specific recounting of the storyline would have been a formidable challenge. By intermission, completely exhausted from the intense concentration, I decided to call it a night.

Shortly after the experience, the theater closed for a couple of years—not for a lack of people who spoke the Calabrian dialect, mind you! I was such a minority in that theater that for once nobody stared, as they figured I must have belonged. What non-Calabrian, non-Calabrian-American, non-Calabrian-Canadian, etc. would have ventured into that production, and stayed? Ironic, but no one paid any attention to me at all that evening.

The cine-theater, once a chic cultural center and meeting

point together with the long-gone *Gran Caffè Siracusa* next door, was grappling with its survival. Apparently, Benetton had to be beaten back in their attempt to convert the space into a mini mall. A very low-key, 'save the theater' campaign was under way, and for a while the only acts presented were on the sidewalk out front, hosted by a variety of the city's finest panhandlers.

Then, one day a new poster appeared, and I decided to give it another shot. This time I did a little reading beforehand, as there was a 10 Euro admission.

Title:	*La brocca rotta a Ferramonti*
	by Francesco Suriano (Calabrian)
Language:	Italian!
Plot:	Prisoners in a WWII internment camp in
	Calabria putting on a comic play entitled
	The Broken Pitcher by Heinrich von Kleist

Okay, by no means upbeat, and I didn't exactly anticipate any laughs from the paradoxical scenario. I couldn't help but remember that the inmates at the Nazi camp in Terezin, Czechoslovakia who had mounted artistic productions for the International Red Cross had just turned out to be actors in the grand scheme. But down in a remote mountain town of southern Italy, who would have thought that Chinese street peddlers from Bologna would have been thrown into the mix?

Long story short, the play was a well done, historical fiction. Ferramonti, the Calabrian camp located in a village called Tarsia in the province of Cosenza, was originally for non-Italian Jews, but eventually housed Italian Jews, anti-Fascists and non-Jews of other nationalities. Inspired by a photograph of a group of costumed prisoners putting on *The Broken Pitcher*, the playwright used a play-within-a-play as a thread around which the characters' individual stories were woven. Minimalist scenery consisting of eight moveable wooden sections that transformed themselves from barrack walls to bunk beds to lecterns created an evocatively desolate backdrop for the actors' rehearsals and the pensive discussions amongst the members of the camp's small theatrical group.

In his program notes, the author presented his work as an homage to and a remembrance of those who had lived this dark memory in Italy's history. He further noted that in certain respects, the Calabrians lived in solidarity with the internees and that the culture experienced inside the camp in its own way served to elevate the general spirit and to defeat the Fascist persecution. In fact (or maybe I should say, according to Wikipedia), the British-Jewish historian Jonathan Steinberg has defined the Ferramonti camp as "the largest kibbutz on the European continent," as the conditions were discretely humane and none of the internees suffered violent treatment or were deported to Germany.

Discretely humane must refer to such activities as the prisoners organizing a school, raising vegetables, and putting on concerts and plays, performances attended by the camp authorities and the local Calabrian population, many of whom, without a doubt, only spoke in dialect. German, Austrian, Polish, Slovakian, and possibly even Chinese actors presenting a German comedy in Italian—what must the audience have thought, over half a century ago, in this far-flung area of one of Italy's most remote regions? When I stumbled into the Calabrian theatrical performance, I at least had a certain familiarity with the representational genre in question.

Historical fiction or just plain fiction? Could Johann Wolfgang von Goethe, the play's first director, have ever imagined such a set of circumstances? I don't need to consult Wikipedia on this one. I know that Herr von Kleist's work was performed at the Ferramonti concentration camp in Tarsia, Calabria because you just can't make something like that up.

11

CRIMINALITY, THE BIGGER PICTURE

'NDRANGHETA, PART 2

> *... matters are not yet in so desperate a situation, as to
> preclude all possibility of restoring these provinces to a
> state of opulence and populousness. If government were
> more attentive to the general good than particular inter-
> ests; if justice were administered with more honesty and
> impartiality by the superior magistrates, and less rapa-
> ciousness of the subalterns; if taxes were more equally
> and judiciously imposed, and more tenderly exacted; if
> the aggrieved peasant had a refuge to fly to in the day
> of oppression, these fertile countries might emerge from
> their present state of desolation, and rich flourishing
> towns might again rise along the now deserted shores.*
> Henry Swinburne, *Travels in the Two Sicilies*

AN ASSEMBLAGE OF CALABRIANS enthusiastically applauded
these words and their translation when I read this passage aloud
at a conference celebrating the writings of English travelers to the
region. Although these lines were composed in 1777, Swinburne's
conclusion regarding the state of Calabria could have been written
yesterday. Certainly, great strides have been made over the past
two hundred years, particularly for the masses, and contrary to
prevailing stereotypical views, the situation is, as Swinburne
assessed, salvageable. Nonetheless, southerners have been
subjected to the lamentations of their northern compatriots since
unification, as if they themselves have done cartwheels over the

historical union or are jumping for joy over their current state of affairs.

The infamous stretch of highway between Salerno and Reggio Calabria, the notorious A3, serves as a classic example. The road was projected in the early 1960s to connect Calabria, for all intents and purposes Italy's third island, with the rest of the peninsula. During the half a century it's been under construction, the local population and its economy have truly suffered from the lack of adequate transportation. Yet, those who may be occasionally inconvenienced when trying to reach a Calabrian beach or the ferry to Sicily, assign culpability to the very individuals who must put up with the hardship as a way of life, as if it were their choice.

When pigeonholing Calabrians, confusion also exists between the *briganti* and the mafia. In most dictionaries, *brigante* translates as bandit. The Calabrian definition, however, would equate more to a Robin Hood figure, a courageous person compelled to the brigand lifestyle in order to survive under an unjust system as described by Swinburne and countless others. Schoolchildren speak of Calabria's most famous *brigante* Giuseppe Musolino with pride. Linking the mafia with such folk heroes is therefore distasteful to Calabrians, most likely a result of the misappropriation and misuse of the word *onore* (honor) by criminal organizations and its continued erroneous application in their regard.

Money is the biggest issue when Italians gripe about Calabria. The fact that many Calabrians have non-potable water coming from their taps, when any liquid drips out at all, is largely of no concern. The solution is to allocate more money and then complain that the funds have been embezzled on the way to their destination. The proposed project remains perpetually unfinished and the cycle repeats itself. No one seems to learn. Calabrians are convinced that most of the money never arrives to the region, and northerners accuse their southern nationals of swindling, or at the very least not having the backbone to stand up to the insidious criminal element that cripples their region. Calabrians then counter with the argument that it seems all too convenient for the politicians in Rome to support the status quo, concluding that they must therefore have a vested interest in enabling the circumstances to continue in the same manner.

Returning to the A3 highway example, as a dispassionate observer I have to question a government that can't manage to build a decent 300-mile road in over fifty years, having spent nearly $10 billion on the project in the twenty-first century alone. Granted, the terrain is challenging. Nevertheless, after all that time, I would personally stop blaming the children and start looking a bit more closely at the parents. The system investigates, makes accusations, holds trials, and then life goes on as before. Every once and a while the highway receives media attention, most often from comedians, and even occasionally by the international press. As if discovering fire, English-speaking newspaper articles report that prosecutors have found evidence of Calabrian contractors charging the government an extra three percent for the mafia's cut. I can't help but asking, "Where's the other ninety-seven percent?"

Water is another problem in Calabria, or to be more precise, getting the precious commodity from its plentiful source to the citizens' taps. Veiled insinuations against certain zones or particular blocks of condominiums at first led me to believe that the root of the problem lay in abusive building practices and with people who hadn't paid their fair share. However, speaking with those who have had to endure the nightmare and from personal experience, I found out that this wasn't the case. The unfortunates had paid in full, constructing their homes with the proper permits, and to add insult to injury, shelled out well above the average, as they were forced to take showers, do laundry and wash dishes during hours in which utilities cost double.

The waterworks is another great Calabrian boondoggle: hundreds of thousands of Euros for damns that haven't turned out a single drop of water after over thirty years, illegal construction in a national park, building in a contaminated area, furnishing communities with water from a polluted reservoir that has trucks rusting at its bottom, tap water not even fit to shower in, and unrepaired aqueducts that leak fifty percent of the region's water supply. In 2004, SoRiCal (*Società delle Risorse Idriche Calabresi*, Calabrian Water Resource Company, a division of the French multinational Veolia) was formed to, unfortunately, keep up the mismanagement. A number of SoRiCal executives have been under investigation, including the president of the company and mayor of Catanzaro, as well as other politicians and those responsible for assigning contracts. Alas, investigations are as frequent as the proclamations of new projects and the predictions for their completion, none resulting in a clean glass of water or even a cup of dirty liquid at certain hours of the day.

The 'Ndrangheta is well known to the police force, as are the individual members of its various clans. The politicians and professionals collaborating with the criminal element, however, are not as apparent. This enemy from within lurks in local, regional and national governments, in all aspects and levels of the bureaucracy as well as in the private sector. During my time in Reggio, a city employee caught stealing several million dollars over the span of a couple of years made a big splash in the news. In the region with the lowest average income, this young woman without any extraordinary skills or accomplishments gave the defense, "I earned it." A few days later, she committed suicide by drinking acid, sitting in her car along the seaside under a surveillance camera. Her suicide note wrapped it up nicely— no need to look any further, all very convenient. The sensation was over quicker than it had begun, but once again I must ask, "Where's the money?"

Town and city governments can be dissolved when found to have ties with or have been infiltrated by the mafia. From 1991 to 2012 over fifty administrative councils were disbanded in Calabria on account of connections with the 'Ndrangheta, the majority of which being in the province of Reggio Calabria and several, two or three times each. More recently in the north of Italy, a number of governments in the provinces of Lombardy, Piedmont and Liguria have also been dissolved for their associations with the Calabrian mafia. In 2012 Reggio Calabria was the first provincial capital to have its council disbanded. To hopefully clean up the contagious elements and get the localities back on their feet again, governing boards are appointed in each of these municipalities for a period of twelve to eighteen months, extendable for up to twenty-four, until elections are held for new councils.

Progress is slow. Fighting back isn't easy. Making an official complaint can bring problems, open up an unexpected can of worms. Counterclaims cost a fortune to combat. For example, innocently filling out a form to report not having received a legitimate reimbursement from the health care system can be countered with an investigation and accusations. According to records, the money was already paid out. The prosecuting attorneys have an excellent case with masterfully forged signatures and even witnesses. After going into significant debt between lawyers and expert testimony, however, the honest citizen prevails. He isn't a *truffatore* (con man). He has been conned. Countersuing isn't recommended or even feasible, though. The criminals have a far-reaching network and unlimited funds. The innocent's luck may have been exhausted, and the next time he seriously hesitates before signing a complaint.

Even in their daily lives, Calabrians are rather cautious of not falling victim of a *truffa* (scam or swindle)—down to the packaging of a simple Christmas present that must go through the mail. They just smiled and shook their heads at the American who would put gifts in mailing envelopes, as everyone knows that those sleeves are so easy to open. Surprisingly, the packages arrived at their destinations, big padded envelopes, each one with only a handful of *torroni* (nougats) that I had thrown in as an afterthought to give relatives back in America a taste of the holidays. The little twenty- to thirty-dollar gifts remained somewhere in Italy, and I needed to be more vigilant in order to avoid the next *truffa*.

The average citizen lives in a state of wariness. From one day to the next, an investigation can expose another bureaucratic *truffa*. Historically, the government and its elected officials haven't safeguarded the population's general interests, so Calabrians don't have much faith in the establishment. Poor roads, an antiquated rail system, inadequate medical facilities, and the butt of jokes to boot. When the bridge crossing the Strait of Messina was still being projected, its uselessness was unwittingly and glibly pointed out by the former Prime Minister Silvio Berlusconi, one of its biggest advocates, "*Costruiremo il ponte di Messina, così se uno ha un grande amore dall'altra parte dello Stretto, potrà andarci anche alle quattro di notte, senza aspettare i traghetti...*" (Let's build the bridge of Messina, so if someone has a great love on the other side of the Strait, he'll be able to get there even at four o'clock in the morning, without having to wait for the ferries...)

Unquestionably, the building of the bridge would have been a boom to the area, just as the A3 and the water company have employed a certain number of Calabrians. However, what use would the bridge have been without the completion of the A3 highway and a general overhaul and modernization of the territory's other roads, rails, power and utilities? 250 million Euros wasted on proposals and studies of a project that was ultimately scrapped, with another 300 million Euros to pay off the contract—money that could have been used on the Calabrian and Silician infrastructures that weren't adequate to support the bridge, anyway. At the very least, the funds could have gone toward upgrading the rail system or improving the ferries and perhaps lowering the exorbitant prices for all the Calabrian and Sicilian lovers impatiently waiting for ferry departures in the middle of the night.

If as Swinburne stated so long ago, Calabria can one day flourish to the point of opulence, the venture will only be possible if tackled with, as he said, the general good in mind. As northern critics are now seeing, the 'Ndrangheta and its tentacles have reached beyond Calabria's borders. The nefarious organization has also infiltrated the political, entrepreneurial and bureaucratic regimes of communities in the north, treacherously spreading its influence and control throughout the country and beyond.

The argument has been made that the people of the south haven't done enough to help themselves. Their way of thinking has been described as *arretrato* (backward), and investigations and persecution of criminals is hampered by *omertà* (the code or conspiracy of silence that protects outlaws). Undoubtedly, many people don't speak up because they are afraid. Others could be defined as having primitive mentalities, supplemented by selfishness and fear. However, Calabria does have brave citizens willing to speak out even at the cost of being completely shunned by their community.

When I first heard Anna Maria Scarfò's story, I almost couldn't believe my ears. The fact that a thirteen-year-old girl was repeatedly raped by a pack of a dozen men for three years, I could imagine in a rural community where both her parents worked as farm laborers. Also, I wouldn't have to stretch the limits of my imagination to see the parish priest to whom Anna Maria went for support and guidance not give the young girl any help whatsoever, looking to cover up the situation and avoid a scandal. I have a little more difficulty wrapping my brain around a religious center refusing the young girl refuge because she wasn't a virgin. Repeatedly threatened with her own death and that of her family if she told anyone what was happening, Anna Maria finally found the courage to go to the *carabinieri* (police) when the gang demanded she bring along her younger sister. Both the law enforcement and a determined attorney came to her aid. With just her family and without even one member of the community at her side, she related her ordeal in court and the rapists were condemned, serving short sentences.

At this point, her story becomes even more incredible for me, but it demonstrates the backwardness and primitive solidarity that is unfortunately a part of the culture amongst certain families and communities. Anna Maria is constantly taunted with nicknames, such as *malanova* (bad news) and *puttana* (whore). Her laundry hung out on the line is soiled with blood, she receives harassing anonymous calls and death threats, no one will hire her or her parents, she is a prisoner in her own home, and her dog is murdered. After a number of years, she is given a police escort as she is literally being stalked by sixteen people, including three of her rapists. The new parish priest refuses to even meet with her.

Why did she stay? A poor woman doesn't easily walk away from the only home she knows. Perhaps she was destined to bring her story to light. She challenged the *omertà* in San Martino, a suburb of Taurianova, and her 2,000 fellow citizens turned their backs. I would like to think that San Martino has decent apples mixed in with the bad, just like in any place. However, bullies, members of the 'Ndrangheta and non, prey on the ignorant and fearful. Anna Maria's struggle serves as an example and hopefully an inspiration to others in the battle against *omertà*.

Another victim of violence, tragically fatal, made his mark on Calabria, the Italian nation and the world. I hadn't ever heard of Nicholas Green before visiting Palazzo Campanella, the Regional Council building in Reggio. The hall dedicated to his memory was hosting an exhibition and the guide spoke of the American boy murdered by the 'Ndrangheta. In 1994, the seven-year-old was on a family vacation, driving along the A3 in a car that was mistaken for another. Nicholas was brutally shot in the head and died the following day. The parents donated his organs, benefitting seven Italians waiting for transplants and winning the hearts of the Italian people for whom organ donation was not a common practice. Since that time, organ donation has quadrupled in Italy and countless schools and parks have been named after little Nicholas. He is a symbol in the fight against criminality and in the hope for a better future.

12

IN THE PROVINCE OF REGGIO CALABRIA

PENTIDATTILO

BOVA

WHEN *IL PROFESSORE* FROM THE *Università per stranieri* (University for Foreigners) spoke, I may have easily responded with the comment, "It's all Greek to me." Indubitably, a non-Italian could have mistaken his singular pronunciation and slurred speech for some form of foreign utterance. Even the ears of native Italians occasionally pricked up like an animal listening to an unfamiliar or frightening sound when forced to interpret his unorthodox delivery. Giving *il professore* the benefit of the doubt, however, I could venture to say that his bizarre elocution had roots in his Greek heritage.

The province of Reggio Calabria clung to the Greek language well past the period of the Byzantines. Historically, the region was esteemed for its fine Greek scholars. Most noteworthy was the fourteenth-century monk Leonzio Pilato who was an important translator and teacher from Seminara, a municipality north of Reggio Calabria. Pilato was the first to translate the *Iliad* and the *Odyssey* of Homer into Latin, translations used by Petrarca and Boccaccio. In more recent times, the area around Bova, southeast of Reggio, held on to its native tongue into the twentieth century and in a few towns up until today. Throughout the rest of southern Calabria, Greek was gradually replaced beginning in the fifteenth century by a Romance dialect, what is referred to as Calabrian. Although dialect is spoken all over Calabria, the variations can be quite striking from one area to another, most notably between the north and the south of the region. These dialects manifest assorted combinations of Latin, Greek, Arab and French influences. Even between Reggio and Locri, the languages have distinct differences. Accents also differ greatly from one area to another.

In a few locations, however, the languages spoken have more in common with Greek, Albanian and even French. In these linguistic pockets, people continue to speak in the tongues of their ancestors, Greek in the province of Reggio Calabria*, Arbërëshe, a variation of an old Albanian language in the provinces of Cosenza, Catanzaro and Crotone, and an Occitan or French-based language in one town of Cosenza. Although spoken only in a handful of communities and at an ever-decreasing rate by young people, these minority languages are officially recognized by the government with laws in place to protect and promote them.

One winter afternoon while zigzagging up a mountain road headed for the picturesque, Greco-Italian community of Bova, two *carabinieri* (policemen) were out with their little red circles on sticks stopping traffic and checking driver's licenses. When the young man took my friend Phil's license and inquisitively read "Nevada" aloud, Phil added "Las Vegas" to give him some context. The officer made a characteristic guttural noise accompanied by a cock of the head and an extended circling of the hand. In translation, he was acknowledging his perceived grandeur of Sin City. Taking the driver's license and AAA's international license back to his squad car, he proceeded to flip through the little multilingual booklet, obviously not zeroing in on anything familiar after about ten quick passes, and returned both licenses to Phil indicating that we were free to go.

Not knowing what to expect in the little town on the top of the hill, I asked the officer if he could recommend a place

---

* Municipalities officially recognized by law as Greek-speaking are Bova, Bova Marina, Condofuri, Melito di Porto Salvo, Roccaforte del Greco and Roghudi. The tiny, entirely Calabrian-Greek community of Gallicianò is a suburb of Condofuri. The minority Greek language is also spoken in a few quarters of Reggio.

to eat in Bova. "*Sì, Al Borgo*," (Yes, "Al Borgo") and he started giving instructions. He then told us to wait a moment, went over and had a short discussion with his colleague inside the patrol car, and returned to say that they'd lead us there. Before pulling away, he returned the license to a woman coming down the hill, who having already been there when we arrived, appeared quite perturbed by the whole procedure. The officers' 4-wheel drive Subaru Forester then led us further up the mountain and stopped in front of a place that looked closed. We watched from our car as instructed as the young policeman knocked on the porch door, called out, waited for a few minutes and crossed the threshold, talking and gesticulating, seemingly in an effort to convince the man in the Adidas workout suit to open for lunch. The only words we overheard were "*due americani*" (two Americans). It was 1:10 p.m.

The little eatery was in a spectacular location on the edge of the Aspromonte National Park overlooking jagged green hills with the sea in the distance. Unfortunately, Etna was shrouded in clouds, but I made a mental note to return on a clear day, as the view was sure to be breathtaking with the volcano so close. More of a summer place with plastic tables and chairs in a glassed-in porch and picnic tables outside, the establishment also had a little store of Calabrian specialties.

The officers put their order in and went off to presumably check more driver's licenses, returning for their mixed grills a little later on—the older officer washing his meal down with a quarter liter of red wine and the younger officer (the driver, one-handed, open-palmed) with a can of Coca-Cola. We decided to have the complete meal at a good value of 16 Euros per person. I can't remember exactly how many plates the antipasti came on, but we had cheeses, sausages, salami, little quiches, and quite an interesting and tasty assortment of vegetables under oil—a few typical kinds such as eggplant and sun-dried tomatoes, and then others, more unusual, such as fava beans and a spiny, winter zucchini. Phil had the pasta with a pork ragù. I chose the subtly earthy goat sauce with a sprinkling of pecorino cheese. A mixed grill of pork and sausages that would have served four to six followed. The succulent meat was served with three sides: *ortiche* (nettles, the jagged leaves and stinging hairs boil up to very delicate greens), grilled eggplant, and an imaginative eggplant parmigiana that was so good, it was almost like a desert. Instead of layering the eggplant, sauce and cheese, the eggplant was fried, mixed together with the other ingredients and baked. We had trouble standing up from the table even though we had barely made a dent on the meat and vegetable course.

At a certain point during the meal, Phil asked me, "Do you think the guy in the warm-up suit is Al Borgo? Sounds like someone from New Jersey." Smiling, I could see the confusion, but "No, it means 'at the village'." After the *carabinieri* left, a table of six northern Italians came in, we presumed sent by the policemen. After all, they had to make it worth "Al Borgo's" while.

A few years later, we ascended the same road to Bova, but in a minivan with a cultural association called Calabria Etnica. The organization was in the midst of a weekend convention and exchange of ideas with Calabrians from all over the region. Returning to the same restaurant, this time with a reservation, we enjoyed another delicious meal with a few jovial participants from Praia a Mare, very north in the region, a resort town on the Tyrrhenian Sea just before the border with Basilicata. Sitting at a table with Calabrians so far removed from the eatery's location gave insight into the Italian perspective of distance. Americans tend to view the food from Italy as one cuisine, called Italian food. In Italy, the frame of reference is much more regional, provincial or even local. The northern Calabrians marveled at every slight variation in the offerings of the day. The *lestopitta* or just *pitta* was by far the most unusual food presented. Although a baked variety also exists in other areas of Calabria, this round, flat pita was deep fried in oil and served with appetizer plates, meat dishes, as well as with honey for dessert. The most exquisite morsel of the day, however, was the ricotta, a heavenly taste experience with a lightness that literally floated on my palate, and on that point the "northerners" were in agreement.

Eating *casereccio* (or *casareccio* = homemade) and food prepared using traditional methods is one of Calabria's highlights, as there is always the chance and often a good possibility that you may stumble on an extraordinary cheese, sausage or other culinary delicacy. Excursions to Bova also include incredible vistas and the Greek cultural allure. Right from the approach, just as the village appears in the distance, perched atop a hilly crest, the first indication of the town's heritage appears on an official street sign:

Comune di Bova
Chora tu vua
ΔΗΜΟΣ ΤΟΥ ΒΟΥΑ

The announcement of the arrival to the Municipality of Bova is posted first in Italian, then in Calabrian Greek (Chòra tu vùa) and finally in Greek. The name in Calabrian dialect is Vùa. Up in town, the newer signs are in reverse with the Italian on the bottom (November 4ᵗʰ Street, for example):

δρόμος 4ης Νοέμβριος
dromo 4 Novembrìu
via 4 Novembre

Part of our Calabria Etnica tour included a visit to the local wine cooperative in the center of the village, as well as pairing their wines with each course. Hoping to eventually receive the DOC status, the communal enterprise produced typical area wines with native grape varieties and aimed to give local growers an economic incentive to cultivate the largely abandoned older vineyards. The wines carried Greek names, and the labels were written in both Calabrian Greek and Italian.

The Greek communities also engage in traditional pastoral

handicrafts in wood, iron and cloth. Of the latter, the artisans work most often in wool, but they are also bringing back the antique weaving of Scotch broom, a skill taken to its height in Longobucco, a town in the Sila Greca mountains of the province of Cosenza.

Today, Bova is sparsely inhabited, although the numbers swell in the summer with many flocking to wander the ancient streets, hike in the environs of the Aspromonte Mountains and to partake in the bounty of its local culinary products. Oddly, a disproportionately large steam locomotive occupies a sizable space in a small piazza. Ironically, its placement honors the railroad for bringing work to its inhabitants, who then moved to the coast and populated the budding Bova Marina, ultimately leaving the older municipality unoccupied and neglected. Wandering through the town and ascending to its peak, we passed several churches, numerous dilapidated houses, a handful of dwellings beautifully renovated and an excellent example of a typical Bova house, a two-story structure made of stone with a substantial, arched-bricked entranceway. The ruins of a Norman castle are at the summit, from which there is a magnificent view of the surrounding countryside.

Later that day, handicrafts from Greek-Calabria and non were on display at Calabria Etnica's headquarters in Reggio's center. Particularly attractive were the ceramics from Seminara, a community noted for producing high quality pottery in a wide range of colors and shapes. They also make fancifully grotesque masks that were (and still are) placed on houses to keep away the *malocchio* (evil eye) and ward off jinxes.

Several handcrafted musical instruments from the folk tradition were also on display: the *organetto* (concertina, a small, button-keyed, accordion-like instrument), *tamburello* (tambourine), *ciaramella* (shawm, predecessor of the oboe), *sonaglio* (rattle) and *zampogna* (bagpipes). Two musicians playing the concertina and tambourine performed several tarantellas. The percussionist worked himself into a trance, intensely concentrating on the repetitive movements required for the execution of this quick folk dance that whirls on and on to infinity. The concertina player also performed on the bagpipes after the longest tuning session I have ever witnessed. While I am admittedly not a bagpipe expert, I find the folk version eminently fascinating, as the musician, historically a shepherd, performs while literally hugging an enormous, puffed-up goat or sheep skin that reaches the length of his body.

Throughout Calabria, folk musicians, youngsters included, perform on holidays and at festivals, hearkening back to the old ways in order to retain a connection with the past. Organizations such as Calabria Etnica work to promote Calabria's rich historical and cultural patrimony, drawing attention to the value of local products and traditions for the betterment of the region. Such cultural societies are helpful when a knowledgeable *carabiniere* isn't available to give culinary recommendations.

SCILLA

IN SPRING, HUGE SWORDFISH HEADS appear on stainless steel tables set up on sidewalks and in windows of fishmongers all over Reggio. The long sword reaching skyward, mouth slightly agape, and dark, vacant eyes make a striking impression—the older the fish, the duller the eyes. Nearby, their large, cylindrical bodies stand by to be sliced into steaks.

The swordfish season continues throughout the summer, in the Strait of Messina and northwards in the Tyrrhenian Sea in the waters off Costa Viola. The so-called Purple Coast extends from just north of Reggio to the town of Palmi and reputably takes its name from the philosopher Plato who described the environs as taking on dramatic reflections and shadings of the color violet at sunset. These coastal towns are popular summer tourist destinations featuring beautiful beaches, rocky cliffs, lush vegetation, and sweeping panoramas of the Isole Eolie (Aeolian

Islands of Sicily). The town of Palmi is noted for its *Casa della Cultura* (House of Culture) with several museums and libraries dedicated to Calabrian heritage, including native sons Francesco Cilea (1866-1950), *verisimo* (realist) opera composer, and writer Leonida Repaci (1898-1985). Nearby Bagnara Calabra is renowned for its handmade confections, in particular the *torrone* (rectangular-shaped almond and honey candy traditionally eaten at Christmas).

As throughout Calabria, towers and castles dot the shoreline. Today merely prized as picturesque, the cliffs that plunge so dramatically into the sea have historically served as lookout points for many purposes, spotting swordfish not the least among them. Jutting out in the center of the town, the rocky promontory of Scilla has been a coastal landmark for epochs, with written accounts dating from the Greeks and Romans. On my first few visits to Scilla, just twenty kilometers north of Reggio, I had to stretch my imagination in order to embrace the fantastical myths and legends associated with such a serenely beautiful coastline. With its imposing castle on the rock dividing the white sandy beach from the quaint fisherman's houses that face the Tyrrhenian's crystalline waters, Scilla is truly Costa Viola's jewel in the crown.

On calm, clear days, the sea glistens with just the slightest ripple; however, during storms powerful waves crash into the seaside dwellings. The Strait of Messina is a dangerous stretch for seafarers. As the legend goes, Scylla and Charybdis, two Greek, mythological sea monsters, live in the waters between Calabria and Sicily. Charybdis creates giant vortexes by swallowing and regurgitating water from his place on the Sicilian side, while Scylla tears apart men and ships from her location under the promontory in the Calabrian town that today bears her name. The Italian expression, *"essere tra Scilla e Cariddi"* (to be between Scylla and Charybdis) is a bit like the English saying, "To be between a rock and a hard place." First told by Homer with versions by Ovid, Virgil and Dante, the myth is sometimes attributed to other geographical locations, although many firmly believe that the legend was created to explain the effects of the treacherous currents between the coasts of Calabria and Sicily.

Despite the perils of the sea, the waters of Scilla have been plied since antiquity. Evidence of swordfish fishing in the area dates back to prehistoric times, a pursuit that served as the town's economic base until supplanted by tourism in recent years. Into the 1950s the fish were caught using a traditional, six and a half-meter (twenty-one-foot), wooden boat with oars. A tall pole in the center with a tiny platform large enough for a man's feet gave the helmsman an elevated position to better view the horizon, four rowers manned the oars and the harpoon thrower launched from the prow. Today, the much larger motorboat measures up to twenty meters (sixty-six feet). The caged lookout tower extends to thirty meters (ninety-eight feet) in the air and the boat is equipped with a long gangplank for the harpoon thrower. Catching the *pesce spada* (swordfish) is often referred to as the *caccia* (chase), an exciting and emotional event for both the fishermen and their followers from the shore.

Back in Scilla's restaurants the swordfish is prepared in many ways, for example: *alla ghiotta*–baked with red onion, garlic, white wine, olive oil and served with a sauce of oil, lemon juice and parsley; *salmoriglio*–grilled steak with a sauce of olive oil, garlic, oregano, lemon juice and parsley; *involtini*–rolled with bread crumbs, grated cheese, garlic, and sometimes capers and sautéed or grilled; *bagnarota* or *stufato*–braised with lemon and capers; *carpaccio*–raw with lemon and oil; and numerous recipes with pasta. Specific ingredients and methods vary with location and cooks, families have their own traditions, and in other regions a recipe may simply be called *pesce spada alla calabrese*.

The fishermen have historically occupied the area called *Chianalea*, a charming neighborhood built right on the sea just north of the castle. Small, colorful fishing boats line the coastline. Narrow alleys off the single, cobbled street lead up and down stone staircases to the old houses and the sea. A few antique, noble residences mix with the simpler structures, many transformed into restaurants and lodgings. Wandering in the lovely quarter, I have seen weathered fishermen working on their nets, an elderly woman hanging out strips of orange peel to dry, and even someone throwing trash into the sea from an upper window.

Summer vacationers flock to the attractive beach on the south side of the castle. Not just for sunbathers and casual swimmers, however, Marina Grande is an entry point for scuba divers. The sea floor drops quickly off the coast of Scilla, and a four- to five-story rock, sharper than that on shore, hosts not mythological monsters, but spectacular sea life, a polychromatic bed of polyps and fan-shaped horny coral that attracts a multitude of fish, crustaceans and mollusks. Scilla's many visitors largely ignore this magical underwater world that lies hidden beneath the limpid, aqua-colored water.

The castle on the rocky outcropping grabs the popular focus, situated in an elevated position in the middle of the town. Its origins are said to go back to the time of Ulysses, who built a temple to Minerva on the spot. Over a few thousand years, indigenous peoples and all manner of conquerors constructed and restructured fortifications on the promontory. Battles and earthquakes have battered its walls, and even Garibaldi slept in the castle in 1860. In addition to an antique swordfish boat on permanent display, several rooms hold regular exhibitions. Nevertheless, the real draw of the castle is its location and the breathtaking views from its walls. The same can be said from any position in Scilla, such as from the San Giorgio quarter on the town's upper level.

Calabrians appreciate not only the broad vistas, but the environment's smaller-scaled allures as well. Along the Costa Viola, I have witnessed high-heeled women precariously scaling old stonewalls to pick capers from the wild plants clinging to the rocks and admirers of unusual or attractive flora surreptitiously slipping a cutting from a public garden under their jackets. Others remain attuned to the area's legends. While building the highway in Scilla, engineers reputably heard the songs of the sirens carried by the wind. Folk tales and traditions have been passed down over countless centuries. For the fishermen, many elements of the swordfish chase have changed; however, certain rituals are maintained as a testament to the time when the local populations lived in symbiosis with the sea. Until today, fishermen scratch the sign of the cross with their fingernails near the fish's right ear, leaving their time-honored mark on the majestic heads propped up on stainless steel tables wherever the fish is sold.

PENTIDATTILO

On advancing, the views of the wondrous crags of Pentedatilo become astonishingly fine and wild, and as the sun set in crimson glory, displayed a truly magnificent and magical scene of romance—the vast mass of pinnacled rock rearing itself alone above its neighbour hills, and forming a landscape which is the beau-ideal of the terrible in Calabrian scenery.

. . . . the appearance of Pentedatilo is perfectly magical, and repays whatever trouble the effort to reach it may so far have cost. Wild spires of stone shoot up into the air, barren and clearly defined, in the form (as its name implies) of a gigantic hand against the sky, and in the crevices and holes of this fearfully savage pyramid the houses of Pentedatilo are wedged, while darkness and terror brood over all the abyss around this, the strangest of human abodes.

Edward Lear, *Journals of a Landscape Painter in Southern Calabria*

I WAS HEADED OFF ON A TRIP TO PENTIDATTILO (also written as Pentedattilo) with the Anglo-Italian Club of Reggio Calabria. A day's activities had been arranged to mark the two-hundredth anniversary of Edward Lear's birth. By this time in my Calabrian sojourn, I was well acquainted with the British artist and writer, whose framed illustrations I had first encountered on the walls of the English school in Locri.

Lear, who is best known for his popularization of the limerick or what he referred to as 'nonsense verse,' was a celebrated author and illustrator in Calabria, particularly for the citizens of the Province of Reggio Calabria. In fact, his book in translation, *Diario di un viaggio a piedi* (Diary of a Journey on Foot) was sold throughout the area. Unfortunately, he never made it to the northern part of the region as his travels in Sicily and Southern Calabria from May to October of 1847 coincided with the local Risorgimento uprising against Bourbon rule. For this reason, the timing of his visit was regarded as suspicious by many of the Calabrians with whom he came in contact, and he felt forced to depart Reggio rather suddenly when he found the city in the hands of revolutionaries.

The club had rented a London, double-decker bus for the excursion, scheduled to lead a procession of vehicles from Piazza Castello (Castle Square) at 9 a.m. to Saline Joniche, a coastal town near Pentidattilo, for the first event in the "Tribute to Edward Lear." Arriving at the piazza shortly before the appointed hour, I naturally was in search of a traditional red bus, looking forward to playing a part in the campy spectacle. But alas, the oversized vehicle had long since been transformed by a nondescript paint job, disguising the characteristic conveyance with an unremarkable neutrality. Oddly, the monstrous *pullman*, as buses are often called in Italian, didn't actually have seating for more than eleven or twelve passengers in its circa 1972 party interior. With a quick glance at the organized transport, most of the group hurried off to drive their own cars, pulling away long before our little band of seven set forth forty-five minutes late— for no apparent reason other than habit. As the cumbersome behemoth negotiated its way through the narrow lanes, locals stopped in their tracks, mouths agape, dumbfounded despite our lackluster pigmentation. Illegal parking necessitated frequent, extended pauses, bringing to mind a trip to Disneyworld, although it wasn't clear as to who had paid for the ride. When we finally reached the highway, I couldn't help but notice my distinguished colleagues ever so discretely lifting their elbows, as the air finally started gusting through the open windows of the un-air conditioned, 1960s bus on that hot, humid June day. Anchored to our places only by means of the chemical reaction between our warm bodies and the Naugahyde seat coverings on the contraption's low-slung couches, we careened toward the southernmost point of the peninsula in one of the least safe vehicles I've ever encountered, arriving extremely late to an event that obviously never had any intention of beginning at its scheduled hour.

The conference room was quite nice and thankfully, in addition to air conditioning and the requisite Italian coffee, had an ample supply of water to replace all that we had lost on our trip there. Although we hadn't traveled on foot as had Edward Lear, it didn't mean that our journey of about twenty-five kilometers (16 miles) was any less exhausting. The symposium eventually got under way with the speakers and dignitaries taking their places at a long table facing the audience, which I found to be encouragingly large for an English literary gathering in Calabria, even considering the fact that no English was to be spoken. The congratulations, which started well over an hour behind time, featured a couple of mayors and the provincial councilor of culture waxing poetic on the importance of the day's proceedings for the local communities. How were we to know that in less than a year the mayor of Melito di Porto Salvo would be arrested for criminal conspiracy with the 'Ndrangheta? Apparently, our day of culture wasn't enough to save him. Nevertheless, these incidents occur frequently in Calabria, showing how difficult it is for progress to be made and why the people exalt anything positive associated with their region—and thus the recognition of Lear and the other British travelers who wrote about their visits. The official lecturers finally began speaking when the entire presentation should have been about to wrap up. In addition to an erudite Italian, two exceedingly knowledgeable, native English speakers contributed the Anglo to the Anglo-Italian Club, infusing their respective Welsh lilt and Irish brogue into their discourses—a multicultural mingling of ideas that was appreciated by the overwhelmingly Italian audience.

Our caravan's next stop was at the Lear monument, erected in 1998 by the Club on SP 22 (Provincial Street 22) directly across the valley from the outcropping of Pentidattilo. It would be difficult to embellish on Lear's vivid characterization of the place, except to say that since he sketched the celebrated rock formation, one of the fingers seems to have gone missing, most likely the result of an earthquake. The abandoned hamlet's stark image does, as Lear wrote, make the trip worth it. Pentidattilo can also be seen from the coast and I never failed to strain my neck in order to get a distant glimpse from the train window whenever I passed Melito di Porto Salvo, its nearest station.

The monument is attractively designed and executed, its light-gray, local stone from the nearby quarry of Capo D'Armi blending with the rocky surroundings. The giant, open book sits upright in a position that allows the visitor to read Lear's brief description of Pentidattilo in English and Italian while absorbing the austere panorama beyond. Between the pages at the sculpture's center bursts a colorful, ceramic bookmark of an agave in full bloom, graceful and pleasing to the eye—a fitting and thoughtful tribute to a writer and artist so respected and beloved by the club and citizens of the province. A few English speakers, including myself, read aloud passages of Lear and other British travelers to Calabria, with Italian translations following.

Many Englishmen have traveled in Calabria and written of their adventures, most notably Henry Swinburne, Edward Lear, George Gissing and the literary classic Norman Douglas. Perhaps owing to the numerous writings by these travelers or to the Anglo-Italian Club's British founders or to the fact that British

English is their standard in schools, I couldn't help but notice the extent to which many of the club members and most Italians who taught and spoke English in the province identified with the British, almost as if the United States was still that revolutionary, upstart colony without any culture or sophistication whatsoever. I found it rather irksome, particularly as the average Calabrian empathized more with the former colonial possessions of the United States, Canada and Australia than they did with Great Britain. When in her closing comments to the readings, my friend Luisa, President of the Club, announced that I was writing a book about Calabria that they would be able to excerpt at their next ceremony, no doubt, a few in the crowd must have thought it quite presumptuous of me to attempt such an undertaking—just like an American!

The release of an injured falcon back into the wild by the forestry department and the consumption of hors d'oeuvres hospitably provided by the town of Saline Joniche concluded the proceedings at the monument. The following stop on the itinerary was the town of Montebello Jonico for a quick tour of the church and a casual lunch with homemade local products in an old stone tower converted into living quarters. A tour of Melito di Porto Salvo, the largest town of the area with about 12,000 inhabitants was projected next, but scrapped for lack of time and we headed straight for Pentidattilo, which has belonged to Melito administratively since the early nineteenth century as a result of the dramatic depopulation subsequent to the devastating earthquake of 1783.

I had already heard the story of the Pentidattilo massacre several times. Calabrians liked to tell the seventeenth-century tale of jealousy and slashing, one noble family pitted against the other in a castle now reduced to an inconsequential ruin. Perhaps the gruesome bloodbath is more easily associated with the *paese fantasma* (ghost town) than any marquis or baron's feudal prosperity. Pentidattilo was completely abandoned by the 1960s, the population having long since settled in Melito Porto Salvo.

However, the forsaken village's unique naturalistic setting has continued to attract the attention of travelers who visit the village primarily in the summer months. Several buildings have even been renovated, a few local artisans have opened tourist shops and a couple of people have made it their home. For a number of years, the ancient burg, a cinematic setting in itself, has hosted an international short film festival. Every August participants fill the small squares and line the staircases for viewings under the night sky.

As we made our way up the well-paved, very steep road from the parking area to the little town, I was reminded that Lear had traversed the province on foot, accompanied by a guide and as he called it, a quadruped to carry his travel necessities, which certainly would have included a good deal of art supplies. Large banks of prickly pears sprouting yellow flowers hugged the rocky terrain, and purple thistles bloomed amongst neglected debris. The quiet village's graded, narrow lanes were pleasant to wander. We rested on the hard church benches while listening to our guide recount the story of the Pentidattilo slaughter in minute detail as part of the town's history. A fountain of local information, the young man also officiated at the ceremony for the Edward Lear bicentennial plaque unveiled that afternoon by the club along the village's main street—an open book in ceramic with a Lear quote in the two languages. I liked the repeated image of the book, as well as their artistic bookmarks. Naturally, a stop-off on the itinerary meant another extended snack, which was gracefully offered by the Melito tourist board.

As we were barreling along a narrow road on our return to Reggio, a club member suddenly shouted out, "Stop! Let's see the Garibaldi house!" With the excuse that the double-decker was too unwieldy to turn around on the cramped street, the driver avoided the stopover, although not without some grumbling. I had gotten a quick look at the faded two-story manor house, and was informed that the Hero of Two Worlds had been there on his first of two landings in Melito. This 1860 *Spedizione dei*

Mille (Expedition of the Thousand) was the mission that caused the collapse of the Kingdom of the Two Sicilies and brought the south into the unified Italy. Garibaldi also took his initial step onto the peninsula at Melito in his unsuccessful campaign to conquer Rome for the new Kingdom of Italy in 1862. Not having the backing he thought, he was wounded and halted in Gambarie in the Aspromonte Mountains near Reggio, today a pleasant, all-season, outdoor escape for city dwellers.

We continued on to Reggio as had Garibaldi on his first escapade from Melito in which his Red Shirts defeated the Bourbons in Piazza Duomo (Cathedral Square). We thought we were on our way to nearby Piazza Castello, but as we got nearer the driver indicated a different drop-off location, eliciting quite an uproar. I joined the fray on principle—we hadn't been told, but no amount of complaining or cajoling would sway him to return to those tight streets on a Saturday night. In the end, we were only a handful of blocks away from our destination, albeit an inconvenience for those who had been tramping around all day in fashionable heels. We didn't have the grit of those early travelers, nor did we have an amenable donkey.

Edward Lear's enthusiasm for the landscape tinged with a nineteenth-century romanticism has won the hearts of Calabrians. His book features fifteen captivating illustrations of the region. Both his idyllic words and images will surely endure.

> Reggio is indeed one vast garden, and doubtless one of the loveliest spots to be seen on earth. A half-ruined castle, beautiful in colour and picturesque in form, overlooks all the long city, the wide straits, and snow-topped Mongibello[†] beyond. Below the castle walls are spread wide groves of orange, lemon, citron, bergamot, and all kinds of such fruit as are called by the Italians "Agrumi" . . .

[†] Mongibello is another name for Mount Etna.

13

IN THE PROVINCE OF VIBO VALENTIA

CAPO VATICANO

TROPEA AND CAPO VATICANO

MY FIRST VISIT TO TROPEA was just a quick stopover. Passing through the province of Vibo Valentia on an excursion, the tour leader announced an hour break in Tropea. Someone shouted out from the back of the bus, "But we need more time to buy onions!" So, we were granted an extra fifteen minutes.

The onions were easily purchasable all over town—from farmers on street corners, outside touristy gift shops and in grocery stores. The luggage compartment under the bus was soon full of plastic sacks with green stalks protruding from their tops. Called a red or purple onion in English, this root vegetable is said to have been introduced to Calabria by the Phoenicians. The variety from Tropea has the IGP designation (*Indicazione geografica protetta*, Protected Geographical Indication) and is greatly prized for its sweet, mild flavor attributed to the area's temperate climate and silty soil. No good Calabrian would visit Tropea without buying several kilos to carry home.

Exported all over the world, the Tropea onion is cultivated manually using traditions handed down over generations. Shops in Tropea specialize in local products made from the onion, such as marinades in oil to top *bruschetti* and a marmalade mixed with sugar, vinegar and spices to accompany cheese or meat. During the winter with only about 7,000 inhabitants, the town center is empty, but the streets are packed during the summer season, as Tropea is one of Calabria's biggest tourist destinations. Noted for its spectacular views and white sand beaches, Tropea overlooks the Tyrrhenian Sea from a cliff on the edge of the promontory that forms the bump on top of Calabria's foot.

This land that bulges out into the sea is called Capo Vaticano, and for my second visit to the area I decided to immerse myself in its natural beauty. Searching the Internet for a place to stay, I discovered that many hotels and the large, all-inclusive vacation complexes were closed most of the year. When traveling alone without a car, I searched for accommodations accessible by train that had a congenial, helpful staff. I found a small, family-run, two-star property in Nicolò di Ricadi that had the sort of reviews I was looking for—excellent food, warm hosts and tranquil location in the country. The hotel opened on Easter weekend with the father in the kitchen, daughter at the front desk, son at the bar and other family members, young and old, dispersed in various occupations. I was their first customer of the season and my clean, brightly decorated room with private bath had a sea view with the Sicilian island of Stromboli in the distance. *Pensione completa* (full room and board) came to forty-three Euros a night with beverages being an extremely reasonable extra. I had chosen wisely. The two-star rating was an enigma.

Situated amidst their fruit and vegetable fields, the hotel-restaurant served their own as well as other local products. Particularly delicious were the homemade antipasti with unusual uses of the onion, and the chef's 'nduja was exquisite. Originally made only in the nearby village of Spilinga, this spicy salami is now found all over Calabria and often tops the *pizza calabrese*. The 'nduja is also spread on *bruschetti* and served on pasta. Made with pork lard, *guanciale* (cheek) and *pancetta* (bacon) mixed with the local *peperoncino* (hot pepper), the salami that is prepared and eaten in Tropea has a creamy consistency with a spicy, intense flavor. I had sampled the 'nduja many times before, but nothing compared to what I consumed in that mom and pop establishment.

While people were scarce in mid-April, wildflowers were not, and the hotel's surrounding countryside was alive with spring color. Dilapidated stone and cement structures were engulfed in weeds and vines blooming in vivid yellows, purples and whites. The blossoming plants flanked the fields and roadsides. Nearby, an abandoned Saracen watchtower that had been converted into a dwelling was unapproachable through the overgrown foliage. Twentieth-century additions hugged its stone walls that hinted at the cape's long history. Farmhands worked in a few of the neatly laid out fields. Several substantial, modern houses with meticulously cared for gardens were closed off from the rambling nature by long fencing. This bucolic Mediterranean terrain was home to the famous onion.

The air was thick with vegetative aromas. I could almost smell the thirty-odd herbs plucked from the area of Capo Vaticano and infused in Calabria's most ubiquitous liquor. The *Vecchio Amaro del Capo* is a very pleasant digestive that is often consumed for its nutritional value (or so I've been told). The dark-colored bitter with a sweet flavor and rich aftertaste of aromatic herbs is produced in a small town in the vicinity. A picture of the cape even graces the bottle's label.

Sitting at a height of 124 meters (407 feet), the white granite promontory known as Capo Vaticano dramatically plunges to the turquoise sea below. Numerous attractive beaches nestle at the bottom of the rocky cliffs, many only reachable by boat or dangerous footpaths. Deserted except for a few young people with a guitar, the *Spiaggia del Tono* (tone beach) that probably took its name from the deafening sounds of the sea, was a steep walk down from my hotel, past empty parking lots and a vast spa complex that occupied an extended seafront area, but was only open a few months a year. I lay on my towel listening to the crashing of the waves that obliterated the strumming just a stone's throw away. The lounge chairs and umbrellas of the summer concessionaires would still be several months away. The *Grotticelle* beach situated on the other side of the point was quieter from nature's standpoint, but had a bit more human activity early in the season.

One sunny morning I hiked to the point of Capo Vaticano, situated between the Gulf of Gioia Tauro to its southern side and the Gulf of Sant'Eufemia to the north. The panorama looking out over the cliffs and down to the sea was absolutely stupendous—the green-gray Mediterranean vegetation clinging to the jagged outcroppings, the clear, sparkling water, the outline of the distant promontories, the Aeolian Islands silhouetted on the horizon. The views from the path near the lighthouse on the cape's rim are truly breathtaking.

Just north in Tropea, nature's beauty is complemented by that of man. As pictured in every guidebook of Calabria, a small, rocky island crowned with an ancient Benedictine sanctuary Santa Maria dell'Isola (Saint Mary of the Island) juts into the sea at the bottom of the cliff. A narrow footpath leading up from the beach to the church completes the picture postcard. Unfortunately, on that Easter weekend, the structure was entirely covered with scaffolding. Several more months would pass before I was to see the church dazzlingly restored, almost too clean for its naturalistic surroundings. Nevertheless, as I gazed out at the tiny island from a piazza up on the town level that day, I felt a rumbling underfoot. The sound and the vibrations steadily increased. Children began to run up the street in the direction of the encroaching, ever-deafening drumbeat, and I naturally followed, with a fast walk. Clearly, the stone buildings weren't constructed to absorb the reverberations of a modern drum, as the town's whole seventeenth-century infrastructure seemed to quiver with the oscillations of the metal snares.

The fast, tarantella rhythm was accompanying the *Ballo dei Giganti* (Dance of the Giants). Two very tall, papier mâché figures were whirling around the street. Mata, with her golden hair, silver tiara and string of pearls wore a rich, brocade dress, while Grifone, bearded and mustached with a darker complexion and hair sported a jacket, bowtie and feathered hat. Often making an appearance at Calabrian festivals, the pair performs a dance of courtship that symbolizes the union of the indigenous people with that of the Moorish. For their part, the puppeteers must execute fast footwork and possess a prodigious endurance, not emerging from their costumes for several hours. Supporting the figurines on wooden frames, the dancers peer out of the puppets' garments from face holes positioned somewhere around the tops of the legs. Naturally, from time to time the puppeteers have something to relate to their partner, conversing independently from the motions of the puppets. Hands also dart and weave out of the openings, as with Italians, the face holes must also accommodate frequent gesticulations.

Fun to watch, the *Giganti* definitely lend a festive atmosphere to celebrations in many Calabrian towns. On that Easter holiday, both locals and visitors followed their dance through the streets. An international tourist destination particularly popular with the Germans, Tropea has a lovely historic center, full of gift shops with gastronomical delicacies from all over the region. Picturesque architecture reflects the town's long history that was often interrupted by incursions and earthquakes.

Evidence of inhabitation in the area goes back to Roman times. The nearby agricultural town of Zungri has an immensely fascinating archeological site from the medieval period that I visited on another occasion. Carved into the foothills of Mount Poro is a complex of cave dwellings that date from the twelfth to the fourteenth centuries. The settlement is made up of one- and two-room houses, a few even have two stories. Windows, arches, air vents for smoke, and inside the individual rooms, different sized and shaped niches have been carved out of the volcanic stone. The units are grouped together and connected by a network of narrow streets and steps as well as a system of water channels and cisterns. Both functional and attractive, the long-abandoned structures with their natural, white walls and stone additions organically blend with their environment. Their inhabitants, in turn, were afforded a magnificent view of the surrounding countryside.

Back out in contemporary Calabria, when confronted with

ugly, illegal construction, I often thought of the cave houses and how, in many ways, their conception and design were so much more advanced. Facing south, they didn't even have the problem of dampness so prevalent in many of the buildings in which I lived and worked. Throw in a diet of sweet red onions washed down by a nutritious herb liquor, and those medieval people may have been living in a Utopia. And with the marriage of the Christian and Muslim worlds as represented by the dancing Mata and Grifone, the community could have relaxed their vigil with regard to the attacks from the sea.

If I were on the Tropea tourist board, I think I'd have the *Giganti* juggling some onions.

VIBO VALENTIA

Calabrians love the sun. Often with just a few clouds overhead, I would hear exclamations such as, "*Che brutta giornata*!" (What an awful day!) So when the days started getting longer and the temperatures began to rise, they would be itching to come out of hibernation. The number of weekly *passeggiate* (walks) increased exponentially, and schools and other organizations embarked on their main period of *gite* (excursions)—scholastic, touristic, cultural, gastronomic, religious, etc.

One early spring weekend, my friend Luisa invited me to tag along on an outing to the provincial capital of Vibo Valentia. She was attending an interregional convention of a religious society called *Movimento Rinascita Cristiana* (Christian Rebirth Movement). The price of the sojourn was very reasonable owing to the fact that the hotel's owner was also a member of the association. As was often the case, however, the schedule seemed to be a little vague, initially departing at 1:00 p.m., then changing to 11:00 a.m., and not knowing if, when or where the bus would stop for lunch. Part of this indecisiveness undoubtedly had to do with the perpetual state of construction on the infamous A3 highway, making the 100-kilometer (62-mile) journey to Vibo Valentia a two-hour affair at best.

I began my day with a hearty breakfast just in case we ran into difficulties along the road. Despite a detour through several small towns, the bus pulled into the center of Vibo in well under three hours and we piled out in search of a slice of pizza, or so I thought. I started following the main group down the deserted pedestrian-only street, when Luisa waved me over in the direction of a nearby piazza to partake in a picnic prepared by one of her associates. We were fortunate, indeed. Her friend had made delicious artichoke sandwiches on homemade bread and had also whipped up a couple of artichoke frittatas that were cut up into tasty, easy-to-eat triangles. In Reggio, I had often seen artichokes being sold in bulk from the backs of pick-up trucks; however, it wasn't until I was able to enjoy the vegetable in such abundance that I realized it would have only taken a handful of customers like our generous picnic chef to quickly clean out the inventory of a rather large rig.

Having finished our nutritious lunch, we checked into the hotel, a modern, well-equipped property with panoramic views of the Gulf of Saint Eufemia. My room was lovely—clean and spacious, looking out across a green plain that extended to the port of Vibo Marina and the sea beyond. Vibo sits up on a hill that has afforded its inhabitants pleasant summer temperatures as well as a prime, defensive vantage point throughout its history. A Norman-Hohenstaufen castle still dominates its topography. Today, the population approaches 34,000, tripled since the period of unification when it was called Monteleone (di Calabria).

In the late afternoon I walked the short distance from the hotel to the town center, leaving the Calabrians, Apulians and Neapolitans with the inspirational cogitations of their guest speakers and joining the throngs of locals on their Saturday evening *passeggiata*. The pedestrian street was hardly recognizable from the desolate thoroughfare of a few hours earlier when businesses were closed and the entire population was taking part in the midday repast. Apart from the families and groups of young and old, the municipality's modest core was comprised of a number of churches, a few aristocratic houses, the city park and a shopping district, all under surveillance of the castle's tall, stone walls on the ridge above.

Populated since prehistoric times, Vibo Valentia was established as Hipponion by the Greeks and under the Romans called Valentia, meaning strength or power for its strategic and economic importance. Caesar and Cicero not only slept there, but also enjoyed the local fish, caught and elaborately processed in the area since the Greek period. Tanks dug into the cliffs and set up on the beaches kept the fish fresh with a system of running water throughout a series of canals. Other basins were used to preserve the fish in salt, to prepare a greatly prized sauce made from the entrails and to even raise fish. Tuna fishing has also been practiced for several thousand years along the *Costa degli Dei* (Coast of the Gods), the name for the seaboard along the geographical bump protruding into the Tyrrhenian Sea in the province of Vibo Valentia.

More recently, Mussolini made a visit to Vibo for the inauguration of a monument in honor of Luigi Razza (1892-1935), politician and Minister of Public Works for a short period before his untimely death in a plane crash. His humble origins in Monteleone di Calabria (today Vibo Valentia) are said to have brought about his sympathetic views with regard to the plight of the peasants and the conditions of the southern laborers forced to move to the north for work. The bronze statue of Razza stands in the center of an imposing, Fascist, marble monument facing the cathedral at the edge of the city park.

For all the grandeur of the Fascist design and the pomp of its execution, the historical and artistic gem on display in Vibo is a tiny sheet of gold that outlines instructions on how to avoid Hades in the afterworld. The *laminetta orfica* (Orphean lamina) is exhibited in the archeological museum attractively housed in the castle. We visited the museum the following day on a guided tour of the town and had the opportunity to view a lovely collection of objects from Magna Graecia including the *laminetta* that was found on the chest of a woman's skeletal remains in a tomb dating from the fifth to fourth century BC. The sixteen-line message was translated on an interpretive sign and directed the deceased not to drink the water from the lake of oblivion, but to approach the guardian and declare the need to drink from the lake of memory. Drinking the water from this exclusive lake would allow the soul of the defunct to leave Hades behind and to be saved as one of the privileged within the religion of Orpheus. Reading the simple, somewhat ordinary instructions for salvation put a human face on the ancient people, concerned with social standing and fresh seafood on earth and at the same time worried about their lives after death.

Back at the hotel, we also focused on fish, enjoying breaded, baked swordfish as the second course at one of our meals, which were all complete and very good particularly in light of the several hundred guests served at one time. Wine was naturally included, although at one table I found myself surrounded by water drinkers, a happenstance unsettling for the priest who was out of arm's length of the wine bottles. When I decided to pick one up and fill our glasses, he was visibly relieved, exclaiming, "Good thing there's an American at the table!"

The weekend passed very pleasantly. Despite the *Rinascita* name, the group was quite sedate, having nothing in common with their proselytizing counterparts in the United States. The born-again Christians, Italian style seemed to be content with philosophizing on what it meant to be a Christian in today's society and focusing on projects of good works. They recognized the precariousness of contemporary life, where one simple choice could change one's entire future course, not unlike the Greeks in the choice of drinking water. Perhaps the first lake or spring, the most obvious option commonly chosen by the masses isn't always the best. A delectable artichoke luncheon may just be the reward.

Over the course of the weekend, Luisa introduced me as her Protestant, American friend, which seemed to be quite a curiosity for the majority. They didn't seem to meet non-Catholics very often. She could have said that I was Shinto, or Orphean for that matter.

PIZZO

ALTHOUGH PIZZO HAS AN IMPOSING CASTLE with an intriguing history, for most Calabrians the town's real importance lies with a gelato dessert called *tartufo*. Bus tours driving along the Tyrrhenian Sea routinely exit the A3 just north of Vibo Valentia for a quick culinary indulgence in this northernmost point on the Costa degli Dei. Those traveling with young ones pull off the road, looking to combine a tour of the castle and its life-size mannequins with the special gelato treat.

The *tartufo* (truffle) is basically a stuffed ice cream ball. The original version is made with chocolate and hazelnut gelato filled with a liqueur-infused fudge sauce and coated with cocoa powder. As I have an aversion to nuts and wasn't in the mood for one of the many variations on the classic, I was forced to choose an exquisite strawberry gelato made from their local berries. And although I could barely breathe from the heavy, meat-based lunch my travel companions and I had just consumed, I was absolutely obliged to eat it, as eating ice cream is what one does in Pizzo—the castle is a bonus. As soon as we hit the main square, the entire bus scattered, filling the gelato shops and cafés as if not having eaten for a week. Luckily, I was caught up in the craze as that gelato had the strongest and at the same time most delicate strawberry flavor I have ever tasted. Clearly, Pizzo doesn't call itself the *città del gelato* (city of gelato) for nothing.

Also known as Pizzo Calabro, the town of 9,000 is built on a rocky promontory that looks out to the sea. Its main piazza is quite pleasant for a short, level *passeggiata*, and branching off, up and down the narrow lanes and staircases, I have attempted on a number of occasions, to work off a few of those ice cream calories. The main square is anchored by the massive rectangular ramparts and cylindrical towers of the castle. Today, this picturesque, Aragon fortification merely adorns an after-gelato stroll, but for nineteenth-century Europe, the execution of Joachim Murat within its walls put Pizzo on the map. The date was October 13th, 1815.

Inside the castle, uniformed dummies reenact the military tribunal of three that sentenced Napoleon's brother-in-law and erstwhile King of Naples (1808-1815) to death by firing squad after his vain attempt to re-conquer his former realm by way of Calabria. Down in the dungeon, a few of his soldiers lounge around in cells. A pile of mangy bedding on which Murat supposedly slept, a little wooden stool which according to a sign was reserved for the derrière of the dethroned ruler during his brief sojourn, and a copy of the farewell letter he wrote to his wife Caroline Bonaparte are exhibited in the upper chamber he occupied in the five days before his death.

Where were the damask curtains, chairs and armchairs? Or the tub Murat had expressly requested in order to take a fragrant bath? On the twentieth anniversary of Murat's death, French writer Alexandre Dumas made a pilgrimage to Pizzo, chronicling these particulars from a firsthand source. Nevertheless, while there may have been a discrepancy with regard to the room's decor, Murat's courage in the face of death was unquestionably agreed upon, as were the details of his final moments.

The courtyard in the castle was small, not seemingly spacious enough for nine soldiers with their rifles poised in firing position, as well as the officials and not to mention the condemned man himself. (I'm always surprised at how such colossal fortifications afford such paltry square footage.) Murat requested to give his own firing orders. On his command, three rifles were discharged, all three shots landing above his head. On his second attempt, once again only three bullets were fired, but he was hit by all three, dying instantly. I imagine at least a few onlookers in the courtyard that afternoon must have been splattered with a good deal of blood.

Twenty years after Murat penned the heartfelt adieu to his wife and children, Dumas hand delivered the letter to Caroline in Florence. Perhaps the postal system was also dubious in the former Italian states and the officials in Pizzo didn't want to trust losing such an important missive—strange, considering that the widow would have undoubtedly been willing to pay an exorbitant sum for its possession, as she had for the watch with her portrait that her husband clutched at his death.

The irony of Murat's ultimate demise is that he was condemned with a law he himself had issued five years earlier against armed bandits in his territory. He hadn't expected it. Upon his capture, he had even ordered two new suits of clothes from tailors that had been brought to his cell from nearby Monteleone (Vibo Valentia). During his short stay in Pizzo, he certainly hadn't tasted the *tartufo* that had yet to be invented, although I would hope that he at least had the opportunity to sample the tuna or other fish for which the city was well noted. Following in his footsteps many years later, Dumas only mentioned a cold chicken, bread and wine, but that was a snack for the condemned man to stave off hunger during the night.

Although not what it once was, the fishing industry has been an important part of the local economy for thousands of years—in particular, tuna. For many centuries up until the 1960s, the method of capture consisted of a series of nets attached to the shoreline that trapped the tuna as they passed by. Obviously, the ban on net fishing has had a dramatic impact on Pizzo. However, two well-known and respected companies with long histories, Sardanelli and Callipo still process tuna and other fish in their factories in Pizzo. Where the fish used to be freshly caught literally along the Costa degli Dei, today the focus is on processing fish for preservation in olive oil. Several of their products even add Calabrian peperoncino to spice up the flavor.

To the extent that processed tuna can be considered gourmet, the fish bottled by these companies in Pizzo definitely falls into that category.

So Pizzo is famous for tuna and gelato. On another trip to the town, I stumbled on an imaginative entrepreneur who had actually combined these disparate foods—thankfully, as a manufacturer, not as ingredients in a recipe. I don't know if by law or culinary decorum, but there was a wall between the side of the retail establishment that sold a range of packaged fish products and the gelato shop set up for both eat-in and takeout.

I was on state road 522 on the north side of Pizzo heading for the *Chiesa di Piedigrotta* (Church of the Piedigrotta), not to be confused with the house of worship by the same name in Naples. According to a legend dating back to the eighteenth century, a band of shipwrecked Neapolitan sailors had carved this small church out of a sandstone grotto in homage to the Madonna of Piedigrotta for having saved their lives. A long staircase leads down to the church from the road above. Sitting directly along the water on a narrow strip of beach, the main entrance has been given a stone façade, while the sides still have the natural exterior—a cave-like appearance with twentieth-century iron bars over the bare window openings. Stepping inside, I was struck with a primitive mysticism as well as by the dampness expected of such a location.

Varying sized chambers and cavities open up from the center nave, full of sculptures mostly created by a local father and son team who began carving figures out of the grotto's natural material in the late nineteenth century. Individual statues and clusters of traditional religious scenes fill the cavern illuminated by filters of natural light. Amongst the few more contemporary sculptures is a man on crutches, an image often seen in Catholic churches; however, in this likeness the character isn't the victim of a tragic accident, but none other than Fidel Castro, missing half a leg and leaning on the crutch of communism. The presumed and in retrospect unattainable hope of the sculptor was that the leader of Cuba would one day walk in Christianity.

While a bit quirky, the Church of the Piedigrotta reflects Calabrian religiosity, an expression of both the personal faith of individuals as well as the collective conviction of the community. Naturally, Pizzo has Catholic churches of more traditional natures and pasts. The town also has other grottos with their own hazy histories and whose legendary usage and occupancy range from Saracen pirates to monk seals. For Dumas writing about his travels to Calabria in 1835 (*Captain Arena*, 1842), Pizzo had been unimportant before Murat's execution and would probably have an inconsequential future, except for that fateful day in which Pizzo became "one of the Homeric stations of the Napoleonic Iliad."

There certainly is a lot to ponder while enjoying a gelato in Pizzo.

14

TWO PROVINCIAL CAPITALS AND A BYZANTINE METROPOLIS

SANTA MARIA DEL PATIRE ABBEY, ROSSANO

CATANZARO

IT IS CURIOUS THAT A SMALL MUNICIPALITY unknown to much of the world could give birth to a word that has transcended international borders and languages, a word that embodies the antithesis of the provincial community from which it derived; however, such is the case with Catanzaro. In 1897 an English writer named George Gissing traveled through Calabria and four years later published a book about his experiences. While in Catanzaro he stayed in a hotel whose proprietor's name was Coriolano Paparazzo. Gissing was particularly taken by the politely determined manner in which the hotelier executed his services, a style of dealing with the public rather common in Calabria, and mentioned his name in his travel narrative *By the Ionian Sea*. Over half a century later, the famous director Federico Fellini in collaboration with Ennio Flaiano was in search of a name that really popped for the character of the photographer in the film *La dolce vita* (1960). Not satisfied with the fruits of their own imaginations, they turned to a book that happened to be at hand and appropriated the colorful surname from the pen of Gissing by way of Catanzaro. Consequently, freelance photographers who aggressively chase after celebrities attempting to obtain candid shots became to be known the world over as paparazzi.

This brush with the international smart set certainly wasn't the first for Catanzaro, as the city was once an important silk center. Already in the late eleventh century, just a few hundred years after

Catanzaro's foundation, skilled workers were raising silkworms and weaving cloth. Their quality textiles were in demand all over Europe from the Renaissance onwards. Production culminated in the eighteenth century when the city had 7,000 silk makers and 1,000 weavers. If there had been a movie industry in that period, the stars and their paparazzi surely would have made their way to Catanzaro for their high-end fabrics. Unfortunately, the decline happened long before any collaboration with Milan could ever have been conceived, as Catanzaro's silk industry fell victim to oppressive governmental policies that rendered their production uncompetitive by the nineteenth century.

Today with approximately 93,000 inhabitants, Catanzaro is Calabria's second most populous city as well as its capital. The historic center retains much of its medieval layout, if not the actual buildings that were largely destroyed by earthquakes. Reminders of Catanzaro's past glories in the silk industry can be found in the names of several old quarters, such as *Gelso Bianco* (White Mulberry) for the area where the trees were cultivated for feeding the silkworms and *La Filanda* (The Spinning Mill), the district where silk was made, a particularly windy zone that helped blow away the strong odor of the naturally occurring silk gum.

That Catanzaro is an extremely windy city is attested to in an old proverb: *Trovare un amico è così raro come un dì senza vento a Catanzaro.* (Finding a friend is as rare as a day without wind in Catanzaro.) Its position high up on a hill, actually three hills, affords views, on a clear day, of both the Ionian and Tyrrhenian seas, but also makes it vulnerable to intense winds. Deep, craggy ravines surround the old town that is characterized by crooked, narrow lanes. I was struck by the seeming modernity of the long bridge that spans the gorge of the Fiumarella riverbed and leads from the periphery to the city center. When inaugurated in 1962, the viaduct designed by the renowned Italian engineer Riccardo Morandi was state of the art and its graceful, single arch continues to appear so amidst Catanzaro's rustic terrain.

Living in the province of Reggio Calabria, I tried not to
fall under the influence of the less than positive opinions many
residents held in regard to Calabria's capital city. "*Catanzaro
sembra più come un paesotto che una città.*" (Catanzaro seems
more like a small town than a city.) "*I Catanzaresi hanno un
accento troppo forte.*" (The people from Catanzaro have an
overbearing accent.) True, Catanzaro doesn't look like a capital,
but then again neither does Tallahassee, Florida, and at least
Catanzaro is centrally located. As for their accent, it is a bit
marked; however, nothing that stands out as compared with the
heavy aspirations of the Tuscan pronunciation or the French "r"
in the Piedmont region, for instance. Any hard feelings that may
exist toward Catanzaro, however, have to do with the dispute over
the location of Calabria's capital that resulted in eight months of
rioting in Reggio.

At first, I was confused by the issue of the capital. I was
told that it had been temporarily moved to Catanzaro after
the 1908 earthquake when Reggio struggled for many years
to get back on its feet. Then, sixty-two years later the troubles
exploded. I would discover that a certain familiarity with Italy's
relatively short history as a unified country was paramount in
understanding the capital discrepancy. On the territorial level,
the regions had been divided up into provinces on the French
model and provincial governments had been in place already
during the Kingdom of Italy. In Calabria, there are the provinces
of Cosenza, Reggio Calabria, Catanzaro and as of 1992 Crotone
and Vibo Valentia that had formerly been a part of Catanzaro.
While the regions were recognized geographically, culturally
and linguistically, as political entities they weren't codified until
after the Second World War with the formal constitution of 1947
under the newly formed Italian Republic. Regional autonomy
wasn't actually put into practice, however, until 1970 when the
first regional councils were elected.

Before that time, a legal capital didn't actually exist, although
encyclopedias and touring guides, for example, routinely listed

Reggio as Calabria's capital city. With the federal government's plan to make Catanzaro the capital, it was the only region in which the largest city wasn't projected as its administrative head. Conversely, in the region of Abruzzo, the initial proposal was to name Pescara, the most populous city, as its capital, but L'Aquila, the historically more important city balked and prevailed. Thus, L'Aquila is the capital, and the concession was made to give Pescara the seat of the regional council, as was also eventually done with Reggio.

Not unusual for Calabria, however, the situation was a bit complicated. I came across historical evidence for the capital rivalry at an exhibition where I found myself confronted with several old maps on which Calabria had been divided in half. Cosenza had been the capital of Calabria Citeriore (Upper Calabria), and Reggio, Catanzaro and even briefly Vibo Valentia had been the capitals at varying times of Calabria Ulteriore (Lower Calabria), which was further divided in the nineteenth century with capitals in both Reggio and Catanzaro. So in 1970 with a good dose of politics in the mix, Catanzaro was offered the capital and Reggio revolted—strikes, protest marches, roadblocks, railroad stoppages, port obstructions and a train bomb in Gioia Tauro. The general civil unrest manifested itself in frequent skirmishes with law enforcement, resulting in clampdowns that ranged from tear gas to armored tanks in the streets, said to have been coordinated by 10,000 members of various police and military forces. The reported number of deaths varies depending on whether the incidents were attributed to the protest or accidents, and hundreds were wounded. In the end, the official capital and the administrative arm of the government went to Catanzaro while Reggio was given the regional council or legislative branch.

The strongest images of the *Moti di Reggio* (Reggio's Revolt) that I came across in the course of my time in Calabria were a cylindrical, metal teargas container a friend had kept as a souvenir and the horrific eyesore of a corroded industrial plant along the coast of Saline Joniche. The colossal graveyard of rusting metal that was seemingly plucked from a futuristic film had been part of Reggio's concessionary package, a gift of promised industry built to the great detriment of the environment and then abandoned before ever having been put into function.

Catanzaro, on the other hand, waited rather calmly through the difficult episode, emerging unscathed as Calabria's official capital with the seat of the region's president and the executive branch of government. The people of Catanzaro had revolted many other times throughout their history, however, and several of these insurrections are documented alongside their military escapades in the city's *Museo Storico Militare* (Museum of Military History) located amidst the lovely greenery of the *Parco della Biodiversità Mediterranea* (Park of Mediterranean Biodiversity). For me, the most interesting exhibit focuses on the *Brigata Catanzaro*, a highly decorated World War I military brigade from Catanzaro. The Calabrian soldiers fighting for several years in the north of Italy for a cause that wasn't their own revolted when they were ordered back to the front lines without proper rest. The rebellion was contained, the instigators were shot and the troops would continue to fight with valor for the rest of the war. Their story is yet another in the long line of a people pushed to their limits.

In the Province of Catanzaro, even the earth is squeezed to its most restricted boundaries. Geographically, the capital city is situated at Calabria's center and narrowest point, where just thirty kilometers (nineteen miles) separate the two seas. Catanzaro is most easily reached by Calabria's largest international airport located within its province at Lamezia Terme on the other side of the slender taper of land. Calabria's third largest city with a population of about 70,000, Lamezia Terme is a destination for many low-cost airline flights and a jump off point for regional tourism.

As with the entire length of Calabria, Catanzaro is close to both the beach with nearby Catanzaro Lido on the Bay of

Squillace and the mountains of Le Serre to the south and La Sila to the north. Also in the area is the birthplace of painter and Knight of Calabria Mattia Preti (1613-1699). Aficionados of late Baroque art never pass up a visit to his hometown of Taverna, north of Catanzaro. Located on the slopes of the Piccola Sila Mountains, the village of about 2,500 inhabitants showcases a good number of Preti's works displayed in several churches and its civic museum.

To truly understand a people, the local food must be sampled. In Catanzaro, the signature dish simmers tripe and veal innards in a tomato sauce spiced with peperoncino. Served atop pita bread, the *Morzello* historically fortified manual laborers and artisans at breakfast and during breaks throughout the workday. I'd suggest ordering it for lunch or dinner.

CROTONE

I HAD HEARD OF THE PYTHAGORAS TRIANGLE. I had even put the theorem into practice on occasion when looking for a shortcut, but I would have to visit Crotone in order to learn of the Pythagoras square. Situated on the Ionian Sea northeast of Catanzaro and surrounded by the fertile, rolling hills of Marchesato, Crotone is a provincial capital and Calabria's fifth largest city with a modest population of 60,000. In Pythagoras' era half a millennium before Christ, Kroton, the city's precursor, was an important polis of Greater Greece, boasting a citizenry numerous enough to be able to send as many as 100,000 soldiers into battle at one time. From a tourist point of view, Crotone has a lot to offer: a long, distinguished history with a wealth of archeological sites; several noteworthy museums; a beautiful beach; a lively *passeggiata* culture; an aquatic nature preserve; and vicinity to the mountains and other historic communities.

I had been looking forward to seeing the lone, Greek column featured in all of the city's publicity materials. However, arriving to the area late in the afternoon, the street signs seemed to impede rather than facilitate locating the Calabrian landmark. As dusk was approaching, my friend Phil and I decided to head downtown in search of a place to stay. A dark, shadowy coastal road led us to the outskirts, from where we easily followed the traffic to the city center. Many centuries before, a good number of Greek columns and their supports had also trailed past peoples to the urban core where the materials were used in the building of the castle and the port.

Although archeologists have uncovered evidence of Crotone's continuous occupation dating from pre-Grecian indigenous people, visually, not much is left from its long history. In the center, the castle is the most significant architectural reminder of Crotone's past. Founded by the Normans and subsequently modified throughout the centuries, the fortification is named after Carlo V (Charles V) who in the sixteenth century expanded the city's privileges and its port, which remains important for local agriculture and industry. Known as Cotrone during Carlo's reign, the name held until the last century when in 1928 it was changed to Crotone.

Once in the city center, we immediately came upon the lovely, nineteenth-century shopping arcade that hearkened back to Kroton's grand temple. Its neo-Doric columns anchored the street that led from the cathedral to the main square: *Piazza Pitagora* — Pythagoras Square! The mathematician better known for his triangles did more than pass through the ancient metropolis, though. Pythagoras (c. 570- c. 490 BC) lived in Kroton for many years, and in 530 BC founded a philosophical school that combined mystical and religious tenets with scientific, mathematical and musical studies. He and his followers were eventually run out of town, and it is believed that Pythagoras ended his days in Metapontum, just up the coast in what is now the region of Basilicata.

As a Greek settlement viewed from a modern perspective, Kroton or Crotone lacks the celebrity attributed to Athens or

Syracuse. And unlike the more famous cities of Greater Greece, such as Paestum near Salerno or Agrigento in Sicily, Crotone doesn't have any gleaming temples in front of which busloads of tourists can congregate for photo-ops. However, Kroton was a flourishing city in its heyday, noted for its physicians and in particular for the physical strength of its citizens. With the top wrestler of the era, Kroton was only second to Sparta in overall number of Olympic victories. The people of Crotone are proud of their ancient proverb, "*Ultimo dei Crotoniati, primo dei Greci.*" (Last amongst the Crotonians, first amongst the Greeks.)

Kroton was founded at the easternmost point of Calabria on the spur that juts into the Ionian Sea. Our visit began in a private tourist office of the modern city that had been built atop thousands of years of history. While there was a perfectly acceptable hotel a stone's throw from Pythagoras' square, we were looking for a more budget-conscious accommodation. The affable young woman in the agency made several phone calls to acquaintances who rented rooms, assuring them, "*Sono signori,*" (Literally, they're gentlefolk—in other words, respectable). Upon arrival we found out how important her assessment was when we realized our hosts had already rented out their main guest quarters and that the lady of the house was giving up her own bed, possibly the most comfortable I've ever slept in. Later, when I asked about the gravity-board in her room, I learned that the poor woman had had countless back operations and as I had suspected, the bed was far from ordinary, particularly in an economical bed and breakfast. Needless to say, she and her son Matteo were lovely people, and to help us navigate the road to their house, they met us directly at the travel agency.

Apparently in Crotone, it wasn't just massive Greek columns that had a tendency to disappear. The unlit coastal road leading into and out of the city was due to missing connective cables, stolen several months earlier, thus leaving the local population in the dark and guessing as to if and when their lights would ever be restored. Finding the accommodation would have been difficult without a guide, although we could have used the lights out in the bay as a point of reference to make a few trigonometric calculations in homage to Pythagoras. Along the drive, we asked Matteo about those mysterious lights on the landscape, what we at first had thought was an enormous cruise ship moored just off the coast. He said that it was a platform for the extraction of methane gas and that the area of Crotone supplied the nation with fifteen percent of the natural resource. So just as the lighting cables had disappeared overnight, a colossal platform had miraculously materialized in their bay courtesy of ENI, the Italian multinational oil and gas company with the very recognizable company logo of the strange, six-legged, fire-breathing black dog on a yellow background.

Local opposition to the methane gas removal counted amongst its issues the area's gradual ground sinking due to the voluminous rate of extraction and the negative socio-economic impact on the community. Matteo emphasized the illicit drilling in and around a protected marine reserve (*Riserva Naturale Marina Capo Rizzuto*). The new rig sat on its boundary, drilled a certain vertical distance into the seabed, and then simply changed angle straight into the preserve. The public outcry seemed ineffectual. The objections came too late. The politicians had shaken hands and the paperwork had already been stamped in Rome. For the citizens of Crotone, the drilling was just another example of Calabria and its people getting a raw deal.

Ironically, the rig had the same name as the lone column's former temple, Hera Lacinia. Perhaps in another 2,500 years when the column will have long since fallen from the vibrations of the drilling and the sinking of the land, tourists will stand on Crotone's shores looking out at the temples of our Modern Era. On our twenty-first century visit, however, we were more interested in the ancient history, and after downing a goodly number of delicious pastries made by our host whose family had been in the bakery business for over a hundred years, we set out to explore Capo Colonna (Cape Column).

The Greeks of Kroton built their most important temple on a cape now named after its surviving column located twelve kilometers (seven and a half miles) south of the city center. Dedicated to Hera, the goddess of fertility, the temple and its sanctuary served as a religious center, a bank, a retreat and a pasture for the deity's sacred oxen. Venerated both for its spiritual significance and its immense riches, the temple was visited by the likes of Hannibal, who in 203 BC left for his campaign in North Africa from Kroton's shores. Today, just one of the forty-eight original Doric columns still stands on the cliff overlooking the sea, sadly protected from contemporary vandals behind a rather innocuous chain-link fence. Area excavations have uncovered other buildings connected with the sanctuary that were utilized for religious celebrations and the collection of donations. In Roman times, the area around the sanctuary was urbanized.

A large archeological park encompasses the column and other Greek remains as well as Roman building foundations that include the layouts of rectangular housing blocks, a bath complex and a brick kiln. The imposing, squared-off *Torre di Nao* (Nao Tower) is also squeezed in amongst the historical monuments. Defensive towers were constructed all along the coast from the Norman period onwards, and in the sixteenth century planned at a distance of about twelve kilometers apart. Today, the varying-shaped round and square fortifications can be viewed with assorted modifications and in diverse states of repair. As an example, the Nao Tower was completed in 1568, losing its function against pirates after about three hundred years and subsequently put into service by French customs, the Italian finance police and as a museum. A few towers were turned into residences, while others were abandoned and stripped for building materials. In whatever their state of conservation, the towers contribute greatly to Calabria's picturesque shores.

In addition to the opportunity of walking amidst the ancient foundations and admiring the archaic construction overgrown with weeds, Crotone also presents two excellent national museums documenting the ancient peoples. The jewel in the crown of the downtown collection is literally a gold crown of laurel leaves. Other precious artifacts dating from the eighth to the fifth centuries BC include decorative bronze and terracotta sculptures. The museum at Capo Colonna highlights architectural fragments and objects found in the sea, and also provides a good overview of the zone.

For millennia, the people of Crotone have had a profound connection with the sacred area where Hera Lacinia's temple once stood, and it is therefore no wonder that the city's patron saint is the Madonna di Capo Colonna. Her miraculous story goes back to 1519 when the Turks tried to burn a painting of the Madonna, throwing it into the sea when it wouldn't catch fire. The picture floated back to shore intact and was found by a fisherman at Capo Colonna. Throughout the year, the Byzantine icon is housed downtown in Crotone's cathedral. Every May during the festival, thousands of the faithful join the procession that starts at one o'clock in the morning from the cathedral and finishes about six hours later at the *Santuario di Santa Maria di Capo Colonna*. This sanctuary is a small church founded a thousand years ago by Basilian monks near the former pagan temple on the edge of the cape. The icon returns to its home in the cathedral by boat against a backdrop of colorful fireworks. In special years, the cortège processes back to the city by land with the painting pulled the distance by an ox-drawn cart.

The spiritual blends with the historical amidst Capo Colonna's natural setting. The promontory is part of a larger area of land with several small capes that protrude into the sea south of Crotone. The zone is full of important historical monuments and excavations from the Bronze Age to the Greeks to the Romans to the Byzantines to the Arabs to Charles V and through the Bourbon period, not to mention the natural inhabitants in the surrounding nature preserve. Called Capo Rizzuto after one of its capes, the marine reserve protects the shallow seabed of the forty-two-kilometer coastline for both archeological and environmental purposes. The unusually named inland town of Isola (island) di Capo Rizzuto is a buzzing center for summer tourism and there is even a small airport nearby. Of course, upon hearing the name of the area, I couldn't help but think of Phil Rizzuto, the legendary American baseball player of Calabrian descent. My hosts, however, hadn't ever heard of the Hall of Fame shortstop, but upon mention of his surname immediately developed an interest in the sport and were ready to swear full allegiance to the New York Yankees.

The Cape Rizzuto Marine Reserve extends past another Calabrian landmark, the Aragon castle of Le Castella. As with the use of the word *isola* for a landlocked town, the application of the feminine plural of *castello* (castle) for this community is also an enigma. However, there isn't any mystery concerning its attraction. Sitting out on its own islet surrounded by the reserve's crystalline waters and connected to the mainland by just a narrow path, the stunning castle is the pride of local and regional tourism. Perhaps its beauty lies in the setting, with the play of light off the many angles of its massive stone walls, or in its design, the round Angevin tower reinforced and surrounded by the irregular Aragon fortification that corresponds to the shape of the slender spit of land on which it rests. It is ironic that this disregarded corner of Italy in the much-disparaged region of Calabria was once considered worthy of such a formidable defensive system.

I considered its long history as I gazed out at the extraordinary vision from my window seat of a local restaurant perched on a ledge of jagged rocks facing the castle. Reflecting on its dramatic presence, I can't say that in that moment I was able to envision Hannibal and his troops camping out on the then bare point of land or turbaned Saracen marauders wielding their curved blades on the beach. I was distracted by the panorama as it was, along with the plate of pasta and glass of local Cirò wine before me. The full-bodied, dry red produced in the nearby town of the same name was Calabria's first DOC wine. The Cirò *rosso* (red) consists of ninety-five percent of the Gaglioppo grape, a vine imported by the ancient Greeks. In fact, wine from the area of Cirò Marina was so highly esteemed by the historic peoples that it was awarded to winning athletes in the original Olympic games.

After lunch, I unexpectedly came face to face with Calabria's history of Arab incursions as I strolled through town. The eyes of a Barbary pirate, complete with flowing mustache and full, elaborate turban glared out at me as I read the inscription under his bronze bust:

Giovan Dionigi Galeni	(his given name)
Kilic Ali – Occhiali	(his Arab name and what he was called in Italian)
Castella – Costantinopoli	(his birth and death places)
Sec XVI	(sixteenth century)

With all the stories of Calabrians building towers and fortresses to combat the Barbary corsairs, their fleeing to the hills and the abandonment of coastal towns, here was a Calabrian who had been captured and enslaved, converted to Islam and become a pirate himself! Leading raids throughout the Mediterranean, he eventually moved up the ranks to Grand Admiral of the Ottoman fleet, dying with enormous riches and 1300 slaves. Clearly, this Calabrian was quite a capable individual, but I couldn't help but think that five hundred years from now when the 'Ndrangheta will hopefully be no more than a parenthesis in Calabrian history, there will be town councils erecting monuments to the thugs.

I preferred Pythagoras Square, although what do I know? Maybe his adversaries had good reason to oppose his strict regimens associated with diet and religion. I would need to look into his stance on Cirò wine.

ROSSANO

BEFORE LIVING IN CALABRIA, I hadn't ever heard of the Codex Purpureus Rossanensis. Nevertheless, a peek at its pages is not only obligatory, but is often the motivation for a visit to Rossano, also called Rossano Calabro, located in the province of Cosenza in northeastern Calabria. For the spiritually inclined, the ancient manuscript is an important, illuminated chronicle of the sacred Gospel. For the historically minded, the rare volume serves to document Calabria's rich past, particularly that of the Byzantine church that flourished in Rossano, giving birth to a pope, an antipope and a couple of saints. Luckily, the town and its environs offer several other interesting attractions to fill out a trip.

We had made a reservation at a local *agriturismo*, and when I called back to get driving instructions, Giuseppe, the amiable proprietor, communicated that his inn was in Rossano's modern section next to the penitentiary. "Better the criminals are behind bars," Phil reassured me as we drove up the Ionian coast towards the civic-minded town, whose population of 37,000 was divided into two main areas of inhabitation. The historic center sat up on a hilltop, while the more recently settled zone, referred to as Rossano Scalo (station), lay between the high ground and the sea. Giuseppe met us next door to the hotel at his brother's gas station/quickie mart/bar, where we would eat our continental breakfast amidst good-natured familial banter.

Maybe our neighbors were on eternal lockdown as we fortunately never heard a peep out of them, and the next morning, well-rested, we set off for the old town, armed with our host's brochures and fortified with his local knowledge as well as an enormous basket of incredibly juicy oranges picked from his orchard out back. Upon arrival, we made our usual mistake of looking at the map and thinking that we could figure out how to drive to our chosen destination along the cramped, twisted roads instead of just parking in the first convenient spot and walking. Thus, after a good deal of frustrating maneuvers that always ended up in the same place, we parked and took a stroll through the rather deserted streets. As all over Calabria, the buildings appeared in various states of repair. Nondescript edifices stood beside the occasional elegant patrician residence. Small shops sold local products and items made in China. A number of churches still preserved Rossano's Byzantine heritage, most notably the attractive, compact Church of San Marco that dates from the tenth century and is similar to the Cattolica di Stilo, laid out in the form of a Greek cross and topped by five cylindrical cupolas.

Rossano flourished from the sixth through eleventh centuries under the Byzantines, functioning as an ecclesiastical, societal, administrative and military center able to withstand numerous enemy attacks and earning the designation *La Bizantina*, still in use today. Clearly, the Italian journalist who first brought the aforementioned Greek manuscript to light in 1846 or the German theologians who presented it on the world stage in 1879 hadn't been stabbing around in the dark as they rummaged through old documents in the sacristy of Rossano's cathedral. Generally believed to date from the sixth century, the Codex Purpureus Rossanensis was most likely composed in the Middle East, possibly at Antioch (today, Antakya in Turkey). The manuscript contains the Gospel of Saint Matthew and most of Saint Mark, along with a partial letter by Eusebius.

As the illuminated manuscript is Rossano's biggest draw, I would have thought that the town fathers would have made it easier to find. Searching all around the cathedral, we didn't see any indication as to the location of the diocesan museum. Next door in what appeared to be an information office, the sole employee brushed us off with his free hand and walked into a back room jabbering away on his cell phone. Nearby, an elderly gentleman in a tiny art gallery directed us down a street and around a corner, where we found the museum locked, albeit well within the posted visiting hours. We returned to the helpful septuagenarian who pointed us to a small shop where we would find a clerk who could open the museum for us. Sure enough, the woman told us she would be there in a few minutes and after a short wait, she and her toddler arrived with the key. Visiting a museum in Calabria on the offseason was as easy as that! The German tourists who arrived half an hour later must have thought how efficient those Calabrians were.

The museum occupies a few rooms full of the usual reliquaries, manuscripts and religious art, but to quote from its website, the "*gemma che da sola fa Museo*" (gem that makes a museum all by itself) is the Codex Pupureus Rossanensis or the Rossano Gospels in common English. Admittedly not having studied Latin, I must say that I was expecting a document with a purple hue, but apparently the word *pupureus* can also mean dark red. The exclusive parchment was a striking rust color, very appealing, with silver and gold Greek lettering on pages of about 30 x 20 centimeters (12 x 8 inches). Of the 188 leaves of vellum, twelve pages with vivid illustrations stood out for the compelling simplicity in which they conveyed the Biblical stories, such as the Resurrection of Lazarus and the Parable of the Good Samaritan. Of course, the book was under glass, but at its side was a freestanding Rolodex containing the images in small poster size, also available in the gift shop.

In the afternoon we continued our exploration of *La Bizantina* with a lovely drive in the country. Our destination was just west of Rossano up a winding, mountain road to the Abbazia Santa Maria del Patire (from the Greek *patèr* or father). Founded in 1095, the abbey grew wealthy under the Normans, possessing a significant library and scriptorium. The religious community flourished until the fifteenth century, when the Italian-Greek monasteries began their decline with the abandonment of the Eastern rite.

Pulling into the parking area, we felt the calm of a more tranquil era. The graceful Basilian-Norman architecture complemented the pristine forest setting. The church's three rounded apses with variegated stone and brick decorative features beckoned across the well-groomed lawn flanked by the arched column remains of the former cloister. Inside, we were drawn to the original, multi-colored mosaics that still covered a large section of the floor. Dating from 1149, the fanciful depictions of real animals, a stag and a lion, lay alongside mythological representations of a griffin, centaur and unicorn. Other interior furnishings were once equally rich, judging from the marble baptismal font made for the church in 1137. Now on display in New York's Metropolitan Museum of Art, the harmonious sculpture is embellished with Greek crosses and a fluid vine motif.

Although the monks are long gone, the abbey still serves as a place to commune with God and nature. We wandered a bit, only coming across the German couple that must have followed us from the diocesan museum. During the summer, I imagined families happily eating at the many picnic tables, escaping the heat of the beach for an afternoon in the abbey's shade. Returning to the car, we were startled by the sudden appearance of a man along the side of the path. The rough-hewn, burly fellow had materialized out of nowhere, and we had the sensation that he had been aware of us longer than we had of him. Feeling a bit cautious in the semi-deserted location, I thought the best tactic would be to engage him in conversation. The exchange would last a lot longer than I anticipated.

"Rra-ahn-jayrrr!" He was trying to tell us what he was doing there. It took us a few moments to realize that he was also demonstrating his knowledge of the English language. Michele was a forest ranger, not the type we were familiar with, dressed in an olive-green uniform, but a come-as-you-are Italian variety. He drove to work in a beat-up, twenty-year-old, compact vehicle and dressed for warmth to sit inside a damp building on the abbey grounds. The former monastery was property of the state, overseen by the territorial forest service. Michele wanted to chat and before we knew it, we were sitting at a picnic table covered with a faded-yellow, daisy-patterned, plastic tablecloth in a smoky, makeshift kitchen. We had been invited into the rangers' private quarters and based on its disheveled, no-nonsense, rustic ambience, it was clear to me that it was a refuge for men.

He invited us to sit down, spread out a piece of newspaper, and began pulling provisions out of the cupboard. Our picnic consisted of *capocollo* (cold cut), *pecorino* (cheese), a few *rosette* (puffed-up rolls with a rose pattern on top) and an enormous jar of king-sized anchovies. His wife had prepared the meaty little fish, first preserved in salt, then desalted and put in oil with peperoncino. To wash it all down, he served his homemade wine from a reused liter bottle with its original "Tavernello" label still attached. Small, casual wine glasses, a wooden cutting board and sharp knife rounded out the accoutrements. Every once in a while Michele went over to the stone fireplace and poked around, seeming to elicit as much smoke as heat. Food, politics, current events—we discussed a host of topics in his cozy home away from home. His most memorable statement had to do with the 'Ndrangheta: In the Province of Cosenza, the Calabrian criminal organization was like a plate of spaghetti with a light, fish sauce, whereas in Reggio Calabria, it was a dish of macaroni drenched in a heavy meat sauce. There wasn't a subject Calabrians couldn't express in terms of food. As for the import of his perspective regarding the 'Ndrangheta, I frequently heard Calabrians from the more northern provinces assert that the criminal organization was less oppressive outside of Reggio.

As authentic as Michele's artisan picnic and philosophical musings were, we needed to save room in our stomachs for our evening meal and took our leave after a pleasant few hours in order to drive out of the woods before dark. Giuseppe had warned us that our dinner was to include an antipasto of eleven *portate* (dishes), two first courses, two seconds with side dishes, fruit, dessert, local liquors, and naturally wine and coffee. He didn't let us down, and while he had a large party to take care of in his restaurant that night, he made sure to frequently come by our table and give us his enthusiastic personal touch. As we left the following morning, he pressed a jar of his establishment's honey into our hands along with a fifteen-pound bag of oranges freshly picked from his trees; going the extra mile to have a successful business, he was a true ambassador for his city.

Our final stop was the *Museo della Liquirizia* (Licorice Museum), an eminently fascinating little museum that tells the story of Rossano's leading entrepreneurs and their licorice production. The museum traces the Amarelli family's history, their enterprise and the precious root of the local, wild licorice plant. The engaging story is presented with a wealth of original documentation and artifacts, from factory machinery to personal, family items.

The Amarellis were already involved with licorice by around 1500, or a short time after the Greek rite was abolished in Calabria. In 1731, they developed a method of extracting the juice from the root and industrialized their operation. Since that time, the factory has produced licorice lozenges, always staying on top of the latest technological advancements while remaining true to their quality origins. The licorice is natural and intense, and has almost nothing in common with the licorice-flavored candy found at movie theater refreshment counters. Amarelli packages its licorice in decorative tins and simple boxes, selling it both in its purest form and blended with other natural ingredients and flavors, added to chocolate and incorporated in alcoholic beverages.

The company's adherence to tradition, innovation and design is apparent from the wholesome products to the design of their containers. Even the onsite factory and smokestack from 1907 can be described as a fine example of industrial archeology. The museum is housed in the Amarelli's historic residence, initially constructed in 1400 and continually occupied by the family and its business until today. While other ventures have come and gone, Amarelli has managed to survive through the Aragons, the Spanish, the Hapsburgs, the French, the Bourbons, the Kingdom and Republic of Italy, and even the 'Ndrangheta.

A number of my middle school students visited the factory and museum on a multiple-day school trip. The same boy whose eyes lit up when talking of his Grandmother's macaroni with goat sauce spoke passionately of Amarelli, certainly one of the region's positive examples. I found the whole operation quite impressive and have, in particular, enjoyed their *liquore alla liquirizia* (licorice liquor), the *sassolini* (literally, "little stones," sugar-coated licorice flavored with anise) that are popular with children, and the tisane of natural licorice roots. I noticed that Amarelli's tour guide didn't mention Greek monks boiling up the roots for a delicate, naturally sweet herbal tea or concocting the stronger digestive for medicinal purposes. However, I imagine the sophisticated culture that thrived in the area appreciated many an infusion or distillation before several noble families in the province of Cosenza began industrialization. Today, Calabrian licorice has been given the PDO (Protected Designation of Origin) status. In addition to candies and alcohol, licorice is frequently utilized in the preparation of pastries and gelato. Calabria's old-world tastes are gaining ground with new-world palates.

15

STRATEGIC POSITIONS

CASTLE, SANTA SEVERINA

THE CASTLES OF SANTA SEVERINA AND CORIGLIANO CALABRO

CALABRIA IS FULL OF CASTLES AND TOWERS. They imbue the landscape with a certain romanticism and make lovely photos. They serve as symbols of towns, cities and even the region. Their histories are long, rather intricate and share a common thread: founded on the site of an earlier structure, attacked, reinforced, destroyed by earthquakes, rebuilt, subjected to new rulers, restructured, passed from one noble family to another, modernized, left to deteriorate and eventually sold, often ending up in public hands. Many castles are merely a suggestion of what they once were, an outline looming on a hill, a defensive tower crumbling under a network of vines. Several have been turned into museums or used for exhibitions and a few have become hotels.

The castles of Santa Severina in the Province of Crotone and Corigliano Calabro in the Province of Cosenza are amongst Calabria's best preserved. Dominating the surrounding valleys from strategic, hilltop vantage points, they proclaim strength as much as exhibit a capacity for resistance. Built as fortifications at the end of the eleventh century by the Norman conqueror, Robert Guiscard, they were subsequently expanded and restructured, used as defensive strongholds and as residences, sold to the state, restored and opened for tours. Having previously visited other castles in the region, I was pleasantly surprised at how much there was to see at these two sites. Of course it's all relative. Just a hint of furnishings is exciting in Calabria, where, if the baron or count hadn't stripped the property of every last stick of furniture, someone else would have.

Santa Severina also boasts one of the region's best-preserved historic centers. Perched on a cliff halfway between the Ionian Sea and the Sila Mountains, the small medieval village presents the characteristic storybook image expected of a European burg. Pulling into the castle's parking area at the bottom of its dry moat, I quickly gained an appreciation for the fortress' imposing inaccessibility. Easy for me to climb up the steps to the main square and cross over the sturdy, arched bridge that had been built to connect the town with the castle when its defensive function had ceased, but without the relatively modern modes of access, the massive, stone walls would have been dauntingly unapproachable, particularly when the drawbridge was raised.

A tour of the formidable, yet attractive castle gave me a sense of the long history that had come to pass behind its walls. For example, an extensive restoration throughout the 1990s indicated that the castle had been erected on the site of a pre-Roman settlement and also revealed the Byzantine structures over which the Norman castle had been built. The exhibit left some of the archeological excavations exposed, showing the remains of a ninth-century church and necropolis, as well as artifacts from the period. In turn, later modifications, such as the sixteenth-century moat and bastions, were carried out through the demolition of a Norman chapel and the alterations of Angevin and Aragon structures.

The life of the nobles who ruled under the feudal system and who periodically lived in the castle was referenced with contemporary reproductions of costumes from the 1500s displayed on the *piano nobile* (noble floor). However, aside from the restoration of the Rococo ceiling paintings and a few canon balls kicking around the unfinished, subterranean corridors, the interior furnishings were non-existent. The castle ended up in the hands of the city in 1904 and was used as a high school for many years.

In recent history, Santa Severina underwent a monumental change in its social structure with the agrarian reform of 1950. Up until that time, large tracts of land in Italy were in the hands of very few. Often, the proprietors were absentee landlords who had a history of squeezing the *contadini* (peasants) for a quick profit without concern for the ultimate productivity of the land or the suffering of their *braccianti* (hired hands). The problem was especially critical in the south. Although the word *contadino* can also be translated as 'farmer,' the term 'peasant' would be more accurate to describe the typical, landless *contadino*. Further, despite the honest work, *contadino* is often used in a derogatory manner to indicate a rough, uneducated, country person.

Many *contadini* lived an impossible reality, having to walk for up to three hours just to reach the plot of land they worked without the right to construct a shelter in its vicinity. At the time of the land reform, eighty percent of the peasants in Santa Severina didn't own a plough, a donkey or have the resources to buy fertilizer. Throughout Italy, general unrest and peasant revolts after the Second World War led to the redistribution of land. The reform had a dual purpose: supplying the *contadini* with the means to earn a living and improving agrarian productivity, particularly in the less cultivated areas of the large estates.

As part of a government plan for the revitalization of the Sila Mountains, for example, its territory extending to the plains of Crotone and the Ionian coast was the first area in Calabria to be evaluated, divided and allocated to its *contadini*. Of an expanse of over 500,000 hectares (1,235,527 acres) under the control of large-scale landowners, 76,000 (187,800) were cut out and allotted to 20,000 *contadini* without farmland. Santa Severina was the first town in which lots were given out. In a grand ceremony filmed for posterity, 1,600 hectares (3954 acres) of land were parceled out to 396 families in the spacious piazza in front of the castle. Everyone was happy and there was a new hope for the future. In fact, the town's population swelled to over 3,000 into the early 1960s, dropping back to about 2,300 into this century. Small family businesses and cooperatives emerged from the reform that changed the face of society, even if it wasn't as successful as had been anticipated. In Santa Severina and other towns in the area such as the much larger San Giovanni in Fiore in the heart of the mountains, tourism has since become an important factor for the economy.

In addition to the castle whose ramparts afford splendid vistas out over the rolling valley as far as Crotone and the sea, Santa Severina's charming center has several historic churches and a diocesan museum. Two noteworthy Eastern Orthodox structures leave a visual reminder of the town's Greek connection and its native son, Pope Zachary (679-752), the last of the Byzantine Papacy. Archeologists have yet to determine its original function or assign a specific date of construction, but the Baptistery most likely dates from the last quarter of the first millennium. The structure is of singular architectural form, small, circular with four extensions in the shape of a Greek cross. From the twelfth-century and equally appealing, the elegant Church of Santa Filomena is an example of the late Byzantine with a mix of Norman decorative elements, including door arches and the slim, sixteen-columned cupola.

When the Normans arrived to build their castle on the cliff of Santa Severina, they were already overlapping more than a thousand years of history. The hill of Corigliano Calabro, on the other hand, had been settled by the Arabs only a hundred years before the Normans came on the scene. The urban center grew under the various counts, dukes and barons of Corigliano. Several kings even had connections with the castle. According to local legend, Charles III (aka Charles the Short), King of Naples, was born in the castle in 1345. Another Charles III, the King of Spain and the Two Sicilies, stayed overnight at the castle in 1735. The last two Kings of Italy spent time in the castle before they were crowned: Victor Emanuel III slept there in 1891, and

Umberto II visited briefly in 1932. Clearly, it was the place to be for many centuries.

Over time, the town grew up around the castle, with an ordinary street and nondescript buildings winding around its perimeter walls. The ducal castle became the property of Corigliano Calabro in 1979, was restored from 1988 to 2002 with funds from the European Union, and subsequently opened to the public. On my visit, I discovered upon arrival to the ticket booth that a reservation had to be made in advance for a guided tour, which would have been contracted separately. Thus, I had to glean all I could from a simple handout of the castle's history as I was escorted through the property by a city employee. The lanky, middle-aged man mutely executed his duties, patiently holding me under observation until I indicated that I was ready to be led to the next point of interest. I didn't see much I could have picked up and walked away with.

The most sumptuous room of the castle was the gilded ballroom that coupled Empire and Venetian Baroque styles and featured lavish mirrors and Bohemian chandeliers. Its eye-catching ceiling fresco was painted around 1870 by Ignazio Perricci who would go on to decorate important rooms in Rome's Quirinale and Palazzo Montecitorio, the President's residence and the seat of the Italian Chamber of Deputies. Entitled "*palcoscenico della vita*" (theater of life), the winsome painting depicted an open sky with local townsfolk in period costumes excitedly looking down over an upper balcony onto the events unfolding below.

The other striking characteristic of the castle, both from a distance and close-up, was the main tower. To the left of the drawbridge, it soared to approximately thirty meters (ninety-eight feet) from the street level to the top of the octagonal turret that had been added to the original, cylindrical Norman fortification. As its function shifted from military to residential, its drawbridge was replaced by a permanent walkway connecting it with the rest of the castle, the walls were fashionably frescoed, and a metal, circular staircase was installed to give access to the commanding view from its upper story.

With careful reading and a bit of imagination, the visit gave me a rough idea of the lifestyle carried on by the Calabrian nobility. Under their control, Corigliano had its ups and downs, suffered from malaria and other epidemics, developed the licorice trade along with nearby Rossano, and eventually planted vast citrus groves, seeing its population gradually grow from 8,000 to nearly 40,000 over the past two centuries. Following unification, "Calabro" was added to its name to avoid confusion with another, smaller Corigliano in Apulia.

After a thousand years in the hands of a very few elite, the castles of Santa Severina and Corigliano Calabro changed direction. The former feudal seats adapted to benefit their entire citizenry, serving as museums to enrich the cultural fabric of their communities. When funds permit, the curious will continue to explore the areas' rich pasts—under ground, beneath surfaces and between pages, as the whole stories have yet to be told, not just by castles and churches, but throughout the surrounding territories. In Santa Severina, evidence of inhabitation goes back to prehistoric, indigenous peoples, with Bronze Age artifacts testifying to the ancient cultivation of olive trees and oil production. Agriculture still thrives, as tomorrow's history will one day chronicle.

At the center of Santa Severina's old village, just a stone's throw from the castle, I met a twenty-first century restaurateur who longed for the days of yore. As I finished my lunch, I was bizarrely "crowned" with a paper diadem reminiscent of a kids' prize at the home of the whopper. Posing alongside me in his multistory hat, the chef encouraged me to smile for the historic photo-op. I did beam—how could I not? I had eaten like a king and would have the picture for proof. I wouldn't have it charged to my credit card, though, as despite all the signs in the window, the machine was *fuori servizio* (out of order), not uncommon in the least.

POLLINO, SILA AND SYBARIS: THE MOUNTAINS AND THEIR ALLUVIAL PLAIN

And why need we mention the Sybarites, among whom bathing men and pourers of water were first introduced in fetters, in order to prevent their going too fast, and to prevent also their scalding the bathers in their haste? And the Sybarites were the first people to forbid those who practice noisy arts from dwelling in their city; such as blacksmiths, and carpenters, and men of similar trades; providing that their slumbers should always be undisturbed. And it used to be unlawful to rear a cock in their city.

And Timaeus relates concerning them, that a citizen of Sybaris once going into the country, seeing the farmers digging, said that he himself felt as if he had broken his bones by the sight; and some one who heard him replied, "I, when I heard you say this, felt as if I had a pain in my side."

Athenaeus, Book 12 of *The Deipnosophists*
(The Banquet of the Learned)
Translated in 1854 by Charles Duke Yonge

WHATEVER BECAME OF THE HEDONISTIC Sybarites who inspired such tales of luxury and whose very name has been appropriated to characterize self-indulgent individuals fond of sensuous extravagance? Athenaeus actually wrote his account seven hundred years after Sybaris was destroyed; and a few millennia after the city's demise, the lowercased sybarite is occasionally still flung about. The ancient Greek writer blamed the city's downfall on the excesses of its citizens, having "taught even their horses to dance at their feasts to the music of the flute. Accordingly the people of Croton, knowing this, and being at war with them . . . played before their horses the tune to which they were accustomed to dance; for the people of Croton also had flute-players in military uniform. And as soon as the horses heard them playing on the flute, they not only began to dance, but ran over to the army of the Crotonians, carrying their riders with them." With such fanciful narratives, the Sybarite legacy was sealed.

Fascination with this lavish imagery persisted, perhaps due in part to the city's disappearance. Crotone at the very least had its remaining column to attest to its former glory, but Sybaris was a lost city of Greater Greece. Once covering an expanse of about 500 hectares (1,236 acres) and inhabited by an estimated population of over 100,000 and by some accounts as many as 300,000, Sybaris had a brief, yet illustrious history. The colony was established in 720 BC, became the most important and powerful polis in Greater Greece, founded other colonies including Poseidonia (Paestum), well known for its surviving temples, and then ceased to exist— all within a span of two hundred years. Sybaris' choice location certainly contributed to its rapid and considerable prosperity. Set on the Ionian Sea between the outlets of two rivers, Sybaris lay on the fertile plain between the Pollino range to its north and the upper plateau of the Sila Mountains to the south in what is present-day northeastern Calabria. Trade developed quickly from its river harbor, and agriculture flourished in the area's rich soil. In addition, the nearby highlands supplied the city with abundant wood, resin, silver and other metals.

I happened upon modern Sibari (Sybaris) during a rainstorm and saw firsthand how water could have been detrimental to the area's long-term success. The Sybarites expertly managed their copious supply with a system of canals that channeled the precious resource to benefit their farming endeavors. Without such activity, however, the area quickly turned into a swamp, breeding malaria-carrying mosquitoes, a grave problem in many seaboard communities before its eradication in the middle of the last century. Pulling off the coastal highway into Sibari's archeological park, I didn't feel very encouraged by the local weather, but I figured that in Calabria, half the battle was actually reaching a destination, so I got out of my rental car and approached the man in the booth. I never was able to establish if the park was actually closed that day or not, but the security guard just sat inside his dry enclosure shaking his head with a smile at the thought of the crazy foreigner even thinking of tramping around the ruins on a day of that sort. Not prepared with hip boots and a bit intimidated by his incredulous expression, I skipped the outdoor remains and examined the interesting collection of artifacts at the indoor museum down the road.

The display took me through the destruction of Sybaris by the Crotonians in 510 BC. I was disappointed that there weren't any relics related to the dancing horses, although there was a piece of a bone flute from the Roman period. As a few sources suggested, perhaps the legendary tales of the Sybarites' lavish lifestyle were concocted by Crotone's overzealous ascetics under the austere leadership of Pythagoras. After a number of years, the Sybarites were able to regroup with some help from Greece, founding a Hellenic community, and later a Latin one. Following the fall of Rome, the civilizations faded into the swamp, buried under layers of silt.

The mystery of Sybaris sparked numerous searches, but the area's first systematic excavations only began in 1967 with the aid of modern instruments. Present-day Sibari grew up in the 1960s as the result of a government drainage project, like that of the Sybarites thousands of years earlier. The high-yielding *Piana di Sibari* (Sybaris Plain) is Calabria's largest flatland, producing olives, rice and citrus, most notably the clementine that has the IGP designation (*Indicazione geografica protetta*, Protected Geographical Indication). Considered a suburb of nearby Cassano all'Ionio, Sibari is also a center of seaside tourism.

The program that literally brought the Sybaris Plain to fruition was part of a larger work project of the Sila range, called

Opera per la Valorizzazione della Sila that included agricultural reforms and addressed reforestation. The goal of providing jobs for the mountain villagers wasn't as successful, however, with massive emigration from the Sila and other inland locations throughout Calabria after the Second World War. The area does have many small farms and family-run businesses that concentrate their efforts on specialized products. Amongst the agricultural offerings of the Sila, their potato stands out with the IGP status. This particularly flavorful variety has an elevated starch content due to its cultivation at altitudes of over 1,000 meters (3,281 feet). The *Caciocavallo Silano*, a cow's milk cheese, has also been recognized with the DOP label (*Denominazione di Origine Protetta* or PDO, Protected Designation of Origin). Easy to spot by its shape, resembling a little sack on a string, this semi-hard cheese is characteristic of southern Italy and is similar to mozzarella in flavor as well as in its stretched-curd production process. The taste is slightly salty, developing a stronger, complex piquancy as it ages. The mountains are also home to many varieties of mushrooms.

The *Parco nazionale della Sila* (National Park of the Sila) was established in 1997 and occupies an area of 73,695 hectares (182,104 acres) in the provinces of Catanzaro, Cosenza and Crotone. Its highest peak arrives at just under 2,000 meters (6,562 feet). Amongst the park's protected species are the *Giganti della Sila* (Giants of the Sila), pine trees that reach forty-five meters (148 feet) in height, two meters (6½ feet) in diameter and 350 years of age. Four artificial lakes created between 1927 and 1956 for hydroelectric energy and as reservoirs also serve as tourist centers with downhill and cross-country skiing in the winter, and trekking and naturalistic pursuits in the warmer months. Tourism has become the focus into the twenty-first century.

San Giovanni in Fiore in the Province of Cosenza is the Sila's main hub and most populous town with 18,000 inhabitants. Laid out on a mountain grade, the old, urban center boasts numerous attractive churches and stately patrician edifices that are unfortunately flanked by a visually contrasting cement sprawl. The original town grew out of an abbey founded by Calabrian theologian and medieval prophet Gioacchino da Fiore (c. 1135-1202), a well-known figure in his day who advised popes and purportedly even Richard the Lionhearted before he embarked on the Third Crusade. His interpretation of the Book of Revelation explored the Holy Trinity in relation to the apocalypse, separating the three entities into time periods: the Father or the Old Testament, the Son or the New Testament, and the Holy Spirit or a New Age in a future where all peoples would unite under an eternal gospel. Many in the church viewed his writings as heresy; others have attempted to make him a saint. Dante Alighieri considered Gioacchino blessed with a prophetic spirit and in the *Divine Comedy* placed him in Paradise together with Thomas Aquinas, whose writings ironically discredited the Calabrian's. A number of Gioacchino's religious drawings and schematics, such as the tree of life and the interlocking circles of the Trinity are on exhibit in the *Abbazia Florense* (San Giovanni in Fiore Abbey). In addition to spiritual offerings, the abbey also hosts the *Museo demologico* (Museum of the Working Class) that shares the everyday lives, in work and society, of the Sila people.

Humans have lived in the Calabrian mountains since prehistoric times. Archeological digs have uncovered evidence of inhabitation in the Sila during the Paleolithic and Neolithic Periods, particularly near the Arvo and Cecita lakes. In the Pollino range to the north, natural caves have provided man and animals convenient shelter for thousands of years. In 1961, 11,000-year-old petroglyphs were discovered in the *Grotto del Romito* (Hermit's Grotto) in the town of Papasidero, located in the northwest corner of Calabria in the *Parco nazionale del Pollino* (Pollino National Park). The carving's most notable figure is of a bull, well-proportioned, graceful and executed with a sure hand. This extinct bovine has since become famous, as the prehistoric rock art has been featured in schoolbooks throughout Italy. Other evidence from the same period has revealed an active obsidian trade with the Aeolian Islands of Sicily. Archeologists have also uncovered the remaining bones of four couples buried in a ceremonious manner, one of which dates back much further, to 16,000 years ago. The site was first settled around 23,000 years ago and has a wealth of Paleolithic artifacts, revealing the eating and social habits of Cro-Magnon man.

As fascinating as early man's dining habits may have been, without a knowledge of agriculture, he wouldn't have been able to have a slice of bread with his steak. Such a meal would be a particularly grave sufferance in the Pollino towns of Altomonte and Cerchiara di Calabria, proud members of the prestigious *Associazione nazionale città del pane* (National Association for the Cities of Bread). Only fifty communities nationwide have thus far proved their adherence to the organization's strict mandate of traditional methods in the baking of their bread. Needless to say, the artisan breads are heavenly. The cheese and sausages of the area are also particularly tasty, as they are throughout the region. The Pollino is especially noted for the quality of an unusual Calabrian cheese, the *butirro*, also called *burrino* or *butirrino*. The fresh, stretched-curd cheese made with cow's milk hides a soft butter at its core. I recommend pairing it with a glass of the Pollino's dry, ruby-red, DOC wine.

The Pollino Mountains mark the border between Calabria and Basilicata, and in 1988 Italy instituted a national park that straddles the two regions. At 192,565 hectares (475,838 acres), this park is the country's largest, with 103,915 hectares (256,780 acres) lying in the Province of Cosenza. Several peaks exceed 2,000 meters with the highest, Serra Dolcedorme, at 2,267 meters (7,438 feet). There are many towns and villages throughout the park whose historical centers are well worth a visit. With 22,500 inhabitants, Castrovillari is the Pollino's largest municipality. It lies in the valley of Mount Pollino, the range's second highest peak, and its architectural landmarks include several lovely churches and one of the better preserved Aragon castles. Amongst the most striking medieval villages of Calabria are the nearby Morano Calabro and the not too distant Altomonte by way of the A3 highway, which I found to be quite comfortable through northern Calabria before it turned toward the coast after Cosenza.

The Pollino also has a number of the region's Albanian communities, established throughout southern Italy between 1470 and 1540 to escape the Turks. Unlike most of their ethnic cousins in Albania, the Italian Albanians haven't converted to Islam, but continue to practice the Greek-Byzantine rite. Arbëreshe, a variation of an old Albanian language, can still be heard, as well as seen on street signs. Weddings and holidays bring out traditional, brightly colored costumes, songs in Arbëreshe and folkdances through the narrow streets of their villages that in the Pollino include Acquaformosa, Civita, San Basile, Lungro, Plataci, Frascineto, San Costantino Albanese and San Paolo Albanese. Calabria has the largest number of citizens with Albanian heritage that are spread out in over thirty towns and villages; the majority live in the Province of Cosenza.

In addition to cultural and religious tourism, the Pollino Mountains offer their own natural beauty. Unfortunately, Calabria's forests have been particularly vulnerable to manmade wildfires, with a handful of malicious individuals putting large ecosystems at risk. Apparently, several Cro-Magnons are still hanging around the area. However, nature is stubborn as the park's flora and fauna can attest: the rare Bosnian pine; wildflowers, fruits and herbs; the wildcat and the Eurasian Eagle-Owl, to name a few. The Pollino also has several nature preserves, such as the spectacular *Gole del Raganello*, a deep canyon with high, rocky walls that can be viewed from the evocatively named *Ponte del diavolo* (Devil's Bridge), high above the river in Civita. Of the park's waterways, the largest river is the Coscile, sometimes called the Sibari, today a tributary of the Crati, Calabria's longest and most voluminous. Sybaris was founded between the mouths of these two rivers, the Coscile from the Pollino and the Crati from the Sila. Although their courses have changed, their nutrients continue to enrich the soil of the alluvial plain.

After the destruction of Sybaris and the ultimate demise of the successive cities founded on the site, the residents fled to higher ground: Cassano all'Ionio, Rossano, Corigliano, and further to the mountains? Pondering on the tales of decadence, I sympathize completely with the Sybarite's desire for a little peace and quiet. I, too, would have favored a law in Reggio prohibiting the overuse of the pneumatic drill. On the culinary front, I have, on occasion, overindulged in Calabria's delectable, cream-filled pastries. And stateside, I have been known to butter the bread of a cheese sandwich, as no one can deny that the more butter slathered on a grilled cheese, the better it tastes. But putting butter *inside* of cheese, well, that's just downright sybaritic!

16

In the Province of Cosenza

Fountain of woman dressed in traditional
clothing, Terme Luigiane, near Guardia
Piemontese

COSENZA

IN MY TIME IN CALABRIA, I heard a lot about the Greeks, a certain amount regarding the Romans, a healthy dose of the Byzantines, a smattering about the Arabs, and occasional references to all of the other conquerors and rulers up to the present. Apart from the Cro-Magnon of Papasidero and the pre-Greco-Roman artifacts exhibited in a few museums, not much was said about the comings and goings of the region's inhabitants before the Greeks arrived—until Cosenza. Here was a city founded by a population living on the peninsula since the Iron Age, a pastoral people under the domination of the Lucani, who ruled the area corresponding to today's Basilicata and northern Calabria. When Lucani's subordinates revolted and formed their own alliance, their former masters named them the Bruzi (Bruttii) or rebels. In 356 BC, the united Bruzi tribes founded their capital on a strategic hill at the confluence of two rivers with the forested Sila plateau to the east and a coastal mountain chain separating the city from the Tyrrhenian Sea to the west. They named it Cosentia, derived from the word *consenso*, meaning consensus.

The Bruzi became a powerful force, attacking Greek cities and gaining control over a considerable territory, but eventually falling to the Romans, the Lombards, Byzantines, Arabs and so forth. Today, Cosenza or the *Città dei Bruzi* (City of the Bruttii) has 70,000 citizens, serves as the capital of Calabria's northernmost province and is the center of a vast metropolitan area of about 270,000. Its early history is chronicled in the *Museo archeologico dei Brettii e degli Enotri* (Archeological Museum of the Bruttii and the Oenotrians), whose artifacts and informational panels help to fill in some of the gaps in Calabria's pre-Roman history. Interestingly, the Oenotrians (1,700 to 720 BC) developed wealthy, civilized communities before the arrival of the Greeks and occupied a territory that extended from Salerno to the Catanzaro isthmus, and very likely down to the tip of the peninsula, before they were absorbed by other tribes. The Bruzi, however, battled with the Greeks and Romans, even aligning themselves with Hannibal and finally Spartacus before their ultimate defeat and submission to Roman authority.

Several centuries later, in 410 AD, Rome was sacked by the Visigoths under the leadership of King Alaric I. But even the Germanic people's most famous king was no match for the devastating malarial conditions along the Calabrian coastline, and shortly after his Roman victory succumbed to the fever in Cosenza. As the legend goes, he was buried in full armor together with his pillaged treasure in the bed of the city's Busento River, whose course was diverted in order to carry out the singular internment. The participating slaves were then killed to keep the location a secret. Since that time innumerable treasure hunters and archeologists have tried to find the spot, but haven't been successful thus far.

Throughout Calabria's history, death by malaria could easily have been swapped for death by earthquake. Unfortunately, there isn't any chemical cure for the geological phenomenon. Luckily, I was spared the seismic tremors and can only testify to their resultant architectural and societal consequences. Alexandre Dumas, on the other hand, lived through an earthquake while visiting Cosenza in 1835 and colorfully described the residents' makeshift encampment on the city's outskirts. The shantytown sheltered those whose homes had collapsed as well as those afraid of being crushed by falling buildings during the aftershocks. The gentry lived out of fancy carriages, attended by their servants in a nineteenth-century-style mobile home park for the privileged. He recounted the experience as though he was merely performing a part in a play:

> In the middle of the night, we were awakened by screams: Earthquake! Earthquake! It seemed that there had been a violent shake that we hadn't felt. We jumped out of our beds that had ended up in the middle of the room and ran to the window. Part of the population wandered through the streets letting forth terrible cries. Everyone else, who like us, had remained in their houses, rushed outside in the picturesque clothing in which they had been surprised.

Although the earthquake took a couple hundred lives, Dumas survived several days of shocks unscathed. Even as a dispassionate observer, however, he was moved by the terrorized peasants falling to their knees, their whole beings wracked with uncontrollable sobs at the local priest's threatening admonishments, correlating society's widespread corruption with God's seismic wrath. It's no wonder that Calabrians are a superstitious people.

Despite the occasional disaster and ever-changing leadership as experienced throughout the region, Cosenza has enjoyed a number of florid periods that are reflected in its charming historic center. Today a modern university town, the city boasted a prestigious academic institution dedicated to philosophical and literary studies already by 1511. The *Accademia Cosentina* has gone through many directional stages right up through the present, but its most important intellectual guidance came from native son Bernardino Telesio (1509-1588). The progressive, late-Renaissance philosopher and forefather of modern empiricism influenced such notables as Thomas Bacon and Calabria's own Tommaso Campanella, demonstrating just how rich Cosenza's intellectual life has been. In addition, the well-known Venetian adventurer and writer Giacomo Casanova, who held a very poor view of Calabria's overall social conditions, was delighted with the genteel lifestyle he found during his brief visit to Cosenza in 1743, recording his thoughts in his memoirs: "Cosenza is a city in which a gentleman can find plenty of amusement; the nobility are wealthy, the women are pretty, and men generally well-informed, because they have been educated in Naples or in Rome."

While some Calabrians still choose to study outside the region, many take advantage of today's options at home. In 1972, Cosenza got its own university, and with approximately 35,000 students, it is Calabria's largest and is recognized in particular for its department of computer science and its comprehensive library. Unlike most Italian colleges that compete for space in downtown locations, the Università della Calabria was constructed well outside the city center and occupies a modern campus with student housing and academic buildings on the same property. The university is actually in Rende, located within Cosenza's greater suburban territory, several kilometers northwest.

Cosenza's city layout is characterized by modern residential, public and industrial nuclei dispersed throughout its territory. The land between these urban hubs is gradually filling in to create one large metropolitan area. At first the construction was haphazard, but city planners are now attempting to proceed in a more systematic manner. On the plus side, the suburban sprawl has allowed the historical town centers of Cosenza and Rende to keep their architectural integrity.

Preserving its medieval layout, old Cosenza presents a maze of narrow streets lined with grandiose patrician houses, churches, convents and other antique edifices. The centerpiece is the simple but elegant Romanesque-Gothic cathedral that embodies the city's long spiritual, artistic and social history. Erected on the site of previous churches completely destroyed by a ruinous earthquake, the present structure was consecrated in 1222 with the Hohenstaufen Emperor Frederick II in attendance. His precious gift of a beautiful *Stauroteca* (reliquary holding a fragment of the true cross) in the shape of a delicate cross in gold with colored enamel decorations and inlaid with precious stones, is exhibited in the Diocesano Museum.

Also restructured in the same period, the ruined Norman-Hohenstaufen castle overlooks the city and surrounding area from the zone's highest hilltop, seemingly unreachable from the neighboring urban clusters and the A3 highway that runs past the city. The Hohenstaufen sovereignty left two other interesting thirteenth-century remembrances in the cathedral, the tombs of Isabella of Aragon who briefly reigned over France and Frederick II's son Henry of Germany who ruled as king for a time in Sicily and then in Germany in a shared capacity with his father, against whom he eventually revolted. Not a match for his father, Henry was dethroned and imprisoned. He died in Calabria during a transfer and was entombed in Cosenza's cathedral. Analysis of his skeleton in 1998 revealed that he had leprosy and was suffering from an advanced stage of the disease when he met his end through a fall—accident, suicide, murder? 750 years after the events transpired, science has uncovered a clue to this mystery, making me think that perhaps some day Alaric's treasure may be found as well.

The cathedral also honors several martyrs who died in the cause for Italian unification. A chapel marks the final resting place of the Calabrian rebels who were executed in Cosenza for their role in the independence campaign waged in collaboration with the well-known Bandiera Brothers in 1844. At the time, the incident garnered much attention for the harsh manner in which the insurrection was dealt with and gave momentum to future revolts that resulted in the formation of a new Italian state.

In 1943 during the Second World War, Cosenza was heavily bombed by the Allies. Many lives were lost, the city and its cathedral were damaged, and the population was reduced to a disastrous economic condition. The terrible conflict was envisioned by Sister Elena Aiello (1895-1961), a local nun who founded the religious institution *Suore Minime della Passione di*

Nostro Signore Gesù Cristo (Little Sisters of the Passion of Jesus Christ Our Lord) in Cosenza. Before Italy entered the war, she wrote a letter to Mussolini warning him that if he didn't do the right thing to save his country, he would be punished by divine justice. Sister Aiello, whose blood of the stigmata was so overflowing as to drench her bed linens, dedicated her life to the poor and abandoned. In 2011 she became the first Calabrian woman to be beatified.

Sister Aiello had her work cut out for her in Cosenza, as did the government and the citizens themselves. During Italy's postwar economic boom, Cosenza's population doubled and spread out into the periphery. Throughout the early twentieth century, a modern section with a number of attractive Fascist structures had already grown up across the Busento River. Today one of its main arteries, Via Mazzini has been turned into a pedestrian zone that features an outdoor sculpture museum, Museo all'aperto Bilotti, named after its benefactor Carlo Bilotti, an Italian-American from Cosenza. The large sculptures by such artists as Mimmo Rotella of Catanzaro, Giorgio De Chirico, Emilio Greco and Salavador Dalì give the zone a sophisticated, contemporary feel, acknowledging a positive present and looking toward a constructive future in a region where the tendency is often to look backwards. The city's National Gallery, housed in the sixteenth-century Palazzo Arnone, also juxtaposes the old with the new, highlighting late-Baroque paintings of Mattia Preti and modern drawings of the Futurist, Umberto Boccioni.

Cosenza has a lot to offer, to both the resident and tourist. The lovely historic center testifies to its cultural past through its artwork, religious institutions, architecture and theaters, and the young university carries forth the intellectual tradition in a vibrant here and now. No doubt the Bruzis selected the city's location for defensive purposes, but I imagine that its proximity to the resources of both the Sila Mountains and the Tyrrhenian Sea wasn't lost on the ancient people. Their descendants are reaping the benefits.

PAOLA

GROUP TOURS ARE POPULAR IN CALABRIA. I would often see flyers stuck to walls and windows in downtown Reggio, many of which advertised trips to religious shrines. Regular pilgrimages were made to the Sanctuary of the Madonna of Tindari in the Province of Messina, the Church of Padre Pio in Puglia and Our Lady of Lourdes in France. Naturally, the faithful also visited the region's countless churches closer to home and attended the numerous religious festivals and processions. Popular mountain destinations for spiritual journeys included the Sanctuary of Our Lady of Polsi in the Aspromonte and the Madonna of the Pollino. When my friend Luisa invited me on an outing to the Sanctuary of Saint Francis of Paola, I decided to dip my toe into religious tourism, Calabrian style.

The bus was to meet us by Luisa's gate at 7:10 on a Sunday morning in early spring. The guide had agreed to the doorstep pickup as it was right on their way. At about 7:30, whoosh, a tour bus sailed past. It was our coach. We ran after it, wildly waving our arms as it continued up the street and finally stopped about a half a kilometer down the road. Not having the contact person's cell phone number, Luisa decided the best tactic would be to stop one of the few passing vehicles. The first driver shook his finger at us. Despite the unusual hour, he seemed to have confused us with the ladies who usually worked that corner. Clearly, he didn't know we were on our way to a religious sanctuary. The second was a scooter. The third yielded success—the father appeared bemused by our plight, the son was grumpy. We got in and the car sped the short distance, pulling around in front of the bus to block any sudden take off.

We made it. As it turned out, Prudenzia, the tour organizer, remembered the pickup, but not the precise location. Perhaps, the confusion was historical, the mistaking of the pile of old Greek stones for the Roman ones that Luisa had used as a point of reference along Via Marina. Things didn't bode well. We were ushered into two seats reserved in the second row. Although there was plenty of space in the back, this positioning was a show of respect as Luisa had brought along a foreign guest. We pulled away, and Prudenzia, hairdresser and tour organizer, grabbed hold of the microphone. I turned to Luisa and said, "She's not speaking in Italian, is she?" And in that moment I had my first clue that the trip was definitely going to be different, at least for me. Actually, it had first come to me as the motor coach flew by us, then again as we approached our leader, and as we entered the bus.

In Calabria, I often heard about how many times and by how many different peoples the territory had been conquered. The watchtowers and castles dotting the coastline served as examples, as did the characteristics of the inhabitants: "Look, she has the blue eyes of the Normans," or, "He's got a Spanish surname." In that bus, I wanted to say, "Listen, we're in an Arabian bazaar!" Prudenzia was yelling into the microphone as if the loudspeaker system didn't exist, and nobody batted an eyelash. I thought that maybe she'd go hoarse after a bit, but not a chance. And she wasn't the only one. I was surrounded by a cacophony that would have stumped even the esteemed French composer Maurice Ravel had he been given the task of orchestrating those raw timbres. Only the likes of shawms, bagpipes and other instruments suitable for the outdoors could have possibly been considered for such a composition. If those women actually knew how they produced such decibels, they might have been able to put their unusual skill to use by, for instance, teaching physical education instructors how to generate the level of resonance needed to soar over the activity in a noisy gymnasium. As it was, their penetrating utterances only served to compete with each other.

So, we were off. I was swimming upstream in dialect. Prudenzia continued with a steady barrage from which there was nowhere to hide. Once on the highway, there was an extended, general prayer in Italian, and we reached our first stop in good time. After having paid for the excursion, Prudenzia was to "offer" us coffee and *cornetti* (croissants) in Gioia Tauro, a large town north of Reggio, which is both an agricultural center situated on the fertile Plain of Gioa Tauro and an important, very active containership port. We pulled off the highway into the modern rest stop, piled off the bus, and consumed the rather tasty pastries that had been stored underneath. We must have been there an hour. Other buses came and went even though the passengers had to take the time to enter the bar for their breakfast. Obviously, I somehow missed the beauty of standing in a parking lot.

Back on the bus, Prudenzia announced that it was time for the rosary: *"AVE MARIA PIENA DI GRAZIA . . . . SANTA MARIA, MADRE DI DIO, PREGA PER NOI PECCATORI!"* Mamma mia! She was literally yelling into the microphone and if the antiphonal responses weren't strong enough, she stopped and scolded. Some of it was sung, lasting thirty to forty minutes. I felt as though I had stumbled into some type of science experiment. I was that animal in the cage, subjected to inordinate noise levels and observed for my reaction: repetitive, zombie-like chanting shrieked through an electrical system, reverberating through the bodies of the captives.

Then, barely stopping for breath, Prudenzia switched back into dialect and regaled the group with off-color jokes. Her responsibilities as tour leader also included saying, "IS EVERYBODY HERE?" each time we got back on the bus. She didn't count or read a list of names, although she was obviously concerned for her foreign guest. The first time we re-boarded, she bellowed, "IS THE AMERICAN HERE?" a few inches from my head. I suppose she didn't want me to miss the howling of the rosary.

More than four hours past the time I had arrived at Luisa's gate, we pulled up to our destination: the Sanctuary of St. Francis of Paola, 186 kilometers (116 miles) north of Reggio. No announcement for the faithful as to the time of the Mass, no overview as to what there was to see. We had an hour and a quarter for our visit because we had taken the scenic route. Most participants scattered rather quickly, but there were a few who just stood in the middle of the sanctuary's enormous piazza looking, understandably, rather lost. Luisa stopped one of the boy scouts marching past in a formation that would have made Mussolini proud and asked about the timing of the religious services. We had time for a quick tour. The grounds were quite lovely, situated high in the hills of Paola, a town of about 17,000 on the Tyrrhenian coast near Cosenza, its provincial capital. Paola's fame rests with the town's Saint Francis (1416-1507), to whom the city gave birth and for whom its lush environs served as a refuge in which he practiced the simple, religious life of a hermit from the age of sixteen. Others followed him and soon a community was formed that eventually developed into the Roman Catholic *Ordine dei Minimi* (Order of Minims).

St. Francis advocated a lifestyle of fasting and penitence, and in addition to the vows of poverty, obedience and chastity, the Minims added living every day as if it were Lent, which meant no meat, not even its byproducts, except in the case of illness. He was a vegan before the word was invented. Of course, a saint isn't made by his culinary choices, and in addition to his holy life, St. Francis performed his share of miracles. He was greatly esteemed by the kings and queens of Europe, and his renown as a miracle worker would eventually force him to leave his Calabrian people. He would be summoned by the French court where he continued to conduct an ascetic existence and lead by example, just amidst completely different circumstances.

His sanctuary was in a tranquil location affording a beautiful panorama from its large piazza. Luisa's first order of the day was to light a candle for her husband, Franco or Francesco, who was named after Calabria's Patron Saint Francesco or Francis of Paola, who had been named after Francis of Assisi. The candle room had quite a turnover. No sooner had a row been lit than an employee snuffed them all out and offhandedly discarded them into a box on the floor. For Franco's sake, I hoped Luisa's prayer lingered a bit longer than the smoke of her candle. However, we didn't have time to dawdle, either, and waltzed through the basilica that had begun as a little church early on in the life of the Minims and gradually expanded over the centuries, as well as the chapel with reliquaries of the saint's bones and clothes. Then, we proceeded down a narrow staircase to an underground, stone passageway with several of the order's original cells over which the church had been built. Back outside, at a spot near the stream that divided the complex, a tour guide pointed out the saint's original grotto where he first retired from the fifteenth-century world. In an area dedicated to his miracles, pilgrims lined up to dip out a ladle of water from a natural spring that had one day burst forth with the touch of the holy man's cane. The visitors were thankfully very hygienic with the ladle, transferring the water to plastic cups and bottles before drinking or sprinkling it on themselves.

The Mass itself was in a large, modern structure that looked more like the setting for an American evangelical worship service than for the followers of a monk who lived as a hermit over half a millennium ago. Completed in the year 2000, the bright, expansive church was decorated with contemporary mosaics and stained glass windows; its interior space featured arched ceiling rafters that resembled a sailing ship, appropriate for the patron saint of sailors and fisherman. While Luisa was taking communion, I took the opportunity to read a bit more about this St. Francis on the church's large display. The story of his encounter with a boatman who refused him passage because he didn't have any money, having given it all away, explained the many images I had seen all over Calabria. The simple monk needed to get across the Strait of Messina so he constructed a makeshift raft and with his coat as a sail, navigated across the channel. (I imagine that this particular St. Francis must also be quite celebrated amongst windsurfers.)

Unable to actually stay for the end of the service, we

hurried back to the bus where the group already seemed to be assembled. As we didn't pull off right away, I thought we must have been waiting for someone, not that anyone had counted those gathered. Upon reflection, however, all of the empty time dallying around the bus that day may have just been due to the fact that both Prudenzia and the bus driver were smokers.

Lunch was in a nearby restaurant overlooking the sea. Dialect prevailed. I forged ahead in Italian, of course, asking the woman to my right how she enjoyed the service. She responded with, "I worship directly with God," which I took to mean that her surroundings weren't important to her. Dead end, but I persevered with a positive comment about the choir to try and get something going. Barely a grunt. Clearly, she wasn't into music, so I remarked on the modernity of the church. Zip, zilch. Maybe she was tired out from the rosary.

The meal was fine, beginning with an appetizer of sliced meats and *crostini* (toasted bread with toppings), followed by lasagne. A few minutes after being served the first course, my gaze was drawn to the left index fingers of the woman on my right and the one diagonally across from me to the left. Why was I looking at their fingers? I felt disoriented. And then I realized, their fingers were red, well past the first knuckle joint, tomato sauce red! They were using their fingers to push the lasagne onto their forks. I was in disbelief. There weren't even any little peas to chase around the plate; baked pasta was easily manageable with one hand. Having great difficulty following the general conversation, I had time to fixate on those sauce-laden forefingers. They were like an accident, a bloody accident, and I couldn't look away. With the meat course of veal and potatoes, the woman diagonally across from me to the right took the opportunity of distinguishing herself. I don't know exactly what it was that displeased her, but at a certain point she spit something onto her plate—directly from her mouth to the dish. A bone, fat, what? She hadn't given a second thought to an action that seemed so disdainful, and neither did her red-fingered tablemates. I looked around for the candid camera. *"Buon Appetito!"* (Enjoy your meal!)

Before boarding the bus after lunch, we once again loitered for a while in the parking lot, this time in the shade of the car park's gorgeous wisteria vine. Not surprisingly, we were quite behind schedule and the stop at Pizzo's Church of the Piedigrotta was cancelled. Tropea was our final stop of the day, and Prudenzia's affinity for the so-called scenic routes brought us to the charming tourist town late in the afternoon with just an hour to stretch our legs before climbing back onto the bus. Our journey home was accompanied by the blare of the Calabrian tarantella, which was apparently the only CD that worked and so it was played over and over, only buoying the prevailing ruckus. With the rosary and the windsurfing, vegan saint behind them, the participants sat back and leaned forward, enjoying each other's company to the fullest—perhaps the main reason for their joining Prudenzia's tour, that and the 5 Euro savings off the usual lunch price.

Our day's excitement hadn't ended yet, however. Shortly after leaving Tropea, panic clutched our leader when she discovered her purse was missing. Up and down the aisles she went, gesticulating and yammering on. We pulled off the road; she searched the luggage compartment. And then, *UN MIRACOLO* (a miracle), the purse was found in the back of the bus. Ha, ha! It had all been a practical joke, which the passengers then tried to repeat on Prudenzia's assistant with the disappearance of her cell phone. After another interminable rest stop, we finally returned to Reggio a little before ten o'clock. In a fifteen-hour excursion, we spent a total of two and a half hours actually at our destinations, another hour and a half eating lunch, and the rest of the time? *SANTA MARIA, MADRE DI DIO, PREGA PER NOI . . .*

GUARDIA PIEMONTESE, TERME LUIGIANE AND DIAMANTE

THE REGIONAL TRAIN WAS DIRECT, it fit my schedule and even cost a little less than the others, but what happened to the air conditioning? Maybe the guy lying on the floor between the compartments was crazy, but on the other hand, that metal flooring might have been the coolest place on the train. Why did the conductor have to disturb him? I had no problem stepping over him in search of fresher air, leaving a crime scene of sweat back on my seat in the other compartment. Now, in addition to compositionally fusing with the synthetic upholstery, a ranting lunatic was banging his head against the seat behind me. CAN'T WE ALL REMAIN CALM?

I was headed for the Terme Luigiane, a spa north of Paola in the Province of Cosenza, and clearly, I couldn't arrive too soon. I was hoping for rest, relaxation and a bit of sinus relief. I was going to take "the cure," although the pampering of an American style beauty farm would have been nice, too, particularly after my two-and-a-half-hour train ordeal. Nevertheless, I had opted for this no-nonsense *terme* (spa) on the recommendation of locals and booked one of the hotels on the property as I was without a vehicle. The reservationist helped me choose the three-star over the four when she waved the single supplement, making the savings too good to pass up.

The hotel's air-conditioned minivan came to my rescue at the station of Guardia Piemontese and took me up the hill to the spa officially situated in the town of Acquappesa. Upon entering the unassuming inn located within the complex's wooded setting, I was greeted like an old friend by the very personable receptionist with whom I had spoken on the phone. As with many small-scale accommodations, I hadn't been asked for a room deposit and was to pay the entire bill upon departure, so I took my key and the next shuttle to the nearby beach, just a handful of zigzags down the hill.

Naturally, a number of the sunbathers at the beach facility had gotten off other shuttles earlier in the day, and I began learning about the spa, whose guests mostly came from Calabria and the surrounding southern regions. I knew that the spa treatments were authorized therapies, the majority of which were financed by the *Servizio Sanitario Nazionale* (National Health Care System) upon presentation of a doctor's prescription. I was surprised to learn, however, that depending on the specific health care plan, many individuals were also entitled to full room and board for the entire period of their treatment at either the three- or four-star hotels attached to the spa. I met people who had come by themselves, groups of friends all with their own prescriptions and married couples, of whom one or both were taking a cure. Some came to the same spa every year and others traveled to different locations throughout Italy. I couldn't help but think how healthy they all appeared. If those people had really arrived ill, the spa waters must have been miraculous, indeed. In addition, most of the treatments were in the morning, leaving the afternoon and evening to enjoy the beach or other sightseeing activity in the area. I was ready to give it a try.

The Luigiane Spa was only open in the summer, coinciding with the typical Italian vacation period. As it was early in the season, the hotel was half empty, and I was given an enormous room with three, extremely comfortable single beds—unusually downy yet supportive for a three-star accommodation. The room was simple and clean, equipped with a basic desk, a good-sized wardrobe, a tiny television set that occasionally got one station, a ceiling fan and a tiled bathroom full of towels as if all the beds were occupied. Air conditioning came with the four stars, but I was comfortable. Interestingly, this lack of what might have been considered a modern convenience was cited as a plus by a number of the older people who had opted in favor of the three-star property for this very reason. With the exception of sweatbox trains, Italians don't like to feel a breeze on the back of the neck, particularly while eating.

Of course, I had signed up for full board and my table, laid for one, was graciously set up along the edge of the dining room from where I had a good view of the restaurant's goings-on, after I made my entrance, that is. I didn't look like everybody else and it obviously didn't go unnoticed. The diners stared as they had on my first day in Locri and continued to do so throughout the week. An old miner, one of the regulars of what I assumed must have been a more serious spa treatment, the pulmonary ventilation, told me with his seemingly boundless energy that he remembered a pair of Americans at the spa a few years earlier. Apparently, we could be counted on one hand.

The food was as unpretentious as its ambience and the people eating it—straightforward, wholesome Italian dishes. Towards the end of the meal, the convivial woman at the table next to mine made public introductions with her neighbors from her seated position. I don't believe Maria had ever met an American before. The next day, this woman from Sibari, the ancient cradle of decadence, began to regale us with colorful jokes in dialect. In fact, southern dialects were more prevalent than Italian in that dining room and at the spa facility, itself, for that matter. The occasional northern doctor sitting at the nearby table reserved for those few medical personnel who cared to wander in for lunch or dinner, clearly didn't understand Maria's witticisms any more than I did before she explained them to me in Italian. "*Dottò, Dottò!*" (Hey Doc!) She was addressing the very tan, bald doctor whose head resembled a shiny seven ball. "Are you a family doctor?" The young physician clearly wanted to be left alone to eat his plate of spaghetti with tomato sauce, although he eventually warmed up and even couldn't help but smile every so often. I would run into that doctor at the spa, but before anything else I would have to go through the *Accettazione* or admissions process on my first morning.

As part of the health system's requirements, patients had to show up with the proper prescription from their own doctor. The admissions procedure consisted of presenting the documentation at the reception desk, being briefly checked out by a doctor on staff and unless reduced for one of various reasons, paying the 50-Euro *ticket* (co-pay) for the two-week treatment. I was obviously an exception to the process as I had arrived without a prescription and would be personally paying for the specific treatments prescribed by the spa's check-in doctor. The main raised eyebrow over my presence was due to its brevity. All of the therapies fit within a two-week period with Sundays off. "But how can everyone possibly react to the twelve applications in the same way? Perhaps some patients may have enough with ten and others may benefit from fifteen," I reasoned with the cordial, female doctor. Maybe my five-day experience wouldn't be as effective, but I was given a medical recommendation based on my brief description of the problem, and without even taking my blood pressure, sent off to the payment desk—cash only. Granted, I wasn't going to be receiving any prescription medication, but I did find one procedure for which the majority of patients never returned for a second application disturbingly stressful.

Donning the white terrycloth robe provided by the hotel and clutching the perforated printout of coupons that corresponded to each of my treatments, I walked the short distance to the THERMAE, a fairly modern structure as the earlier edifices had succumbed to a series of earthquakes and mudslides. The spa's mineral water has been known since ancient times, noted by such personages as the Roman, Pliny the Elder and Saint Francis of Paola. Today, Terme Luigiane is Calabria's most widely recognized spa amongst those of Spezzano Albanese, Cassano allo Jonio (called Sibarite), Lamezia Terme (Caronte), Antominima, Galatro (Fonti Sant'Elia) and Cerchiara di Calabria (Grotta delle Ninfe). Each spa is distinguished by the chemical composition of its water or mud. Luigiane is renowned for its thermal water that flows forth at 43-47° Celsius (109.4-116.6° F) and is characterized by a sulfur and salt-bromide content. In fact, its mineral water has the highest percentage of sulfur in all of Italy. Thus, the subtle, rotten egg smell in the air and on the skin, but it's like eating a lot of onions or garlic—not a problem if everyone is doing it.

Luigiane's therapeutic treatments are indicated for rheumatism and arthritis, chronic afflictions of the ear, nose and throat, respiratory diseases, skin maladies, and gynecological disorders. The therapies highlight the importance of sulfur to the body, purporting the theory that the treatment methods allow for the greater absorption of this necessary element, thus compensating for or preventing a deficiency that can lead to a chemical imbalance and disease. Applications concentrate contact with the skin, respiratory system, mucous membranes and the digestive system. In addition to the official treatments, those in the know fill up their water bottles at a local fountain to round off the complete body cure.

My personal focus was the ear, nose and throat, which required various ways of inhaling sulfurous vapors and gas. Upon entering the hallway that led to the inhalation rooms, I was immediately struck by the fact that many ailments ending in "ite" corresponding to "itis" in English were rather popular in Calabria: *rinite, sinusite, faringite, tonsilite, adenoidite* and *laringite*. Oh, the humanity! The majority of patients claimed to be there for preventative measures, driving over for the day from surrounding communities or staying off the property and arriving in very casual summer wear. The smattering of robes pit the atmosphere of an overcrowded proletarian clinic against a relaxing holistic sanatorium. The very common clinic easily won out. I took a number and waited in cramped rooms with the all too occasional whining child. In my short time at the spa I only witnessed one senior collapse, ostensibly due to low blood pressure, which I thought was pretty good considering all of those ailing people undergoing procedures in hot, overcrowded conditions.

When finally called, I filed into one of the narrow, aerosol rooms, set up like a library study hall with rows of numbered cubicles, but fitted with tubes and large, shallow, rectangular sinks instead of desktops. Once a row was complete, the assistant began the flow of sulfurous gas and I breathed it through my nose one day and by mouth the next by way of little, throwaway plastic attachments put on the end of the hose. After a short rest, I moved on to the inhalation room, arranged in the same manner, but with a shorter, wider tube coming directly out of the partition. With shower caps in place to protect our hair from the humidity, we were like guppies at feeding time—open-mouthed, inhaling the hot, sulfurous steam that flowed from the yellowed tubes. Following another break, I proceeded to the *humage* treatment, which was carried out in a room with a large, square, glass container full of a greenish-yellow, bubbling liquid. A controlled number of people were admitted to the small chamber that was saturated with sulfurous gas, released through the gurgling of the thermal water. This particular therapy lent itself to conversation as it was practiced in a small group, and between the initial waiting time, ministrations and breaks, over a half hour easily passed in the company of the same handful of people. One pleasant, young history teacher who had a number of serious nasal issues swore by the spa's *humage* and confirmed the general consensus that the waters of Acquappesa were by far the most effective in Calabria.

Between the atmosphere, the individual treatments and my physical reaction to them, I had the sense that I was really working on my cure. Two therapies, however, gave me the willies and I was glad that the check-in doctor had taken the wait-and-see approach and initially signed me up for one of each to see how I handled them. The tympanic insufflation was my only procedure that had to be performed by a qualified physician, and as it turned out, the seven-ball doctor from the dining room was an ear, nose and throat specialist. However, looking at my form, he said that my first visit had to be done by his colleague. So although I had more confidence in the seven ball who had a work hard and play hard look about him, I had to be seen by his associate who just looked as though he had played hard. I don't think I can be blamed for not wanting to see my doctor's wife-beater T-shirt as he blew sulfurous thermal gas up my nose, through my Eustachian tube and into my inner ear. CLOSE THE WHITE COAT OR PUT ON SOME SCRUBS. I understood that there wasn't any air conditioning and that his attire in no way diminished his technical abilities, but I would have preferred a little more decorum. He, in turn, would have been happier not fielding all of my questions in pursuit of the procedure's merits.

Such an interaction wasn't possible at the nasal irrigation station down the hall as the attendant was just a pleasant young woman who had been trained to show the patient how to position the head over the sink and hold the tube of sulfurous water that flowed from the tank above, into one nostril and out the other. Perhaps the space behind my forehead, nose and cheeks was too clogged to allow the liquid to pass. My sinuses exploded with pain, my head ached for the rest of the day, and I was shocked when, an hour later, I caught a glimpse of my beet-red face that finally gave the locals something worth staring at. I persevered and completed the procedure that morning, but had no intention of a repetition.

The cure certainly wasn't easy and it was time consuming, as well. I also had appointments for what was called galvanic electrotherapy for swollen, tired feet. For this dubious treatment I was in the company of a decidedly plump nun from Sicily, one of the many ecclesiastics seen along the corridors of the spa, which I supposed indicated that the days of self-flagellation were well behind us. She didn't seem to be a particularly upbeat or saintly woman, although with some prodding we were able to engage in basic conversation as we sat together, hooked by colorful cords to tabletop machines with green-lit numbers. Her electrodes were attached to her back, while mine served to galvanize the mineral water in a small, plastic basin, ostensibly imbuing my feet with an electrifying energy. I don't know that the galvanic electrotherapy did anything for the inner workings of my feet, but the procedure did help to smooth them out a bit.

Strolling back to the hotel in my robe and sandals after my second morning of therapy, I realized, however, that my system was reacting positively to the sulfurous bombardment. My head was draining; it felt lighter and I was breathing more easily. The dining room was full when I arrived; the patients were hungry after a morning of treatments. Maria and her roommate had invited me to join their table and as I sat down, I noticed that the waiter had altered the place marker to reflect the change: *2 INPS + una persona*. At first glance, I read "2 imps" and thought that not only did those two ladies have sparkles in their eyes, but they were actually fairies. Then I realized that INPS was one of Italy's countless acronyms and we were characterized as 2 *Istituto Nazionale della Previdenza Sociale* or Social Security Service and one person. I was surprised that it didn't say "+ *un'americana*," which meant I was to be treated like any other person who wasn't a member of INPS, Italy's principal governmental institution with the responsibility of pensions, insurance and other social services. Although Italy is a country with socialized medicine and everyone is entitled to the same healthcare treatment, differences vary amongst the institutions that collect and distribute the contributions, thus INPS patients were eligible for food and lodging while undergoing their treatments. The reasoning behind the table designation was a mystery to me, as we all seemed to be treated like people regardless of the indications on the place cards.

My lively, new impish friends also invited me to join them at the spa's nightly dances frequented by the same older set that filled their hotels. The overly confident young *animatori* (entertainers at tourist locations whose job is to inspire the guests to fully participate in the activities in order to maximize the vacationers' fun factor) were brimming with energy, if not practical knowledge. Their sequined top hats, logoed T-shirts, toothy smiles and solid grounding in line dancing, very popular at large Italian weddings, were of no use to the older Italian men in their dress shirts and leather dance shoes. An American, however, fully cognizant of her less than proficient dance step quickly became the focus of many an Italian gentleman looking to twirl her around the dance floor. Alas, with only one of me to go around, Maria mercifully stepped in as the *animatori* faltered and whipped up the crowd to produce the unified group dancing the young people had attempted to organize, and a good time was had by all.

On another evening, I signed up for an excursion to the northerly town of Diamante, known for its seaside tourism and its central position on the *Riviera dei Cedri*. The *cedro* or citron (not to be confused with the word's other meaning, that of cedar tree) is another of Calabria's marvels. Difficult to cultivate, the Diamante citron, the variety raised in the area, is a large oval citrus fruit with an extremely thick, bumpy skin. Although I have eaten the fruit itself, which consists of a small, center pulp and a very wide, edible pith that isn't bitter like other citruses, the citron's principal culinary usage has traditionally been in its candied zest. This unusual fruit also plays an important part on Succoth, the Jewish fall festival that commemorates the sheltering of the Israelis in the wilderness. Once a year, Jewish food inspectors, principally from Israel and the United States, descend on such towns as Santa Maria del Cedro in order to select the most perfect citrons for their rituals according to ancient religious law.

The participants on my tour bus, however, were more interested in the culinary uses of the citron, particularly in the local pastry, gelato, granita, liquor, marmalade and its infusion in extra virgin olive oil. I enjoyed a refreshing cup of the delicately aromatic citron gelato as I joined the waterfront *passeggiata*, crowded on an early summer weeknight when the population swelled many times beyond the locality's approximately 5,000 residents.

Diamante's murals provided the impetus for countless conversations amongst strollers along the interior streets. Begun in 1981, the more than one hundred images painted by artists from Italy and around the world covered the walls of buildings throughout the historic center. The colorful murals ranged in both aesthetic style and subject matter from classic depictions of fisherman to contemporary illustrations that accompanied written expressions of a philosophical nature.

Walking the streets and visiting the shops, I quickly learned that Diamante wasn't known only for the citron, but also had particularly close ties with the peperoncino, imported from the New World and thoroughly embraced by Calabrians throughout the region. Home to the *Accademia Italiana del peperoncino* (Italian Peperoncino Academy) that boasts international associates from New York to Tokyo, Diamante has hosted an annual festival dedicated to the peperoncino every September for over twenty years and its stores sell the spicy product in all imaginable forms—even gelato! Proponents of the little red pepper, *cancarillo, pipazzu, pipi vruscente* and *diavulillo* in various regional dialects, have praised its many health benefits for centuries. Thus, in the Italian region renowned for its production of the peperoncino and in particular the yield from the Tyrrhenian coast between Amantea and Diamante, I found its consumption in light of its beneficial properties with regard to the cardiovascular system completely appropriate to my total body cure. A discriminating bar of dark chocolate with overtones of spicy peperoncino made a great snack to bolster oneself between treatments.

A shorter excursion from the spa presented itself one afternoon in a ride up to the town of Guardia Piemontese. Perched on a hill above the bath complex, the community of roughly 2,000 inhabitants was settled sometime between the thirteenth and early fourteenth centuries by *Valdesi* (Waldensians), adherents to a Protestant movement that originated in France. As the town's name implies, the group came from Italy's Piedmont area. A few centuries after the Waldensians' peaceful arrival, however, their protestant religion was squelched by the Inquisition, as highlighted by the *Porta del Sangue* (Blood Gate) from which the blood of the inhabitants was said to have flowed in 1561 and through which we entered the partially walled village for a pleasant walk through the historic center's medieval lanes.

For this outing, my tablemates and I were escorted by our very sociable waiter, who not only lived in one of the old stone houses, but spoke the native residents' Occitan language, referred to as *guardiolo*. Presently, Guardia Piemontese is the only Calabrian pocket of this minority European language, spoken in communities in the extreme northwest of Italy, France, Spain and Monaco. At one time, speaking the language was forbidden in Calabria, thus it was eradicated long ago from the few other localities in the Province of Cosenza where Waldensians had settled. Today, the street signs in Guardia Piemontese are in the two languages, such as Thermal Bath Street:

Via Terme (Italian)
Via dei Banh Chaut (Occitan)

Although Guardia Piemontese's elevated position turned out to be no match for religious persecutors, the location was deemed an ideal vantage point for defensive towers constructed both half a millennium before and after the massacre. The picturesque circular edifice of stone built prior to the arrival of the Piedmont Protestants as a sentry post for Saracen ships sat on the crest of the hill beside a cylindrical eyesore made of concrete from the Second World War. We weren't confronted with any attackers on that cloudless summer day, just a lovely shoreline and coastal settlements beyond Calabria's classic, irregular ridges that are so prone to the earth's motion in the form of mudslides and quakes.

The green forests enveloping those hills provided a tranquil backdrop for the spa's large, outdoor thermal pools filled with warm, greenish water. Not having thought to throw in a few rheumatoid symptoms at my meeting with the check-in doctor, I felt a bit left out of the official mud treatments at the clinic, so I indulged in several applications of the aesthetic variety in the open air. The green ooze was great for the skin, as advertised, although I didn't notice its additional claim with regard to weight loss. But then again, I hadn't come anywhere close to the magical twelve applications.

My time at the spa was brief, but beneficial. I had achieved my goal. Even after my short stay, I felt more relaxed and I was breathing easier. My skin smelled of rotten eggs, and I had met a number of warm people who hadn't noticed. Amidst all that sulfur, I was also immersed in the salt of the earth.

I departed from the platform of Guardia Piemontese Marina to the strains of the local band as they led the procession of their patron saint Maria Goretti, popular with humble folk. A couple hundred faithful in sunglasses and respectful summer garb followed the life-size statue down the main street as I boarded the train that was, thankfully, comfortably air-conditioned.

17

VISITING CALABRIA'S NEIGHBORS

SASSI DI MATERA, BASILICATA

VULCANO

SO CLOSE, YET SO FAR . . . I had seen the outlines of the Aeolian Islands many times from Calabria's coast north of Reggio, but outside the summer tourist season, popping over for a weekend getaway would take careful planning. The volcanic archipelago lay in the Tyrrhenian Sea to Sicily's northeast and was principally made up of seven islands, from largest to smallest: Lipari, Salina, Vulcano, Stromboli, Filicudi, Alicudi and Panarea. For my first visit, I chose Vulcano, mainly because it was the closest to Reggio and one of the easiest to reach. While hydrofoils from Reggio to Messina ran throughout the day all year long, the service to the Aeolians was much more limited and boats only made the trip once a day during the winter season, which actually encompassed spring and fall, as well. Additionally, if the sea was too rough, the hydrofoils didn't leave the port at all. A train to nearby Villa San Giovanni, ferry to Messina, followed by a train to Milazzo from where another ferry could be taken to the islands was the alternative, and despite the rigmarole, often the most secure. However, I settled on the simpler route and while the skies were overcast, the sea remained calm enough for the two-hour journey including a stop in Messina for the dropping off and picking up of passengers. The boat was practically empty.

Pulling into Vulcano's dock, I was struck by the wide palette of browns coloring the island's unusually shaped rock formations. The omnipresent sulfur smell was equally impressive. Upon checking into my bed and breakfast, I would discover that the local spa was still closed for the 'winter.' I had been looking forward to comfortably lounging in and around the geothermic pools, a pastime that seemed more inviting in cooler weather. Nevertheless, the proprietor of my B&B informed me that the mud pit was accessible year round, as was the aforementioned, all-pervasive odor.

Near the port, just a short walk away, the pit was empty with a small rope barring entrance to the oatmeal-gray pond. Across the street, a few women chatted at a snack bar and I inquired about the mud. One of the women walked me back over, stepped across the rope and explained the mud bath procedure. The attendant had probably wanted to go home early, she said. So, I went back to my room, put a suit on under my clothes and returned. The pool was very shallow, not all that warm and extremely slippery. I decided not to submerge or go near the bubbling hot spots, but reached down and scooped up the slimy mud from the bottom smearing it on my arms and legs. There was a slight burning sensation every so often and when I scraped the mud off, following the instructions on the posted signs, my skin was amazingly soft if not a little blotchy.

I thanked the woman as I walked away, and she asked me if I wanted to go up the volcano the following morning with a friend visiting from Switzerland. I could meet her in a little while and join them to watch the sunset on the black sand beach. Okay, I replied.

When I returned to the snack bar, two toddlers were playing with a twelve-year-old on the picnic tables and my new friend Gabi was talking with a tall Swiss woman from the French-speaking region. After introductions, I realized that we were going to drive to the beach. The only vehicle in the vicinity seemed rather small for the group; however, its compact size and numerous dents made less of an impact on me than the homemade license plate. Incredibly, as we were piling into the car, Gabi complimented her son on having done such a nice job on the tag. The day before, the little group had been pulled over for driving without license plates, which had been stolen in Catania three months earlier. Gabi had reported the theft, but never had the tags replaced. How much time could that calligraphy project possibly buy her? Never mind the child safety seats, where was the candid camera?

I, for one, felt reckless as we pulled up to the black sand beach, testimony of volcanoes gone by. Rough-hewn rocky outcroppings flanked the bay whose seascape framed other islands in the archipelago and provided a perfect backdrop for the red sunset. A few young locals drank beer as they watched the sky change colors; my group was more the milk set. Unruly screaming signaled the dinner hour and an invitation to Gabi's.

Her vacation home on the island was built in the traditional Aeolian style, quadratic shape constructed of lava stone painted white, terraced and situated amidst oleander and prickly pear cactus plants. We cooked and ate in her patio-kitchen, a simple pasta with a sauce made of goat's milk ricotta.

The next morning as my new Swiss friend and I started out at the bottom of the volcano, I realized that she was a serious hiker. I gasped for air as we strode past a group of Germans, all decked out with their fancy walking sticks, backpacks and shoes. How had I overlooked the fact that her thigh was the length of a standard baseball bat? As we approached the top, I covered my mouth to protect my lungs from the hot sulfurous vapors escaping from the fissures—no guardrails or signage to keep me from falling into the abyss or to at least steer me in the right direction. Winded, on shaky legs, I felt as though I had been transported to some otherworldly planet, albeit together with the cadre of hikers behind us. The peak was so barren, so austere, but a spectacular panorama unfolded as we stepped back and looked out over the volcano's rim. I imagined the hand of a god-like Mars, hurling his spear to form the surrounding islands. However, the deity in question was actually Vulkan, the blacksmith, as I was on the island of Vulcano, the home of the immortal smithy who would lend his Roman name to all the volcanoes of the world.

As we were descending, I envied the handful of Italians

beginning their leisurely ascent after several cups of coffee and a mid-morning pastry. I would have trouble walking for three days. Although I normally wouldn't have needed the purported rheumatic curative properties of the mud pit, after the hike, I decided a little heat on my legs couldn't hurt. That afternoon, the attendant was available to collect the 2-Euro entrance, and I joined the pond's solitary client, a friendly, rather sturdy, German-speaking Swiss woman with bright red hair in a high mound atop her head. She came to Vulcano several times a year.

I slithered to a seated position in my 5-Euro, throwaway bikini that barely covered, as Gabi hadn't been able to negotiate a fitting into the sales price at the little shop near the snack bar. No problem, really—the suit and any other clothing that came in contact with the muddy water would have to be disposed of anyway, as no amount of bleach was a match for that sulfur smell. The soles of my feet felt like a baby's bottom. Heck, my *bottom* was as soft as a baby's. Off-season travel definitely had its advantages.

MATERA

MY STOMACH DIDN'T FEEL RIGHT, but I was awake, so I took a shower and stumbled out to the bus, which fortunately was leaving from the main train station, practically right outside my front door at the time. It was dark. I arrived at 4:35 for the 4:40 scheduled departure. I thought I was the last to present myself, but then an Italian couple showed up at 4:42, apologetically taking their seats amidst the scowls. Where was I? Who were these punctual travelers?

A few weeks earlier I received a forwarded email message from the secretary of the school where I was working. The Russian teacher, who wasn't overwhelmed by the local demand for language lessons, was circulating information about an excursion to Matera, a provincial capital in Basilicata, the small region nestled between Calabria and Apulia. I had wanted to see the ancient cave dwellings known as the *Sassi di Matera* for some time. The catch was that the excursion was all in one day—391 kilometers (243 miles) each way.

I hadn't slept at all. Vera, the tour leader, introduced our bus drivers: Antonio and Vassily, "who speaks our language." The majority of the group was Ukrainian, although they spoke Russian amongst themselves, as it was the language of their schooling and the one with which they felt the most comfortable. They were one of Italy's numerous groups of immigrant workers, many of whom cleaned houses, took care of the old and young, and performed other physical labor. When I boarded the bus, I had two seats to myself. At the penultimate pickup point, however, a rather large woman who had already begun to sweat in her sleeveless shirt got on and plopped down next to me, boisterously chatting away in Vasilly's language with her two grown daughters in the seats behind us. With my knees already butt up against the seat in front of me, I knew that I wasn't going to be able to withstand the pressure from the ever-encroaching recliner together with that of the soft, warm thigh that was impinging on my lateral space as well, so I escaped to the last row, which I shared with a young Italian woman and where I was able to catch a few winks that would enable me to get through the day's exhausting journey.

We pulled into Matera at around 10:30 with three very short rest stops during which I spent all of my time waiting on the bathroom line. Somehow, the others were able to smoke a cigarette, drink a thimble-full of coffee, circumvent the queue, and return to the coach ahead of me. Arriving at Matera's tour bus parking lot, Vera took the lead without hesitation, stepping out at a clip, then stopping after about five minutes and admitting to not knowing where she was going. Apparently, *"con la guida"* (with a guide), as the trip had been presented, must have referred to her reading aloud a paragraph about the *Sassi* on the bus. Her recitation went something like this, *"Bushka shyveskaza Mel Gibson dasvadanya papushka vadushka Mel Gibson djezhe zachod sashazsky chaikovsky mussoursky sayevich Monica Bellucci Mel Gibson . . . . "* Gibson's film *The Passion of the Christ* was clearly crucial to our appreciation of the historic site.

We were wandering through the traditional, European-looking part of the town. The patrician houses, churches and piazzas all looked normal, quite lovely, in fact. Perhaps for that reason, when finally coming upon one of the terraces that overlooked the *Sassi*, which sat at a lower level having been constructed on the slope of a ravine, the historical chasm between the two very different social realities of Matera's citizenry was all the more startling. The monochromatic jumble of modest structures blankly stared out at me from the gray landscape, occasionally broken by a white satellite dish of someone who had apparently returned to live in the ghost town. The houses were partially carved out of stone and partially fabricated. Blocks of high-rises poked out of the hill in the distance to the right, built to accommodate the community's 15,000 inhabitants when a federal sanitation law required their relocation in 1952. Since 1993, the area encompassing the ancient structures, referred to as the *Sassi di Matera*, (literally, Stones of Matera) has been on the list of UNESCO's World Heritage Sites.

Left abandoned for many years, the cluster of dwellings and churches has provided the backdrop for over forty films. Signs marked the Stations of the Cross from Gibson's movie, and tourists eagerly posed in front of the landmarks. Craft and gift shops occupied several buildings. A few churches and a peasant house carved out of the calcareous rock were on display. In the latter, a cutout in the floor revealed the town's ancient cistern system, canals hewn out of the stone underneath the habitations. Medieval wall paintings decorated the churches' stone interiors. Even more archaic were the caves on the opposite hill, an ashen-green, treeless slope marked with curved entrances sculpted out of the whitish stone. The gorge had been inhabited since the Neolithic period. Today, the city of Matera, population 60,000, sits atop the canyon from which it has developed.

In Italian, the word *bello* can be used to describe just about everything. In English, I would often have to modify its application. The *Sassi* have an eerie beauty, captivating as an image, but perhaps more so from an anthropological point of view. The unusual place has sheltered hundreds of families, thousands of people bound together along the sides of the gorge that has protected generations over centuries and even millennia.

On my return to the bus I discovered the main pedestrian street of Matera, a very attractive thoroughfare with many historic buildings of a different type—elegant, gentrified. When I arrived at the bus at three minutes to one, the Ukrainians were already in their seats impatiently waiting to take off. I could have lingered in the area for several days, but our collective stomachs called. Lunch was originally slated as an outdoor barbeque but was changed to a sit-down location 20 minutes away. Almost an hour later we pulled into Montescaglioso, apparently at a distance of only fifteen kilometers. As throughout southern Italy, Montescaglioso's formal history dates back to the Greek period and a number of noteworthy artifacts have been found in the area. Part of the town's present territory has been united with that of Matera to form a large archeological and nature park called *Parco delle chiese rupestri del Materano* (Park of Matera's Cave Churches).

Our lunch that day was in a restaurant with *"Carne Equina"* painted in big white letters on its large plate glass window along with a picture of a horse balancing on its two back legs, just in case there was any doubt as to the local specialty. Never having eaten horsemeat before, my young Italian friends looked a bit concerned. I had at least tried a horse meatball in a restaurant in Catania a few years earlier—for me, a very sweet taste that transmitted an odd, cloying sensation.

Our all-inclusive, 10-Euro lunch started off with a tasty bruschetta, then a simple dish of pasta with tomato sauce, followed by a plate of grilled meat that we thought was meant to be shared when the waitress first put it down. It was enough meat to choke a horse, to use a potentially indelicate expression considering the context. That amount of raw meat couldn't have been bought at the supermarket for 10 Euros. There was a large horse hamburger and the rest was pork: several skewers, a cutlet, sausages, etc.—all quite good. Unfortunately, after my difficult, sleepless night I wasn't really able to do justice to the plate. I finally had to ask the waiter to remove it with effusive apologies, as regardless of the positioning of my knife and fork, the dish remained before me as I clearly hadn't consumed enough to warrant of its disposal. A decent red house wine, bottled water, a green salad and espresso were included in the meal. And it seemed that the packaged ice cream cones the Ukrainians were nonchalantly pulling out of the freezer were also part of the meal. Vera could have been stronger on the informational aspect of her tour, but she sure knew how to satisfy her clients' stomachs at an economically advantageous price.

We never saw the programmed castles or museum, which looked inviting on the excursion's flyer but weren't ever mentioned that day. Instead, we were brought to Montescaglioso's Benedictine Abbey of San Michele Arcangelo that had the usual pleasant cloister and an exhibition room with a few nineteenth and twentieth-century articles. My new Italian friends and I posed for pictures in the angle of the mock-Fascist schoolroom.

Before lunch, Vera had asked for a show of hands of those who would like to buy a loaf of the local bread. The bakery needed a bit of time to prepare for the Sunday afternoon demand. Consequently, we made an unscheduled bread stop, as well, before heading back to Reggio. The loaves were about the size of a 1½-year-old child for 2 Euros each. I bought one for my friend Luisa.

On the return to Reggio I chatted in the back seat with the Italian girls, an architect and an art restorer. We had some nice views of the Ionian coast northeast of Locri, arriving back in Reggio a little after 11, exhausted, laden with bags of bread and the paraphernalia packed for the day's excursion. Vera announced her upcoming trips. The one to Pompei with a 2 a.m. departure sounded particularly enticing . . . The *Sassi* were *belli*, but I think I learned my lesson. *Do svidaniya!*

Or perhaps better said in the Matera dialect: *Ci sckëjtë 'ngjlë 'mboccë së chegghjë.* (Who spits in the air, takes it in the face.)

18

Journey's End

Cornetto filled with fresh pastry cream

REFLECTIONS

Calabria is not a land to traverse alone. It is too wistful and stricken; too deficient in those externals that conduce to comfort. Its charms do not appeal to the eye of romance, and the man who would perambulate Magna Graecia as he does the Alps would soon regret his choice. One needs something of that "human element".
. . . The joys of Calabria are not to be bought, like those of Switzerland, for gold.

Norman Douglas, *Old Calabria*

"BUT WHY CALABRIA?" Certainly, the mother-tongue English teacher in Rome or Florence or even Naples, a city that has received its share of bad press, didn't have to answer that same question over and over again. I often found myself defending the region to the locals who couldn't believe someone without Calabrian blood would have had any reason to linger longer than an extended summer vacation. Back in 1969, British travel writer H. V. Morton recorded much stronger sentiments in *A Traveller in Southern Italy*: "There are Italians in Lombardy and Tuscany who shudder to this day at the very name of Calabria, and would as soon think of spending a holiday there as in the Congo." Harsh, but true, these words could have been written yesterday. It is therefore ironic that Italy's very name has its roots in a region so often regarded with disdain.

Aristotle recorded the origin of Italy's name in his *Politics*:

"The learned say that Italo, one of the inhabitants of that region became king of Oenotria, and that the Oenotrians changed their antique name to Itali, and that from him, the whole European peninsula between the Gulfs of Squillace and Lamezia, a distance of a half day's walk from one to the other, took the name Italy." These gulfs Aristotle mentioned are on either side of Calabria's center, surrounding the isthmus that separates the Ionian and Tyrrhenian Seas. Thus, from Italo, a late Iron Age Calabrian, the whole of the peninsula eventually took its name.

Wherever I went in Calabria or whatever I read about it, I never ceased to be amazed by its wealth of history. Today, this erstwhile Mediterranean hub is off the beaten path of the average tourist, as it was for the English on their famous Grand Tours of the continent; however, a number of adventurous British travelers did make pilgrimages to Italo's homeland, leaving behind colorful accounts of their impressions. When I finally began reading a few of the books that the Anglo-Italian Club of Reggio Calabria put up on a pedestal, I was surprised by many a description of the region and its native inhabitants. Twenty-first century political correctness certainly has taken a bite out of the travel writer's humorous anecdote. Alongside many laugh-out-loud scenarios, however, authors such as Norman Douglas and George Gissing, obviously endeavored to tell it like it was, and in so doing, revealed both the good with the bad, giving a real sense of the time and place. While some Calabrians may take umbrage at certain passages, most take the books for what they are, appreciating the effort many of these individuals made to visit the region and the time they took to acquaint themselves with the local culture. For Calabrians, the general consensus seemed to be that it was better to be talked about, in whatever fashion, than to be ignored.

Just as travel on poor roads and antiquated trains isn't easy today, and daily life is rife with challenges such as the frequent lack of adequate heating and the occasional absence of running water, centuries earlier, exploring the region and its mountain towns was truly a formidable prospect. The early British travelers were made of hardy stuff, traversing great distances on foot and occasionally even sleeping under the stars. Many were cautioned to move about only with armed escorts to protect them from the legendary brigands for which Calabria was infamous, but the great majority of these intrepid globe-trotters refused such assistance, managing to explore even the most notorious areas without any criminal encounters whatsoever. Under normal circumstances, contemporary travelers won't run into any outlaws, either; however, evidence of their activity will be all around them, such as in the illegal construction, unfinished expressways and a very high unemployment rate. Notwithstanding, the tourist will also encounter guest accommodations, for instance, as conventional as in any other Italian location for comparably rated properties.

Italians the entire length of the peninsula lament over the lack of opportunities for young people, low wages and the excessive joblessness. In Calabria, these problems are exacerbated to the point of being an ordinary component of daily life. Nevertheless, they resent being viewed as a burden by northerners and often point to unification as a negative turning point for their economy. The commemoration of the 150th anniversary of Italian unity wasn't celebrated all that joyously in Calabria, where Garibaldi isn't universally hailed as a hero. Despite the fact that Reggio's main pedestrian street, Corso Garibaldi, bears his name, many Calabrians view the unification as its downfall, seeing his statue as no more than a perch for the city's pigeons. The largely accepted notion that Calabria was only agrarian and completely devoid of industry before unification is distressful for those who point out, for example, the region's historic mining along with its associated metal and steel industries. Popular conception sees the centralized government's abandonment of such production in favor of northern manufacture, forcing their people to emigrate to the north and abroad for survival. Of course, everything wasn't rosy for the average peasant before unification, either, but

Calabrians feel that they have been too severely judged on an unfair playing field.

My friend Luisa's nephew is an enterprising young man, an architect who has sought out work opportunities in his field, submitted proposals, been awarded contracts. He recently decided to start a business on family property, constructing a small facility for kite surfers on a beach location excellent for the sport. He hoped to start making some money on his investment in his second year of operation, but that wasn't to be, as before the season began, everything not nailed down was stolen and the following day everything else was completely destroyed. Of course, this sort of thing can occur anywhere, but it happens too frequently in Calabria. His friends encouraged him to rebuild, invest in better security. Nearby, a similar venture with little tiki huts had mysteriously burned down a few years earlier and the disheartened proprietor never rebuilt. Is it worth it? Criminals seem to operate without impunity, and this is one of Calabria's troublesome realities.

Should the young man abandon his hometown and join his cousins in the north or in parts farther flung? Many have certainly done so before him and have thrived, as locals will readily point out. Calabrians pride themselves on their cleverness. A friend once told me of an illiterate, old woman who owned a small grocery store in his village. At the time he was learning how to read and write in school, he realized that the shopkeeper could do neither and asked her how she kept track of the tabs she ran on her customers. She pulled little burlap bags with different colored bows out of a drawer and spilled the contents of one of them onto the counter. It contained an assortment of beans, and she explained that a fava bean was worth 100 lire, a navy bean 50, chickpea 10 and lentil 5. She had devised a simple, practical system without ever knowing how to write. Today, her granddaughter carries on the business with a computer.

Calabrians respect a quick wit. Unfortunately, this innate attribute has enabled them to survive, but hasn't been of service in conquering their enemies at home. The characteristic does result in a more interesting conversation than one might expect amongst ordinary circumstances, as I noted with the club of rough and ready Campari drinkers in a casual restaurant I frequented. In fact, over a century ago Gissing remarked on this same quality in a comparison between middle-class English and Italians based on café conversations in which the Calabrians "exchanged genuine thoughts, reasoned lucidly on the surface of abstract subjects" and had "an innate respect for things of the mind." Based on his encounters in a Catanzaro bar, he pronounced the Italians far superior to his countrymen with regard to intellectual discourse.

Norman Douglas also referred to the philosophical view of life in his classic *Old Calabria* (1915), citing cultured Calabrians' "subtle detachment and contempt of illusions—whence their time-honoured renown as abstract thinkers and speculators." On the other hand, he eloquently cautioned against the over-reliance on rhetoric and its "elegant partisan non-truth," that resulted in "a constitutional horror of a bald fact, because *there it is*, and there is nothing to be done with it. It is too crude a thing for cultured men to handle. If a local barrister were forced to state in court a plain fact, without varnish, he would die of cerebral congestion; the judge, of boredom." The Italians do have a way with words and their embellishment thereof. During my time in Calabria, I couldn't help but notice that appearance was usually more important than substance—beautifully crafted sentences, high-dollar words, a delicate dance around the subject—they were masters of the protracted introductory remark and the art of persuasive speaking.

As is a general trait of the very sociable Italian people, family ties are extremely close in Calabria. Traditions are still quite strong. Childhood friendships last a lifetime, even when career paths might take classmates in completely different directions. The home village and hometown have meaning, a destination in the mass migration that takes place on holidays and for summer vacations by the Calabrians who have relocated to the north or immigrated to other countries.

The sons of American immigrants have also written books about Calabria, accounts of a completely different nature from the British travel narratives. The descendants tend to be much narrower in their focus, looking for something very specific as they search for their roots. The most notable is Gay Talese's *Unto the Sons*, a monumental immigrant saga that traces his familial history back to his ancestral home of Maida, a small town in the province of Catanzaro. But as Edward Lear noted over 150 years ago, "this land of pictorial and poetical interest has had but few explorers; fewer still have published their experiences."

Italy has so much to offer its visitors that Calabria rarely makes the list. Certainly not on today's Grand Tour or, in modern parlance, on Italy's Top Three of Rome, Florence and Venice, or the Top Five that may add Milan or Naples/Pompeii, or even any of the ubiquitous Top Ten lists. I watched cruise ships regularly sail through the Strait, docking across the water in Messina from where their passengers were bused to Taormina, and on rare occasion shuttled over to Reggio to see the Bronzes. In 2012 Reggio hosted its first cruise ship, and dockings in Tropea and Corigliano Calabro were celebrated the following year, with regional plans to develop regular ports of call in these cities as well as in Crotone and Vibo Valentia.

Many of these initial cruisers were undoubtedly surprised by what they discovered, not knowing what to expect with such an itinerary. As observed by Lear, even today, "The very name of Calabria has in it no little romance," and unlike any other region, "holds out such promise of interest, or so inspires us before we have set foot within it . . . . But – Calabria! – No sooner is the word uttered than a new world arises before the mind's eye, – torrents, fastnesses, all the prodigality of mountain scenery, – caves, brigands, and pointed hats . . . – costumes and character, – horrors and magnificence without end." Alas, today, the wonderful pointed hats and costumes of yesteryear can only be seen in a museum or exhibition, unless one stumbles into the right village at an opportune moment. And certainly, one hopes never to confront the horrors of a devastating earthquake or the savagery of the mafia; however, these reputations and fears dangle out there, adding a mystery of the unknown. Moreover, of the entire Italian peninsula, Calabria is the region most at seismic risk, a factor that has not only damaged the landscape, but has harmed its psyche as well as its attractiveness for investors.

Many view Calabria's future in tourism and cottage industries, such as small agricultural businesses that produce natural, high quality food and wine based on local, time-honored methods. Creative artisans also continue to work in their fields, striving to expand an interest in traditional crafts of ceramics, textile and metal. Several masters have been recognized internationally, such as the jeweler Gerardo Sacco (b. 1940) from Crotone, who has received accolades for his creations worn by celebrities ranging from Liz Taylor to Monica Bellucci. And the most famous artist of recent times is the fashion designer Gianni Versace (1946-1997), whose craft was handed down from his mother, a seamstress and stylist who had a boutique on Reggio's Via Tommaso Gulli, from which the aspiring couturier could stick out his head and see the cathedral to the left and the Strait of Messina to the right. Leaving for Milan to make his place in the international fashion world, Versace no doubt carried with him the culture and spirit of his hometown.

While Reggio has its share of elegant stores, delightful in which to window-shop the lines of Sacco and Versace, Calabria's true pleasures, as expressed by Douglas, cannot be measured in gold. A lovely pedestrian street may enhance the *passeggiata*, but the true joys of Calabria are its simple pleasures. It is a place where a slice of pecorino cheese or sausage can still be savored as people have done for centuries. The tastes are simple yet complex, to be enjoyed in company, seemingly simple, yet equally complex.

IN PREPARATION FOR MY DEPARTURE

Perhaps also because at the moment of leaving Calabria, despite everything we had suffered we began to feel connected to these people who were so odd as to be studied for their primitive resolve and to the land so vivid to behold in its eternal devastation. Whatever it was, we went away from this beautiful city, so hospitable even in the very midst of its calamity, not once but a good two times, with profound sadness; after we lost sight of it, we retraced our steps to bid one last farewell.
Alexandre Dumas, *Captain Arena*

"Is there anything I can do to convince you to stay?" "Yes, you can get me a work permit." I hadn't planned on not returning to my teaching job; it just came out. I had evidently had enough. I understood the difficulties of running a business, but I had hoped my employer would have put forth a bit more effort with regard to straightening out my legal status. Two issues were at the core of the predicament: the difficulty of obtaining a work visa and the lack of funds to pay the proper taxes on legitimately registered employees. The school hadn't ever attempted to take care of the paperwork, however thorny a process it may have been, knowing they didn't have the money to back it up. Even considering Italy's low pay rate, I was in essence donating my time to the school a few days a week and I was tired of doing so in a cold, damp room.

I felt sad. Despite the inconveniences, the place and its people had gotten under my skin. Dumas had sensed it, that primitive resolve, a staunchness of temperament acquired amidst the stark landscape's tough realities.

This characteristic determination in its unadorned simplicity brings to mind the story of the banana. For a while when I lived only a few kilometers from the school in Reggio, I walked, as the bus was unreliable and jarring. My classes usually started in the afternoon and I taught through the evening, so businesses were closed except for the bars and a small fruit and vegetable stand. One day, I realized I had forgotten to bring a snack to tide me over to dinner and for the first time stopped at the small, family market. As I approached the bananas in the case just inside the doorway, the proprietor suddenly appeared, indicating that he would take care of the fruit gathering. I said that I would like one banana. He stared at me curiously and after a few seconds, pulled one banana off a bunch and put it on the counter. "*Poi?*" (Then?) "*Solo una banana, grazie.*" (Just one banana, thank you.) More inquisitive staring. The other man and woman, perhaps members of the family, who were sitting and talking in the back of the little storefront, fell silent and turned in our direction. I began getting out coins and the storekeeper shook his head as if he couldn't possibly consider taking money for just one banana. I tried to insist, as I knew I wasn't ever going to want any more than one or at most two pieces of fruit at a time from his establishment, but in the end I just had to thank him and leave the three Calabrians marveling at the foreigner who had attempted to purchase one, lone banana.

As with the work permit, more than one factor was at play in that exchange. To begin with, his code of ethics wouldn't have allowed him to take money for such a small object, particularly from a female customer on her initial visit to his store. He was bound to offer it for free, to show his hospitality. In bars throughout Calabria, friends and acquaintances tripped over each other to pick up the tab for the coffee. "*Offro io!*" (It's on me.) This phrase, once uttered, cannot be argued with at the risk of offending or damaging pride. The other side of the banana was that of the good businessman. He had caught me in his web, binding me to return and spend money in his store. Unfortunately, he had bound me not to ever return to his shop because I couldn't again enter without buying more than the one banana.

Without the means or even the interest in modern marketing, such proprietors hook their clients the old-fashioned way. Likewise with other forms of communication, Calabrians don't leave important issues to chance. If they have something to say, they say it. They aren't shy. History has proven the importance of seizing the rare opportunity immediately upon presentation. The more eloquent may take half an hour to set forth a formal thesis, elucidating all of its particulars in the most florid of manners, leaving no doubt as to their intent in an extraordinarily roundabout fashion, while someone less educated will blurt out a phrase in dialect accompanied by an abrupt physical gesture so that the theatrical aspect alone would have transmitted the message even to those not familiar with the particular patois.

After four years in Calabria, I realized that I had learned to speak up, to hold my place in the bars' and pastry shops' imaginary lines. Strangely enough, despite the high ratio of these establishments in proportion to the population, they seemed to thrive, not at all reflecting the stereotypical image of a struggling south. Where coffee and pastry were concerned, the people didn't hold back, maybe because the social experience could be bought for a mere 80¢ for *un caffè* (an espresso) or about a Euro for *un cappuccino*. I would certainly miss those delectable *pasticcini* (pastries), such as the assortments of pop-in-your-mouth *mignon* (miniatures) that appeared on trays in homes and businesses at the slightest mention of a celebration, very often washed down with a bottle of *spumante* that always seemed to be at hand. I made sure to have my fill of the delicacies, however caloric, before returning to the states, as the region's *pasticcerie* (pastry shops) produced some of the most scrumptious in the country. Even the omnipresent *cornetto* (croissant), poised under glass in bars throughout Italy, is particularly noteworthy in Calabria. My favorite was filled with a divine, fresh pastry cream. *Mamma mia, che buono!* (Oh my, how good!)

During the summer, a *granita* with brioche made a refreshing breakfast. Usually served in a clear glass with a spoon, this semi-frozen treat is made of sugar, water and either fruit juice, most often strawberry or lemon, or another ingredient such as almond, coffee or chocolate. The brioche features prominently in another popular summer extravagance—an ice cream sandwich that, at a glance, resembles the form of a large hamburger with bun; the classic sweet roll topped by a little ball of the same dough is filled to order with the gelato flavor or flavors of choice. In keeping with the regionalism of Italian food, the Sicilians claim origins to both the *granita* and gelato sandwich; however, with Reggio's vicinity, I can say that its specialty shops and bars serve up a deliciously faithful culinary indulgence.

Perhaps my vivid memory of Calabria's numerous bars is based on their cultural importance, reinforced by the lasting impression of their popularity left by my summer departure. In warm weather the gelato patrons spill out onto the streets from both the bars and gelato shops; the walkways are splattered with puddles of the melted dessert. Proprietors set up tables under sidewalk canopies, and large eating areas are opened along Via Marina for al fresco snacking and dining along the strait. Likewise, the beach concessionaires return, their structures dominating most of downtown's lower-level shoreline.

Sitting in a lovely, open-air *gelateria* (ice-cream parlor) with a friend on the eve of my departure, I felt as though I had become part of the tradition. Our young server placed two very appealing oversized goblets of gelato before us but sped away before I could ask him to take our picture, so I hailed an older, more distinguished waiter just behind him. He looked at Donatella and me, and with a big smile pronounced our gelato unworthy of our beauty and whisked our dishes back inside. He hadn't been pleased with his more youthful colleague's creations and returned with a fanciful cornucopia of gelato and fresh fruit topped with whipped cream and cookies, a work of art that tasted as good as it looked—now, all just a wonderful memory, as we discovered my battery had lost its charge.

In Calabria, rewards were proffered when least expected, perhaps simple compensation for the daily struggles or just a greater appreciation for humble pleasures: gazing at Sicily's hilly coastline beyond the waters of the strait while enjoying a dish of gelato on a lazy Sunday afternoon, meeting friends for a quick morning coffee, encountering acquaintances in the course of a *passeggiata*, sharing a meal with family and friends at home or dining in a casual pizzeria. When the opportunity presented itself to smell the roses or the pasta sauce, the people didn't hesitate. Although at times I hoped to see more action in combating the day-to-day inconveniences, coping with them did help to fine-tune the collective sense of humor. Change was encumbered by apathy due to the ineffectiveness of previous attempts to alter the system and by fear, either of losing a job in a society with extremely high unemployment or of conflict with criminality or other powerful entities. In dialect, "*Cangianu i sonaturi, ma 'a musica è sempre 'a stessa.*" (The players change, but the music is always the same.)

Ridiculous situations persisted for no better reason than that they could. I was farmed out one morning a week to teach in a nearby pre-school, a private institution with a large enrollment and a high ratio of students to teachers. The school had countless toilets designed to the specifications of Sleeping Beauty's dwarves—all functioning. Shortly after I arrived, I noticed that a bucket had been placed next to the commode in the teacher's sole bathroom and quickly learned that it was to be used for flushing. There's nothing quite like struggling to get a large, plastic pail under a sink's faucet and then whipping the water into the toilet of a communal bathroom. Months passed. The brazenfaced proprietor continued to collect tuition and the teachers carried on instructing the pupils in great numbers. Strangely, those educators were amongst the most pleasant I've ever met, but I couldn't help wondering if I were in the European Community or some remote African community.

The people didn't always speak up, not to the proper authorities at any rate, and as an *extracomunitaria* (non EU member) I didn't either. My position was awkward and I was leaving it, turning to wave one last goodbye, catching a final glimpse to carry with me and having one ultimate gelato for the road.

AIRPORT FAREWELLS

I HAD ARRIVED IN LOCRI WITH one suitcase, carrying it back and forth to the United States each year, and I would make my final departure with that same bag. My acquisitions beyond its capacity were packed up in boxes and stored at my friend Luisa's. I wasn't ready to make a clean break; I knew I would return fairly soon, but I just wasn't sure exactly when or for how long.

Luisa served my final luncheon in her formal dining room with its massive, handcrafted, nineteenth-century mahogany furniture her mother-in-law had brought from the Piedmont when she had married into the Calabrian family. Contrary to the more routine migratory patterns, the occasional northerner did, in fact, relocate to the south, as well. On that warm afternoon, the open French doors beckoned a pleasant summer breeze, billowing the long, lace curtains under the stately chamber's five-meter (16½-foot) ceiling. We were in six alongside her husband Franco and her nephew visiting from Rome with his two children. I had eaten so many wonderful meals in that room that I couldn't say what we had on that particular day, but surely at the very least, a plate of pasta, a meat course with vegetables, potatoes and a salad, cheese, fruit and dessert, all served in abundant portions.

I reminisced on my first visit in which Luisa had graciously invited a friend and me, two perfect strangers, inside her home as we admired her stately art-nouveau residence from the street. Serving us fruit juice and cookies in what could only be called a parlor for its old-world refinement, Luisa shared a little history of the house, built in the 1920s when Reggio was finally getting back on its feet after the devastating 1908 earthquake and the privations of the First World War. She and her husband had welcomed me into their home and hearts, in a short time embracing me not as a guest but as though I were part of the family. I would miss these warm people. Even Venerdì, their mixed breed German shepherd "Friday," eyeing my suitcase by the door, hung his head that day.

Along the short ride to the airport, I caught a last glimpse of the benevolent smile radiating from the round face of Padre Catanoso on the faded remains of a poster clinging to the side of a building. Luisa's father had provided medical services to this holy man, Calabria's most recent saint and undoubtedly my closest connection to any godly personage, which I figured couldn't hurt.

As Reggio was cumulatively resting after lunch, the streets were empty and we arrived at the *Aereoporto dello Stretto* "Tito Minniti" in less than a quarter of an hour. The airport lies along the strait south of the city center and was named after an aviator and Second Italo-Ethiopian War hero from the provincial village of Placanica. The small terminal handles a modest number of passengers, although the first time I found myself in the middle of the crowd at the arrivals door, I wondered at the airplane's dimensions before realizing that each traveler was being met by his entire extended family.

On my final departure day, surrounded as I was by my Calabrian family, I felt as though I had truly arrived. As I had often witnessed, my little assemblage occupied a good deal of space and engaged in the type of overlapping, animated conversation into which an outsider would have had to exercise a certain effort in order to interject a thought. Sadly, the moment to go through security came all too soon and the rounds of hugs and kisses, with a few damp eyes, quickly passed with my last turn and wave to the group of warm faces enthusiastically returning the gesture from the other side of the metal detector. I had been lucky to find such friendship, to have stumbled on Calabria and its people.

I didn't have long to ponder these thoughts before the flight was called and I walked the fifty yards across the tarmac with a view of the strait and the haze of Mount Etna at the end of the runway. I had a short flight to Rome, so different from my initial arrival on the overnight train to Locri. I felt as though I had jumped forward half a century, and in terms of experiences, perhaps I had. However, the primitive conveyance that had brought me to Calabria had played its part in setting the scene, breaking the ice for the challenges that would follow. I had learned a great deal and appreciated the modern efficiency of my flight that day more than I would have ever imagined.

My journey to Calabria had begun in Rieti where I received the fateful email from the English school in Locri, and I would transition out of my Calabrian adventure with a short visit to the home of my dear friends in this provincial capital outside of Rome. It was always a pleasure to spend time with them in a town that I had come to value not only for its copious supply of running water, but for the fact that the precious commodity could be drunk directly from the tap. Notwithstanding, my friends weren't wasteful, and I noted that they ran their dishwasher and laundry machine at night, during off-peak hours, an arrangement that seemed such a luxury after my recent experience.

My return to the United States had one last European stop, just for an overnight layover to take advantage of the best available ticket price. I landed safely in Frankfurt, Germany, found the efficient train that brought me within a block of my accommodation, rested comfortably in the bed and breakfast, returned to the airport the next morning and went through security in record time. I waited my turn at passport control and handed my American passport to the policeman. He flipped back and forth through the document, looking for the stamp of my entrance into Germany or the European Union amidst the many faded and partial governmental impressions.

He was in search of a date within the ninety-day tourist window and began to talk of my being in Europe illegally. I said that I was sorry, but I had been in Italy, adding, "Perhaps the Italians didn't stamp my passport." "Yours wouldn't be the first," he tersely replied and began cursing the population. I could see that I had pushed the right button, as the Germans were particularly exasperated with their southern neighbors at that time due to their various financial crises. I felt scared but looked him directly in the eyes and made up a date and story of my most recent entry. He asked to see the airplane receipt, but it had been an electronic ticket, which I had thrown away. "Do you have an Italian hotel receipt?" "Certainly, in my checked luggage. I'm returning from my vacation at a Calabrian spa." I felt as though I was in a scene from a film. Looking fit in his European-cut uniform, the officer had the type of chiseled jaw-line that indicated he knew how to use the pistol at the ready in his underarm holster.

I wanted to explain that I hadn't profited from any European largess, paying through the nose for my American health insurance and putting every Euro cent I had earned back into their economy. Of course, none of that had anything to do with the rules.

In the end, he shrugged his shoulders and brought down the stamp. After all, my flight was going directly to the United States. I was returning home, enveloped in a host of warm memories and armed with a newfound knowledge that would accompany me for the rest of my life. I needed time to gather my thoughts and reflect on all that I had seen and done. Then, after a bit of rest, I would set out to write my story of Calabria.

CPSIA information can be obtained at www.ICGtesting.com
Printed in the USA
BVOW08s0629200416

444902BV00002B/91/P